GOVERNING THE
WORLD ECONOMY

Willem Molle

Routledge
Taylor & Francis Group

LONDON AND NEW YORK

First published 2014
by Routledge
2 Park Square, Milton Park, Abingdon, Oxon OX14 4RN

and by Routledge
711 Third Avenue, New York, NY 10017

Routledge is an imprint of the Taylor & Francis Group, an informa business

© 2014 Willem Molle

British Library Cataloguing in Publication Data
A catalogue record for this book is available from the British Library

Library of Congress Cataloging-in-Publication Data
Molle, Willem.
Governing the world economy / Willem Molle.
pages cm
1. International economic relations. 2. Financial institutions, International.
3. International agencies. 4. Economic history–21st century. I. Title.
HF1359.M628 2013
337–dc23
2012045365

ISBN: 978–0–415–83303–5 (hbk)
ISBN: 978–0–415–83304–2 (pbk)
ISBN: 978–0–203–42875–7 (ebk)

Typeset in Bembo
by Keystroke, Station Road, Codsall, Wolverhampton

Printed and bound in the United States of America by
Edwards Brothers Malloy

CONTENTS

FIGURES

TABLES

BOXES

PREFACE

The global problem

The world is confronted with many problems. The recurrent storms on the financial markets have ravaged many countries. Poverty is still widespread, notwithstanding decades of massive development aid. The environment is at risk, as witness the loss of biodiversity and ongoing global warming.

In the future, many of the persistent problems are likely to be exacerbated. Conflicts over access to resources such as energy, water and clean air loom large. There will be an increasing pressure of migration, by people fleeing in massive numbers, regions plagued by lack of resources and internal conflicts. Social fabrics constructed over centuries are in danger as increased globalization increases the shocks while decreasing the capacity of national governments to protect their citizens.

These problems demand rapid and consistent action by policymakers. However, the major institutions charged with world governance have not been able to deliver good results in the past, such as the World Trade Organization, the World Bank and the Organisation for Economic Co-operation and Development. Neither do they seem to be ready to formulate adequate answers to future challenges. In many of these organizations the process of finding solutions has become stuck. The reason is generally that the interests of the major partners are too diversified for them to reach multilateral agreements setting uniform rules and requiring strict compliance with those rules.

So, alternative solutions need to be searched for. These are likely to be highly diversified in their subject, country coverage and governance methods. It means that the developments in the future will be characterized by many fuzzy and complex interactions between flexible groups of actors seeking agreements on the solutions for the most pressing old and new problems. Progress will become rather unpredictable and will depend on time-, place- and subject-specific cases of convergence of interests. This need not be only negative. Flexible solutions have the advantage that they can be easily adapted if the conditions change. And one may expect many sudden and profound changes to happen frequently in the future.

The need for a new book

The major changes depicted in the previous section have been documented in many articles and books for specific domains. However, a good overview covering the major policy areas is missing. My book *Global Economic Institutions* (Molle 2003) did provide a systematic view of the different global regimes for trade, finance and the environment. However, it is no longer adequate, for two reasons. First, since its publication many things have changed in the world economy and in its institutional system (e.g. the mechanisms to handle a financial crisis). Second, many new insights into the dynamics of institutional development have been delivered by the recent literature. So, the text needed updating. However, a mere update would not have been sufficient to make the book adequate for present and future needs. It would not have dealt with the continuous misgivings about the (lack of) effectiveness of the major institutions. So, attention had to shift from "what is" (major organizations) to "what works" (governance). In practice this implied a new book instead of a revised book.

Writing a book is a very demanding exercise. So, before setting out on the task it seemed advisable to check whether others had already delivered a text that would satisfy the demand. There are indeed a few very interesting studies that have been published since my previous book (see, for instance, Tabb 2004; Deacon 2007; Siebert 2009; Mattli and Woods 2009). However, they do not provide the well-structured systematic analysis that has been much appreciated in my previous book. Neither do they put the accent on the economic aspects of governance. So, I have set out to write a new book with a different focus. To that end I have started to delete the parts of the text that were little used; next I have thoroughly restructured the remaining material and finally I have added much new material. I have tested different versions of this new text during my course for students at Erasmus University, and I have had the benefit of critical comments on the manuscript from colleagues that are well known experts in the different subjects the book covers.

Audience

The book addresses two main categories of readers. The first consists of the increasing number of students who are taking courses in international economics, business, political economy and public administration. They will learn how institutions develop as they devise solutions to new challenges. Moreover they will be able to compare the practices of major organizations that function in the most important socio-economic policy fields. Finally they will learn to examine critically the strengths and weaknesses of the governance methods of the major international organizations in meeting challenges, and to evaluate the desirability and chances of improvement.

Second, the book is written for all those professionally interested in the governance aspects of the global economy in the widest sense. It addresses varied professionals such as national and international civil servants, staff members of international firms, researchers and consultants, journalists, and members of organizations that represent the interests of business or civil society (NGOs). They will all be helped in preparing strategies, policies and actions by a broad view on and a critical assessment of the factors that shape the effectiveness of global institutional arrangements in the most important socio-economic policy areas.

Structure

To best serve the two groups of readers, the material of the book has been organized and presented in the following manner:

- Individual chapters have been written in such a way that they can be studied without having to go through the complete preceding text.
- The first chapters introduce the basic notions and the format of analysis. This format is rigorously applied in the chapters dealing with the diverse policy areas. It will permit comparisons of the most salient features of the various regimes to be made in the final chapter and relevant conclusions drawn.
- The structure of the individual sections highlights the main features and arguments by presenting them as bullet points. I apply this method to present arguments pro and con, to list relevant characteristics, etc.
- The key findings of each chapter are given in the summary section at the end of the chapter.
- To facilitate access to the material and arguments presented, I have refrained from using mathematics and have written the text in such a way that it can be studied by those with only a basic knowledge of economics.
- For those wishing to make a deeper and more complete study of specific subjects, ample references to more specific literature are given.[1] This comes in the place of a separate section on "further reading" that many textbooks place at the end of each chapter.

ACKNOWLEDGEMENTS

In writing this book I have been supported by many, in particular students and colleagues.

Over the past years my students at Erasmus University, Rotterdam have made many critical comments on earlier versions of the text.

Many colleagues have contributed by discussing the analysis made and the arguments put forward and by critically checking specific parts of the written text, on which they are experts and I am not. I am particularly indebted to two colleagues. First to Alan Winters of Sussex University, who made many suggestions for adapting the draft text of the chapters on trade, development and evaluation. Second to Caspar de Vries of Erasmus University, who scrutinized the draft text of the chapter on financial stability.

I am also grateful to the members of the commission "The shifting balance of economic power" of the Social Economic Advisory Council of the Netherlands, for very stimulating discussions on the changing global context that will shape the future development of the major multilateral institutions.

I thank them all for their contributions to my effort. Their comments have helped me to keep focus, avoid errors, fill gaps, clarify arguments and improve consistency. Of course, I am solely to blame for the remaining shortcomings.

ABBREVIATIONS

ACTA   Anti-Counterfeiting Trade Agreement
ADB   Asian Development Bank
AFTA   ASEAN Free Trade Area
ASEAN   Association of Southeast Asian Nations
BCBS   Basel Committee on Banking Supervision
BIS   Bank of International Settlements
BoG   Board of Governors
CAP   Common Agricultural Policy
CB   central bank
DAC   Development Assistance Committee (of the Organisation for
            Economic Co-operation and Development)
DDA   Doha Development Agenda
DSP   Dispute Settlement Procedure
EB   Executive Board
EBRD   European Bank for Reconstruction and Development
EC   European Commission
ECOWAS   Economic Community of West African States
EDF   European Development Fund
EEC   European Economic Community
EU   European Union
FCCC   Framework Convention on Climate Change
FDI   Foreign Direct Investment
FSB   Financial Stability Board
FTA   free trade agreement
GATS   General Agreement on Trade in Services
GATT   General Agreement on Tariffs and Trade
GB   Governing Body

GDP	gross domestic product
GEF	Global Environment Facility
GPG	global public good
GSP	Generalized System of Preferences
IADB	Inter-American Development Bank
IAIS	International Association of Insurance Supervisors
IASB	International Accounting Standards Board
IATA	International Air Transport Association
IBRD	International Bank for Reconstruction and Development
ICANN	Internet Corporation of Assigned Names and Numbers
ICAO	International Civil Aviation Organization
ICC	International Chamber of Commerce
ICJ	International Court of Justice
IDA	International Development Association
IETF	Internet Engineering Task Force
IGF	Internet Governance Forum
IIA	international investment agreement
ILC	International Labour Conference
ILO	International Labour Organization
IMF	International Monetary Fund
IMO	International Maritime Organization
IO	International Organization
IOSCO	International Organization of Securities Commissions
ITU	International Telecommunications Union
KP	Kyoto Protocol
LDCs	less developed countries
MAC	multilateral agreement on competition
MAI	multilateral agreement on investment
MDGs	Millennium Development Goals
MEA	multilateral environmental agreement
MFN	most favoured nation
MIGA	Multilateral Investment Guarantee Agency
MNF	multinational firm
MTN	multilateral trade negotiation
NAFTA	North American Free Trade Agreement
NGO	non-governmental organization
ODA	Official Development Assistance
OECD	Organisation for Economic Co-operation and Development
OEEC	Organisation for European Economic Co-operation
OPEC	Organization of the Petroleum Exporting Countries
PCD	Policy Coherence for Development
PTA	preferential trade agreement
RTA	regional trade agreement
SAARC	South Asian Association for Regional Cooperation

SADC	Southern African Development Community
S&D	special and differential treatment
SDR	Special Drawing Rights
TRIM	Trade Related Investment Measure
TRIP	Trade-Related Aspects of Intellectual Property
UN	United Nations Educational, Scientific and Cultural Organization
UNCCC	United Nations Convention on Climate Change
UNCED	United Nations Conference on Environment and Development
UNCTAD	United Nations Conference on Trade and Development
UNDP	United Nations Development Programme
UNEP	United Nations Environment Programme
UNESCO	United Nations Educational, Scientific and Cultural Organization
UNFCCC	United Nations Framework Convention on Climate Change
WB	World Bank
WEO	World Environment Organization (proposed)
WTO	World Trade Organization

1

INTRODUCTION

1.1 The need for global economic institutions

1.1.1 Globalization trends

During the past half-century, "globalization" has become a very pervasive tendency. It increasingly involves all parts of the world, including emerging economies such as China and India and many developing countries. It is increasingly invading all segments of business (from manufacturing to logistics, research and development, management, etc.). This growing interconnectedness and fragmentation is largely induced by a considerable decrease in transport cost (both sea and air) and communication costs (mainly because of the Internet).

Many consider that globalization has increased the vulnerability of individual people and whole economies to shocks and decreased the capacity of private and public actors to deal effectively with these. They are looking for solutions.

1.1.2 Private actors

People tend to take it for granted that private international economic transactions can be effected without problems and at low cost. However, the possibility of engaging in such international transactions depends critically on the pre-existence of a number of international institutions – or at least of the effective coordination of relevant national institutions. To illustrate this, we need but mention the rules that govern the electronic payments operations of the international banking system. They permit a businessperson from, say, Brazil to travel to, say, Thailand and pay the expenses involved by using a credit card.

With the increasing complexity of the economy on the one hand and the increase in the *number* of international transactions on the other hand, the need for more specialized international institutions has become apparent. In part, such institutions can be set up and run by the private sector. Banks, for instance, have developed many protocols for efficiently executing transactions among each other. But often the private sector is not best equipped to take on such roles.

1.1.3 Public actors

In modern market economies the state generally assumes the role of setting up institutions that govern transactions. National states provide public goods; these goods will not be produced by the private sector because their use cannot be restricted to those who are prepared to pay for them. Examples are a good legal system, protection against risks (e.g. flooding) and the care for environmental sustainability. However, with increasing integration of national economies the capacity of nations to do this effectively has been eroded. A good example is the reliability and stability of the financial system. The provision of this public good has been realized on the national level by the public setting of standards for access to the trade and the public surveillance of the operations of financial institutions.

But due to the increasing internationalization financial institutions can withdraw from national control by channelling their operations via countries with a lenient surveillance regime. This creates a system risk, because if something goes wrong, the negative effects will be felt in all countries that participate in such financial transactions. So, there is a need for institutions that can provide the public good of financial stability on a higher geographical level. To some extent this can be done on the regional level, where neighbouring countries come together to cope with problems that transcend national competences. A case in point is the European Union. However, the European Union is rather exceptional; there are no other cases where regional integration in financial matters has developed so far. It means that for the effective coping with the provision of international public goods, truly global institutions are needed. For instance, the reliability of the world financial system requires an international institution with a truly global dimension.

1.1.4 International organizations

The combined inadequacies of the private sector and the national public sector to cope with many issues that cross national borders have incited governments to cooperate to come to multilateral agreements. In many cases these have taken the form of international institutions. The first ones to emerge were organizations created to deal with technical problems, such as the International Telegraph Union (created in 1865). After the First World War an attempt was made to come to more encompassing organizations, resulting in the creation of the League of Nations. This organization created several subsidiaries, of which the most significant is the International Labour Organization (see Chapter 9). However, the severe crisis of the 1930s prevented all these initiatives from coming to maturity. It also showed the world the negative sides of protectionism.

After the Second World War, bold and imaginative action was taken to create a number of institutions. Paramount among these is the United Nations, dealing mostly with peace and security. But important organizations were also created to govern the global economy. These include the so-called Bretton Woods organizations – the International Monetary Fund (IMF) and World Bank – and the General Agreement on Tariffs and Trade (GATT), which later developed into the World Trade Organization (WTO).

In the course of the second part of the twentieth century these organizations were gradually adapted to meet new demands, extended their coverage in terms of members and in many cases strengthened their governance methods. New organizations have been created when major new needs have become apparent, for instance in matters of environmental protection. However, this setting up of multilateral formal institutions with a remit very much inspired by Western norms has come under stress in recent years.

1.2 Recent shifts in conditions

1.2.1 For global governance in general

During the past decade the global economy has gone through a very severe crisis. Moreover, major new players have come to the fore. Consequently, there have been profound shifts in the way major players seek to cope with global economic problems, putting much strain on the governance of the global socio-economic system. The most salient features are shifts in:

- *The relation between regulation and liberalization.* In recent decades the dominant paradigm has been the retreat of the public sector under the influence of what many call market fundamentalism. However, this has shown its negative side: a case in point is the financial sector where inadequate regulation in some developed countries has resulted in the financial crisis that began around 2008. It has, in turn, led to a considerable increase in the total government debt with considerable negative impact on tax payers. This case has revealed the inappropriateness of this paradigm even to its former believers.
- *The relation between public and private.* In the past the dominant private players in the international economic game were multinational firms based in Western countries. The major trade regimes have all been designed to preserve fair competition between such firms on national and international markets. In many emerging economies, publicly owned enterprises have a considerable share in the economy. They are very strong in countries such as China, and play an increasing role in the international strategies of their governments. This does endanger fair competition on the global level. Moreover, sovereign wealth funds have shown that they are capable of influencing international relations very considerably; geopolitical considerations in those cases may overtake the present rules of the game.

- *The relation between multilateral and national.* The number of relevant players has increased. In the past the United States and the European Union dominated the scene; now, a large group of emerging economies (mainly the BRICS countries)[1] have taken their place in world governance, and many others, including the major developing countries, are claiming their place. With that extension of the number, the diversity of interests of the relevant players has greatly increased. It means that the difficulty of reaching agreement in multilateral negotiations has increased and that future progress is likely to be slow.
- *The relation between formal and informal.* The model of the second half of the twentieth century was based on a firm belief in the advantages of formal institutions – organizations with clear written constitutions and rules. The practice of recent decades has shown that in many areas established formal organizations may show signs of fossilization: they no longer adapt to new consumer needs, technical possibilities and power balances. So, to avoid ill-adapted institutions there has been a move away from formal institutions towards more flexible and informal forms, such as customer-based light organizations (e.g. the Internet), informal gatherings of government leaders (e.g. the G20) or cooperation in networks of both public and private actors (e.g. in the environment).

The architecture of global institutions responsible for delivering public goods has to take all these factors into account in order to be able to cope with the challenges of increasing international exchange in an increasingly complex world.

1.2.2 For specific regimes in particular

The factors discussed in the previous section were of a general character and affect all types of international institutions. In addition to these, a number of major changes can be observed in the conditions for further development of global regimes in specific fields:

- *Trade, investment and production.* For centuries the global situation was characterized by an economic epicentre in the few developed countries in the North Atlantic area. In the past decades this dominance has been eroded. The share of the new emerging countries and many developing countries in total trade and foreign direct investment has considerably increased. We can illustrate this with foreign direct investment (FDI) figures for both origin and destination. While incoming FDI used to be concentrated on developed countries, by 2010 more than half of total FDI went to developing and emerging market countries. A similar development holds for outgoing FDI: emerging countries have started to invest massively in developing and developed countries alike.
- *Financial services.* The vulnerability of the financial institutional system has increased, owing to a lack of transparency of the exposure of individual insti-

tutions to a multitude of risks. Moreover, owing to the lack of quality surveillance, private debt and risk have become public debt and risk as governments had to intervene in order to avoid a collapse of the system. The financial crisis has contributed to the shift in economic dominance. Indeed, it has hit in particular the most developed parts of the world, namely the United States and the European Union. In terms of *financial stability* the origins of the recent crisis have not been in the developing world but in the developed world. Indeed the crisis sparked off in the United States, the centre of the global financial system, which until recently even refused any IMF surveillance. Moreover, in Europe, where weaknesses of the financial sector (Spain) or the public sector (Greece) have resulted in near sovereign default of these countries. This shows that past patterns have been revolutionized.

- For *development aid* a fundamental change in tendencies can be observed. Traditionally, the developed world underwent high growth, while the growth in developing countries tended to be inhibited by a multitude of factors. In the past, this trend led to an increase in disparity. In recent decades, however, this tendency has been reversed: growth in many developing countries is now very high, while growth in the developed world has tended to stagnate. The result is a considerable reduction of poverty and a lower disparity in world incomes. The diversity of national situations is thus tending to make obsolete the traditional development aid in terms of objective (0.7 per cent of GDP of the rich countries) and methods (traditional standard Western). Completely new forms of world solidarity and mutual support for balanced national and global growth will have to be worked out.
- *Resources.* The very high economic growth coupled with demographic growth of many emerging and developing countries leads to increasing pressure on existing scarce resources (clean air, water, materials and food). Climate change means that weather conditions are becoming more and more unpredictable, leading to increasing costs in coping with droughts, floods, hurricanes, etc. Considering the combined effects of scarcity in resources, geopolitics and climate change, one may foresee sudden disruptions of supply, leading to high inflation and unemployment. So, preservation of the environment and sustainable development are becoming more and more urgent.
- *Employment and social aspects of development.* With increasing wealth levels in many countries of the world, there is also increasing demand regarding the qualitative aspects of work and for the solidarity aspects of workers' protection.

This shows that past patterns have been revolutionized in all these segments of global governance and that there are major challenges that demand new answers.

1.3 Objectives and structure of this book

1.3.1 Objectives

The problems that have been described in the previous sections have been the object of many studies. This literature refers to a very large variety of theoretical notions, uses a panoply of often largely overlapping definitions, often goes into great detail and is often sector-specific. In other words, for most readers with a general interest in the subject it is not adequate. The present book seeks to fill the gap.

Its *objective* is to present solutions to the problems of world governance on the basis of the results of theoretical and empirical analysis. It sets out to clarify issues, to present a clear structure and to adopt a common approach for all areas of economic, environmental and social policy. It acknowledges different views. It substantiates the positions presented by referring to authoritative studies made into the subject. Where relevant, it does not hide many persistent uncertainties. It takes a comprehensive view of economic prosperity, covering not only growth of incomes and productivity (mainly through better allocation and stabilization) but also issues such as fair distribution of income (solidarity by development aid), a good quality of life (environmental sustainability) and social progress (decent work). So, the book presents a framework for thinking about global governance issues and their application to different socio-economic policy fields.

This book thus has as its *focus* three main features of the global governance system. It will:

1. introduce the fundamental factors that shape institutions, concentrating on adaptation to changes in their environment (in other words, the book focuses on the rationale and dynamics of global institutions);
2. describe the way in which the major global economic institutions function – in particular, the governance methods they use to deliver public goods effectively;
3. discuss proposals for changes in the total system design so as to cope better with present inadequacies and future challenges.

1.3.2 Structure

The structure of the book (see Figure 1.1) follows closely the three focus points just presented.

Part I of the book deals with the *development of the socio-economic institutions in a global context*. This part provides the main toolkit with which I analyse the specific problems set out in Part II.

I start (in Chapter 2) by showing that globalization affects negatively the ability of national states to influence policy outcomes. There is a growing need for global institutions to recover collectively what has been lost individually. Next we turn our attention to the solutions that need to be found for such problems. To that

Part	Chapter	Subject
I		DEFINING PROBLEMS AND SEARCHING FOR SOLUTIONS
	2	– Creating institutions to deliver global public goods
	3	– International organizations
	4	– Governance and compliance: methods and instruments
II	5–9	IMPLEMENTING SOLUTIONS (PRACTICE)
III		COPING WITH INSUFFICIENCIES
	10	– Complements
	11	– Evaluation and outlook
	12	– Outlook

In Part II row, boxes: Trade, Finance, Etc., Labour; Social protection

FIGURE 1.1 Map of the book's content.

end, I define the main product that the global economic institutions deliver, namely a global public good. I shall show how problems of collective action lead on the one hand to the creation of a set of specialist agencies, each of them coping with a specific problem. On the other hand they lead to the creation of institutions with a limited number of members (clubs). Moreover, I define in this chapter different types of institutions and discuss their dynamics (the main factors that determine their development).

In Chapter 3 I define the concept of international organizations. Moreover, I briefly describe the architecture of the system of international organizations as a whole. I subsequently present the specialist organizations that are part of the UN system and have worldwide coverage. Next, I present the organizations that have more of a club character, in particular the G20 and the Organisation for Economic Co-operation and Development (OECD). Next, I deal briefly with regional institutions; these mostly concern trade. To make the picture complete, we examine the global organizations of private business and of non-governmental organizations.

Finally (in Chapter 4), we examine the ways in which international organizations can put their policies into effect. That is, I demonstrate the toolkit of instruments that are in principle available for making national governments and private actors comply with international rules. In the same chapter I define some basic concepts that make it possible to check the effectiveness of the actions of international institutions.

In Part II of the book we go into *the structure and functioning of the global system of economic regimes*. I devote a separate chapter to each of the most important economic problems the world is confronted with. Individual chapters present the main features of the development of an important regime, such as trade, finance and the environment. Each chapter has a similar structure in five sections. The first is on the causes of the problem and its remedies. The next section covers such aspects as the sort of public good that needs to be provided in order to cope with the problems. Here I also define the basic objectives that are to be pursued. The third section is on the emergence of the organizations that have to make sure that this good is provided. The fourth section covers aspects of the toolkit of instruments of the most important of these organizations. A final section gives an evaluation of the past performance (achievements), the inadequacies of the present and suggestions for the future improvements of this specific regime.

This set-up can be illustrated by the international financial and monetary system. The main problem here is monetary instability leading to recurrent crises. So, the world is in need of stability, defined as the possibility of avoiding crises and of solving them if they do occur. Several organizations, such as the OECD and the G20, assume some responsibilities in this respect. However, the main responsibility has been entrusted to the International Monetary Fund (IMF). It uses surveillance techniques to prevent crises and gives loans to countries that are victims of crises. Both roles have been strengthened to cope with the considerable problems major countries are now confronted with due to the crisis.

Part III contains a discussion of *essential complements of the present system* and a *general evaluation* of the results of the analyses presented in the previous chapters and an *outlook to the future*.

The first chapter of this part of the book (Chapter 10) presents some initiatives that have been taken to construct the missing links in the system. These mainly concern regimes for production factors (capital/investment and labour/migration) and for market order (competition). We also discuss here the Internet, where an increasing number of transactions of all sorts take place.

The second chapter (Chapter 11) is devoted to a broad-ranging evaluation of the dynamics of the global institutional system. In that chapter I make critical assessments of each of the major elements of our analytical format: problem, public good, organization, governance method, results. This comparative analysis shows that the "system" is inadequate for dealing with a number of important problems.

To round off I discuss, in the final chapter, proposals for future change of the system as a whole, taking into account the discussions about the improvements of individual regimes. Contrary to the previous chapters that were all firmly based on the results of theoretical and empirical studies, this chapter has a much more speculative character.

1.4 Main results

On the basis of the analyses made in the various chapters of this book, I arrive at the following major conclusions:

- Notwithstanding constant adaptations of the present international organizations to new challenges, the present situation is not adequate.
- This is the case for organizations taken individually with respect to their specific field of competence. On many points they do not respond adequately to present needs.
- It is also the case for the organizations taken collectively, as they do not provide a consistent and comprehensive world government; they are a patchwork, not a system.
- Improvements will be very difficult to realize. Theoretical arguments and historical examples show that change is inhibited by many factors. Given the changes discussed in section 1.2, we may not expect new large-scale multilateral agreements to emerge, but the future will probably be marked by the development of a multitude of small-scale and partial arrangements of a very diverse nature.

PART I

Defining problems and searching for solutions

2

CREATING INSTITUTIONS TO DELIVER GLOBAL PUBLIC GOODS

2.1 Introduction

Fundamental forces, such as technological change, drive globalization. It implies an increased interdependence of the national economies and causes a decreased capacity of national governments to deal with problems. Indeed due to global-ization they have lost a number of their instruments while some of their remaining instruments have lost their effectiveness. In the next section we describe these phenomena and argue that to recover collectively what has been lost individually national governments have to create international institutions.

International institutions have the objective to cope with global problems, or in other words to deliver global public goods. We will continue the analysis of this chapter by presenting the specific characteristics of public goods in comparison with other types of goods.

The creation of institutions that are capable of delivering public goods effectively is not easy. So, we will analyse questions such as who should take action, what would motivate actors, what forms of action are likely to be chosen, etc. Essential here is the collective character of the action. To gain a better understanding of this aspect I describe the logic of group formation, the way groups tend to be formed and the most likely outcomes: the formation of groups of limited size and of specialist nature.

Institutions have to be better defined in order to arrive at operational concepts. In the fourth main section I present a layered view of institutions; I deal in particular with the basic principles and governance (here used in the sense of implementation of policies).

The most general form in which institutions appear is generally called a regime. I define in the final section the rationale, the forms, the dynamics and the com-pliance mechanisms of regimes.

I round off the chapter with a short summary of the main findings.

2.2 Globalization of the economy demands international institutions

2.2.1 Globalization

Globalization is the gradual evolution of the cross-border activities of economic actors that span the globe. These activities encompass mostly those of three categories of players.

Firms' involvement in globalization mostly concerns international trade in goods and services and investment in production in other countries. It also concerns international collaboration for the purpose of product development, production, sourcing, transporting, financing and marketing. For example, the management of a Canadian shoe firm makes a direct investment by opening a production site in the Philippines, or an international bank allows a Japanese salesman to pay for car rental in Argentina by credit card.

Individual persons migrate internationally to seek better living conditions. They diversify their investments internationally in order to seek higher returns. They spread their consumption internationally, for instance by long-distance tourism. For example, an Afghan intellectual migrates to the European Union as a refugee, or a French student uses the Internet to buy a specialist book she needs for her thesis while studying in the United States.

Non-governmental organizations articulate the needs of the civil society. They have traditionally done so on a national level. However, as problems in one country impact increasingly on the life of citizens in other countries, NGOs have internationalized. A case in point is climate change. The global dimension of such problems has meant that environmental NGOs have organized themselves on an international scale and act accordingly.

People tend to take it for granted that private international economic transactions can be carried out without problems and at low cost. However, this is far from self-evident. The possibility of engaging in such transactions depends critically on the pre-existence of a number of international institutions – or at least on the effective coordination of relevant national institutions. So, an international sales agreement between, for instance, a Chinese subsidiary of a European manufacturer implies, minimally, a set of common notions of property and contract. With the increase in technological possibilities, the complexity of the economy and the number of international transactions, the need for better and, often, more specialized international institutions has become apparent. To illustrate this, it is only necessary to mention the rules that govern the electronic payments operations of the international banking system or the rules that govern the use of trade measures such as import duties, export subsidies, etc.

2.2.2 Technology: very long-term decrease in distance cost

Over time, globalization has increased considerably. There are many factors that have contributed to this increase. However, the major one has been the development of technology. Indeed, major innovations in technology have led to an explosion of productivity and to a considerable reduction in transport and communication costs.

Productivity was influenced by the main inventions that characterized the industrial revolution: the steam engine and the mechanization of production. Later there followed the development of automation. Energy efficiency has played a major role here (compare the switch from coal to oil and electricity). The structure of production has also changed fundamentally from agriculture via manufacturing to information. In order to reap the ensuing economies of scale, production in large series became necessary. This required in turn large markets. Where national markets were too small, the opening up of foreign markets became imperative.

The *decrease in transport costs* over time has been very significant. Present transport costs are only a fraction of what they used to be only a few decades ago. Thus, the quality of the services that are delivered by the transport sector has increased considerably over time. For passenger transport, one need but think of the increase in frequency of passenger flights and the comfort of the modern jet aircraft compared to the old propeller plane. For transport of goods we mention the far greater reliability and speed of modern container transport compared to that in traditional general cargo ships.

The cost of *information* and communication has also shown a decreasing long-term trend. The cost of a unit of computing power fell by 99 per cent between 1960 and 1990. Access to the Internet has reduced the cost of information dramatically. This has made it possible to offer a whole range of new services and to increase considerably the quality of the service (compare, for instance, the old-fashioned telegraph with the new broadband access to the Internet via smartphones).

Increasing costs of research and development and increasing economies of scale for production and marketing (brand names) are factors pushing towards a larger scale. Globalization permits firms to recover their costs on volumes of sale extending far beyond the size of even large national markets. The decrease in the cost of transport and the liberalization of international transactions have permitted the spatial split of different stages in the production process and a split between production and consumption. The recent revolution in the information processing and telecommunications sector has reinforced this tendency, as it has made it possible to extend the capacities of management to coordinate complex international production and marketing systems.

All this has contributed to the very high growth in the volumes of trade, direct investment, financial transactions, etc.

2.2.3 System competition

So, due to the factors described in the previous section national governments have to face an increasingly *international business community* that is less and less inclined to adapt to a multitude of specific national rules. Multinational firms have the capacity to choose among several countries where to locate their economic activity. They will choose their location on the basis of a set of criteria. Among these are cost considerations. National regimes concerning labour market regulation, taxes, the environment, etc. influence these costs, and hence location.

Investors that do not like the national regime they have to comply with can remove themselves from this regime by turning to some other location. So, there will be competition between countries. It will induce governments to comply with investors' wishes by adapting national institutions, regimes and policies. This may have considerable welfare effects. Some of them may be felt as neutral – for instance, the switch to a new set of technical standards. Other aspects are felt as negative – for instance, the lowering of labour or environmental standards. But standards are only one aspect of the whole system, in which social security, innovation, dispute settlement, competition, taxes, infrastructure, etc. all have their place. Good governance in all these fields is essential to attract multinational firms (MNFs). However, it is also needed to allow indigenous firms to flourish.

2.2.4 Loss of effective policy instruments

To give effect to their policies, governments use several instruments, including regulation and financial means. Globalization restricts the range of instruments available. This applies to several segments of policy-making. The most obvious one is trade policy: to provide MNFs with an open regime, governments have given up the use of many *trade instruments*. Monetary policy is another case in point: under integrated financial markets, most countries lack the resources to shelter from the effects of a crisis (e.g. by introducing capital controls). In this way, globalization has increased the vulnerability of national states (in particular, small, open developing economies) to external shocks.

This loss of intervention capacity due to internationalization is reinforced by a tendency towards *denationalization and privatization*. Examples of the first are monetary instruments that are now in the hands of independent national central banks. Examples of the second are telecom and energy markets that have been liberalized, with the result that many possibilities of government leverage have now vanished.

Although many see this loss of intervention capacity as a problem, one has to see the extent to which this is indeed a problem in economic terms. To answer that question one has to check first how economically efficient the forgone national regulations were. If the result of the check is positive (meaning that regulation reflected the basic preferences in society, for instance maintaining a balanced social security system), the loss of that regulation may imply a welfare loss. However, if the regulation reflected only the interests of special groups of rent seekers who wished to protect their privileged situations (for instance, trade unions having obtained high salaries for workers in sheltered industries), deregulation may actually have a positive welfare result.

2.2.5 The new role for national governments and international institutions

In the light of the challenges of globalization, governments need to find new ways to devise their internal institutions and their participation in international institutions. In the past, there was an important strand of thought that wanted to solve this loss of national governance power by curbing the international activities of the private sector. However, all unilateral measures to separate the national economy from the world economy do imply loss of benefits in terms of economic growth. Moreover, the effectiveness of this "go-it-alone" approach is likely to be limited, as a single country would have to make bilateral deals with a variety of partners. To do so would be practically impossible, so the present conditions oblige national governments to be open to the world economy and to orient their efforts towards the improvement of international competitiveness. This implies action both on the national and international level.

On the *national level* governments have to organize efficient product and service markets, sufficiently flexible labour markets, equitable income redistribution, stable macroeconomic and monetary conditions, adequate social standards, reliable institutions and good governance.

On the *international level*, institutions have to be created to cope with problems that can no longer be effectively dealt with nationally (Molle 2008a). In this way, governments can recover collectively what they have lost individually in matters of effective economic governance. In general, this is done with one of the following objectives:

- To improve the positive effects of globalized economic activity by setting the rules of the game. This takes away much uncertainty and conflict. An example is the regulating of trade and settling of trade disputes by the World Trade Organization.
- To reduce the negative effects. This can be done by either prevention (e.g. the setting of emission standards for preventing further global warming) or cure (e.g. alleviating poverty by development aid from the World Bank).

2.3 Global public goods

2.3.1 A general scheme

International institutions also supply a number of *global public goods*. Global public goods (GPGs) are a specific case of public goods. To define them, I will first of all define public goods in general. This can best be done by comparing them to the characteristics of other types of goods (see Table 2.1). In the two top rows I present the two key criteria for distinguishing categories of goods. In the next layer I specify the way the use is organized (allocation or rationing), while finally in the bottom layer I indicate the order by which the supply and demand decisions are taken. We

TABLE 2.1 Types of property and conditions of provision and allocation

Type/characteristics	Private	Common	Club	Public
Excludable	Yes	No	Yes	No
Rivalrous	Yes	Yes	No	No
Provision (supply)	Private (autonomous)	Collective resources	Collective resources	Public funds
Allocation (demand)	Private (autonomous)	Internal rules	Internal rules	Rules, price subsidies

Source: Adapted from Kasper and Streit (1998, p. 180).

will go in more detail into the various aspects of each of the rows of this scheme in the following sections.

2.3.2 The criteria for making a typology

Differences in rivalry and excludability determine the various categories of goods. I shall define briefly the categories given in each of the columns of Table 2.1 and place them in an international context.

The *private good* is the most complete expression of property. It can be traded on markets. The owner can sell it to somebody else; this transaction implies that the buyer becomes owner and that the seller receives money in return. Ownership implies that the use of the private good can be exclusively restricted to the owner. Another aspect is rivalry: if the owner uses the good (e.g. consumption of petrol in his or her car), somebody else cannot. With the growth of the global economy, ever more goods are exchanged on the international scale.

The concept of *public good* is just the opposite. Here we see that the consumption of the good is non-rivalrous, in that consumers cannot be excluded from its use. Decisions on the production and allocation are made by public choice. Let us take the example of peace. Suppose the security of a country is protected externally by its army and internally by its police force. The state of security that results from it is a public good. It is non-excludable, as every citizen will enjoy its advantages. Moreover, it is non-rivalrous in the sense that the use of it by citizens living in a border area does not in any way affect the benefits for the citizens living in a central area.

Public goods can be provided at different levels. Traditionally, the *nation-state* has taken responsibility for the supply and sometimes also for the production of such goods. A good example is the reliability and stability of the financial system. The production of this good is realized on the national level by the public setting of standards for access to the financial services trade (e.g. banking) and the public surveillance of the operations of financial institutions.

The increasing openness and complexity of international relations mean that an increasing number of public goods have to be defined on the *global level*. The definition of a global public good specifies the three words that compose the notion.[1] The element "global" causes means that major parts of the world are concerned.[2] The element "public" is fairly well defined as opposite to the other types in the table. The word "good" is often defined with respect to its opposite; the absence of solutions for the problems cited may produce a global *public "bad"*. For example, a stable financial and monetary order on the global level, can be considered as a public good, as any country or economic actor can benefit from it without its being depleted. This example shows that global public goods will often have a systemic character.

Common pool resources are property that is available to multiple users (maybe rivals) who cannot be excluded from use. A case in point is the use of common grasslands, where every member of a village community can herd his or her sheep. The problem is that common goods are subject to depletion (commons) or to congestion (urban roads). On the international level[3] we can define the stock of natural resources as a global common. All nations can use this stock (an example is clean air). The problem with the use of the commons is that it is in everyone's private interest to maximize its use, yet collectively this behaviour leads to a situation where the stock of clean air is depleted.

Club goods are excludable in the sense that non-members of the club have no access to them; an example is the use of a tennis court. If sufficient facilities are available, the use of the court is largely non-rivalrous. If not, there will be a problem of congestion. Decisions about provision and use are taken by the club. An international club good will occur where a limited number of governments get together to solve a problem. A case in point here is the International Energy Agency, which was created in the mid-1970s by the major oil-importing countries with the objective of safeguarding the provision with oil to all members in the event of politically determined limitations in supply by the oil-producing countries.

Common pool, club and public goods together form a category that is often labelled *collective goods* because their provision and allocation demand some sort of collective action – that is, action by groups of individuals, states or other private or public organizations (see further section 2.4).

2.3.3 The production/supply side

The organization of the production of the various types of good is quite different (see the penultimate row of Table 2.1). This can be illustrated as follows:

- *Private*. Each private party decides autonomously how he or she will use resources to make sure the good is produced. If this is to be on a relatively large scale, firms are usually no longer owned by individuals but become incorporated.
- *Public good*. Supply of the good is done by the public sector. The mobilization of the funds needed is a problem in itself (taxation). The logical corollary of non-excludability is compulsory membership. Society at large will then decide

on an equitable way of burden-sharing. In some cases (see hereafter) the conditions are such that public goods are not only provided but also produced by the public sector. In other cases the private sector may be asked to take part in the production under contract from the public sector.

- *Common.* Supply is by nature (e.g. grass on common pastures). Often the maintenance of such commons comes at a cost; here we see that the limited group that is entitled to the use of the commons has to put up collectively the necessary funds.
- *Club.* Supply is made possible by the mobilization of group funds. The way in which these resources are mobilized will depend on the type of club. Some sort of members' contribution system is elaborated, often in line with the objective of the club and the use members make of the club good.

The production of all types of good is the result of the cooperation of many actors, both private and public. On the one hand, private goods can only be efficiently produced in the event that public goods are provided. An example here is the legal and adjudication system that is needed for arbitration and settlement in disputes of private parties. So, the provision of public goods is a prerequisite for efficient production of private goods. On the other hand, public (and club and common goods) can only be efficiently produced with the help of the private sector. Indeed, all three may use the possibilities of procurement with private suppliers to increase efficiency. That means that they buy private goods on the market (e.g. military equipment for defence, or laboratory equipment for scientific research).

2.3.4 The allocation/use side

The categorization of the various goods made in the previous subsections has a significant bearing on the way in which the use is organized (see the bottom row of Table 2.1). This has a particular importance on the global level.

- *Private.* A private actor is completely free to decide on the use he or she thinks fit. The actor will use markets to come to transactions such as sales and hire. The same applies to the international level, where firms enter into contracts with each other and establish international firms to facilitate operations.
- *Public.* For a pure public good, there is no rationing of demand. The defence system of a country provides security that can be used by everyone without problems to others. The global public good of climate stability will be available for everybody, irrespective of the use they make of it. In cases where government agencies provide the public good (e.g. fire brigades), access to use is regulated by collective choice and political processes. On the international level we do not yet observe rules of this type being worked out.
- *Common.* Use is regulated by internal procedures; these are often of a traditional type. The rules of the use of the global commons have to be determined by the

collective action of national governments. Many cases can be given of international institutions created for that purpose.[4] Often the problem is attacked by partly transforming global common goods into "private" or "club" goods: a case in point is the allocation of sea resources to coastal states in a zone of 200 miles.

- *Club.* Here some sort of rule is set by internal institutions to avoid problems. To illustrate this, one can cite the "first come, first use" rule for the use of a court by members of a tennis club. To take an example on the international level, the International Energy Agency has worked out rules to distribute the available oil over each participating country in the event of supply disruption.

2.4 Collective action

2.4.1 Which actors?

Global public goods (GPGs) demand action by national governments. They have to deal with the problems back home, are aware of the limitations regarding the action that can be taken and have the necessary legitimacy to act on the international as well as the domestic level. However, collective action by governments has to involve other actors, mainly NGOs and private business. This leads to complicated two-level games. On the national level, governments have a negotiation interface for the definition of their negotiating position in international fora and for the acceptance of the ensuing international agreement. On the international level, governments negotiate with their partners to come to an agreement. These international intergovernmental negotiations are often paralleled by negotiations between national NGOs and MNFs and their international umbrella organizations.

2.4.2 What objectives?

The second problem of collective action is the uncertainty as to the objective to be reached. In many instances the participants can agree on objectives on a very high level of abstraction. However, the more the formulation of those GPGs is done in specific terms the more controversy occurs. Moreover, complications arise as the actors will not limit the negotiation to formulate objectives and design the type of institution to deliver it. On the contrary, many negotiators have strong views about the type of instruments that the new institution should have at its disposal to deliver the public goods effectively. Diverging preferences on these scores often complicate the coming to agreement.

The whole idea that international organizations are created for the provision of public goods and that they operate in the "public interest" has been criticized by the Public Choice school as a normative theory. This school's adherents view the actions of international institutions as collusions of national governments against majorities in their own countries made possible because the voters have very high information cost. They moreover suggest that there is a big risk that the actions of international organizations will become subservient to the interests of big international pressure groups (such as MNFs) because for the latter the lobbying costs have decreased. Finally, it has been suggested that the risk that bureaucrats will pursue their own objectives of budget maximization and effort minimization applies a fortiori to international institutions (see, for example, Fratianni and Pattison 1982; Frey 1984; Vaubel 1986).

These factors have certainly played a role in the emergence and evolution of a number of international organizations (IOs). However, this book will consider that although these phenomena are distortions of the basic picture, they do not alter it fundamentally. So, we will continue to work with the notion that international organizations are formed to pursue a clear objective, one that can be formulated in terms of public goods.

2.4.3 What ambition level?

The basic hypothesis for the analysis of the formation of collective action groups is that the members have each concluded that it is in their interest to form coalitions to bring about change. In other words, they have done their cost–benefit analysis of different options and they will negotiate with those interests in mind. However, in a considerable number of cases the situation is not so clear-cut. We live in a world of great complexity and we frequently have to take decisions without being able to judge either the conditions that will prevail in future or the real costs and benefits of different options. This creates the problem of bounded rationality[5].

Negotiations between the different actors will then tend to lead to a result where a number of actors will agree while they are convinced that the cost–benefit relation for them is positive. Now, it may be that this group is limited and that the benefits for that group would be much larger if others agreed as well. This is, for instance, the case for trade liberalization and for action against global warming. The question then comes up: what could be done to rebalance the cost–benefit situation for the countries that are hesitant or unwilling to participate? We can illustrate this with a game in trade matters. Often a blockage in negotiations may be related to a special interest group. Now, the granting of a specific derogation to liberalization to a country that hesitates might come at a small cost to the core group yet permit large benefits to be reaped for all. This makes it possible for a deal to be made at a higher ambition level for overall tariff cuts thanks to a series of exceptions for special cases for products and countries.

The outcome of such a deal may be *optimized further* by:

- stipulating that the derogation has a *temporary* character and will expire automatically after some pre-fixed period sufficient for the country that has obtained the derogation to restructure its economy;
- accepting *discrimination*: this may result in different ambition levels for different types of countries (e.g. emission reduction targets under the climate change agreement; see Chapter 8);

- determining clearly the *quantitative size* of the specific case at hand; in such a way the occurrence of further distortions can be avoided;
- specifying the instruments that may be used to effectuate the agreed exception, e.g. in trade matters a higher tariff or a quantitative restriction (see Chapter 5);
- *making side payments*: by providing advantages on other scores (e.g. see Chapter 7, "Development aid"), the benefit:cost ratio for hesitating countries can be improved.

2.4.4 Trust in partners?

One of the problems with international agreements is that they can rarely be fully specified. As was explained in section 2.3, the problem with global collective goods is that, once provided, there is no possibility of excluding those who have not participated in their creation. This will lead some countries to adopt an attitude of waiting to see whether others will take the burden for the collective action.

This free rider risk persists even among parties to an agreement. A case in point may be the *mutual obligation of countries to invest in pollution abatement*. Imagine that one party to an agreement has made an early start and fulfilled its part of the contract by adapting its power stations and by obliging its industry to limit emissions by investing in clean technology. The other country can then choose to do nothing; it thereby limits its investment cost and increases its competitiveness because it has lower production cost and it benefits from a cleaner environment. The risk of a partner adopting such an attitude may prevent a country that is willing to comply with the obligations from taking action. Such distrust may prevent many such cooperative deals from materializing at all.

2.5 The likely results of collective action

2.5.1 GPG-specific solutions

In basic theory collective action follows very clear rational and economic rules (Olson 1965).[6] Actors calculate whether the benefit:cost ratio of his or her efforts will be positive or not for him or her. If it is positive, that actor has an interest in participating in a collective action. The first step, then, is to identify partners for whom a similar positive benefit:cost ratio is likely to prevail. The next step is to define the common interest and to convince other potential partners that they stand to gain by cooperating to realize that common interest. All this involves cost to those engaging in collective action. Now, the chances that such costs will be accepted by partners and hence that a collective action will be successfully organized is higher (1) the clearer the benefit to the group, (2) the smaller the cost of group formation, and (3) the more equitable the distribution of cost and benefits over partners.

Unfortunately these conditions rarely obtain. For many public goods there is an imbalance between the potential benefits and the cost of collective action for individual partners. Indeed, if the cost of action is high compared to the benefit for an individual actor, there will be very little incentive to start a collective action. This problem of inertia is bigger under a number of conditions. One is a case in which the positive effects are likely to take a long time to materialize. Another is a case where there is a high degree of uncertainty as to the likely distribution of the benefits.

One basic consequence of these complications is *high specificity of international agreements*. An international agreement leading to the set-up of an institution charged with the provision of a global public good will only come about in those cases where the constellation is favourable: that means agreement on clear objectives and clear net advantages for major players. Now, because the basic interests, the relevant cost:benefit ratios and the distributional consequences are very different from one GPG to another, actors tend to negotiate for each good separately. As a consequence a wide diversity of coexisting specialist global institutions has emerged.

The advantage of this situation is that tailor made solutions can be found for specific problems. However there are also disadvantages. One is the lack of consistency between interrelated subjects dealt with in separate organizations (see Chapter 11). Another is the danger that the institution will be *captured by special interest groups*, often consisting of powerful firms. Notably, organizations that make extensive use of the governance methods of regulation and finance (see Chapter 4 for definitions) are at risk. Cases in point are the World Trade Organization (WTO) for trade, the International Monetary Fund (IMF) for financial stability and the World Bank for development. Leaving technocrats under the influence of business to deal with issues without adequate public oversight can lead to very problematic situations creating considerable welfare losses (Mattli and Woods 2009).

2.5.2 Clubs are trumps!

The next question that has to be considered is *how many parties* will be involved in the negotiations and are likely to become signatories to the agreement.[7] A limited number is likely to be the most common case (see Eden and Hampson 1997). A small group can more easily define a common interest, while the cost of getting organized can be kept within limits. Moreover, a small group has more possibilities of coercion during the process of negotiation and of compliance once the agreement is concluded.

Notably, if the costs and benefits are not clear for each potential signatory, it is not a good strategy to involve them all right from the start. In these cases a small (vanguard) group of influential countries that have a very strong interest in results will shape the agreement. They will not run the risk that the extension of the number will lead to a weaker and more ambiguous commitment, and they will accept that a number of countries will be free-riding on the benefits of their efforts. Moreover, the marginal cost and benefit of one more country joining the group may be small. Countries that see a benefit in joining will do so afterwards.

In some cases, where collective action proves difficult even for a small group, the stalemate can be broken by the determined action of a single major player for whom the reward would be sufficient to pay the cost. Such actions then change the cost–benefit conditions for the other players, who may then be more inclined to join their efforts too. Examples of a hegemony that weighs very heavily on the willingness of others to participate are very common (Eggertsson 1990: 312–314).

The dynamics of club formation may lead to outcomes for the whole world that are at odds with the principles of fairness or equity. Indeed, a small but powerful action group that knows how to define and articulate its views may define the public good in terms of its own interest. Now, a larger group may very well have a more important interest, but as it cannot come to collective action, it will see its wider interest being subordinated to that of the small group. Consider, for instance, a situation in the world where a small group has set the rules of a regime in its favour. As setting up an alternative organization is not feasible, others will tend to adhere to such a regime (notwithstanding the fact that to them it is only second best) in order to grasp at least part of the benefits that an international regime provides. A case in point is the membership by less developed countries (LDCs) in the WTO and the IMF. LDCs complain that the rules of these bodies, which have been set by the most developed countries, are in the interest of firms in the developed countries and are not conducive to poverty reduction and balanced growth in the developing countries. The articulation and defence of such wider interest is often taken up by NGOs, a fact that justifies their funding from public sources and by charities and foundations.

The consequence of this preference for clubs is that in many cases regime formation follows the route of *regionalism* rather than globalism (examples include the European Union and the North American Free Trade Agreement). Such regional agreements have the advantage of providing public (club) goods to part of the world and so are better than nothing. Moreover, they serve as pilots for global solutions that may emerge at a later stage.

2.5.3 Large groups: difficult but feasible

Getting collective action going is difficult in cases when there is no close relation between the users and the providers of the good. This will lead to a problem of undersupply of collective goods. On the national level the standard solution to this problem is production by the public sector and cost-sharing by taxation. This can easily be done because over the centuries countries have developed elaborate institutions with strong coercive powers. However, on the global level the *supply problem* is quite different from the one at the national level. On the global level there is no structure like a sovereign state. So, a new organization (or a set of new organizations) has to be created. Here all the problems of collective action involving very many governments come up. Hence the following prediction:

> The larger the group the farther it will fall short of providing an optimal supply of a collective good, and very large groups normally will not, in the absence of coercion of separate, outside incentives, provide themselves with even minimal amounts of a collective good.
>
> *(Olson 1965: 48)*

The picture may be different if the provision of a new GPG can be entrusted to an organization that already exists. In this case the cost of organizing collective action is decreasing as there is a framework in which negotiations can be done and there will be less uncertainty as to the cost benefit relation and the position of potential partners. An example of such a situation in daily life is an automobile association that was set up to provide support in the event of mechanical problems but has started selling insurance and providing tourist bookings to its members. An example in the case of international institutions is the WTO, which was created to decrease tariffs on industrial goods but over time has assumed new tasks in trade policy matters relating to services and intellectual property.

2.6 Factors of change for institutions at different layers[8]

2.6.1 Some definitions

There is much confusion as to the definition of "institution". Various authors use the word to mean different things and use different words to mean similar things. I have selected here the definition that is used by one of the most influential authors in this respect: "Institutions are defined as the humanly devised constraints that structure political, economic and social interactions. They consist of both informal constraints (sanctions, taboos, customs, traditions, and codes of conduct), and formal rules (constitutions, laws, property rights)" (North 1991: 97).[9] Important in this respect are not only the rules themselves but also the way in which they are applied or enforced; so, aspects of implementation and compliance. The main rationale of institutions is that they reduce or remove uncertainty as to the behaviour of partners in the interaction.

The problem with the term "institution" as it is defined here is that it is too broad to be of use in concrete operational situations. Many attempts have been made to arrive at more precise concepts for specific institutions. Fairly generally accepted in economics and in international relations is the broad concept of *regime* (see section 2.7), which covers quite a variety of forms. More specific is the concept of *organization*, which we come back to in the next chapter.

Institutions can be defined at several levels: the different layers influence each other (see Table 2.2). I will deal with each of the layers one by one in separate subsections.

2.6.2 Social embeddedness

At the highest or "meta" level, institutions indicate the norms, traditions and values of a society, which are often related to fundamental phenomena such as religion and tradition. Meta-institutions tend to give guidance to the actions of individuals and organizations. This may show up in differences in ideology, for instance between liberalism and communism. It may also show up in national cultural features, for example in the rather individualistic values that characterize the United States, the more social or equity-oriented values of the European Union or the more collectivistic (group, organization) values that characterize Japanese society. An example of a common (some say universal) value on the international level is the respect for deals (contracts). However, one has to be careful with the notion "universal". What may seem universal values to Western people, such as democracy, free markets, limited government, human rights, individualism and the rule of law, may meet with widespread scepticism and sometimes even intense opposition, in other cultures.[10]

2.6.3 Principles

At the second level, institutions provide the rules of the game that economic actors play. These take the form of principles. Meta-institutions described in the previous subsection influence the elaboration of institutions on this layer. I shall give some examples. The fundamental ideological values of liberalism will lead to the understanding that economic actors have to compete in a market, which leads to the adoption of the most favoured nation principle in trade relations (see Chapter 5). The consideration that humanity is the custodian of the global environmental patrimony (which has to be handed over intact to future generations) will lead to the adoption of the precautionary principle in environmental matters (see Chapter 8).

Differences in values and ideologies will make cooperation for regime development difficult. In the past this has been the case for trade, for example: the differences between the ideologies of centrally planned and free enterprise countries precluded the realization of a global regime on trade based on the most favoured nation principle. Nowadays this distinction has lost most of its relevance, but on other scores such differences remain. For instance, the principles that guide competition are very different. The United States and the European Union are now rather strict against dominant positions; a country such as Korea has rules that are rather lenient. Such differences do limit the possibilities of arriving at an international regime on competition (see Chapter 10). The Internet is another case of a "culture clash", where strong differences in values deeply influence the discussions about the creation of a regime (see Chapter 10).

2.6.4 Governance structures

The concept of "governance" is used with a considerable variety of meanings.[11] In this book it means the way in which an institution uses its instruments to realize its objectives – in other words, how, by whom and to what end these forces should and can be controlled to achieve specific ends (Kirton and Furstenberg 2001: 3).

The top levels of values and principles influence the governance level. I can illustrate this with two examples. The shift in ideology towards more liberalism has brought about a shift in the role of the state. Whereas formerly a state might have opted for the use of the instrument of prohibition in environmental matters (e.g. prohibiting the use of certain fuels by public power stations), market-oriented instruments (such as the use of tradable permits) may now be preferred. The adoption of the "polluter pays" principle in environmental matters determined the choice of charging the users of energy via carbon taxes rather than via the general tax system.

2.6.5 Allocation mechanisms

At the lowest (fourth) level we move from discrete structural analysis to marginal analysis. At this level we find the way in which things are actually allocated, given the situations that prevail at the three higher levels. At the level of international regimes the allocation of pollution permits by the national authority of one of the signatory states of the Kyoto Protocol (see Chapter 8) may be cited.

TABLE 2.2 A layered view of institutions

Level	Type	Frequency (years)	Purpose
1	**Embeddedness:** values, customs, traditions, norms, religion ↓ ↑	10^2 to 10^3	Non-calculative; spontaneous
2	**Principles,** concepts (property, etc.), functions (polity, judiciary, bureaucracy) ↓ ↑	10 to 10^2	Get the basics right
3	**Governance:** play of the game (aligning governance structures with transactions) ↓ ↑	1 to 10	Get the implementation right
4	**Allocation** (prices and quantities; incentive alignment)	Continuous	Get the marginal conditions right

Source: Adapted from Williamson (1998: 26).

2.6.6 Dynamics

Institutions are not universal and they are not created for eternity. They emerge at certain moments in time and under certain circumstances as a reaction to specific needs, and they adapt as a consequence of changes in their environment. The frequency of change is dependent on the place in the four-layered structure (see the middle column of Table 2.2).

The higher the level of the institution, the lower the frequency at which it changes. Values (social embeddedness) change only very slowly, over a period of centuries or sometimes millennia. So, if on this level differences inhibit international collective action, progress will be almost nil. Principles (rules of the game) tend to be stable for at least decades, sometimes for centuries. So, if differences between countries exist at this level, one may at best hope for slow progress. Governance, by comparison, is less stable; it tends to last only several years to a few decades. Differences on this level may be relatively easy to overcome, as opinions will change as evidence on best practices becomes forthcoming. Finally, on the level of allocation, decisions are part of an almost continuous process, so differences between countries are likely to be resolved relatively easily.

International institutions that are successful in realizing public goods at low cost will become valued. The opposite is also true: institutions that are not effective and efficient will lose support. However, because the cost of collective action to realize a change in international institutions is high, once created they will tend to continue to operate even under conditions that would not be sufficiently benign to bring about their creation.

2.7 Regimes

2.7.1 Definitions[12]

The inclusion of the highest level of the hierarchy in the definition of "institutions" is impractical for many purposes. For that reason, scholars have tried to find a better operational term that is nevertheless sufficiently broad to cover a considerable variety of forms that have developed over time. Many have adopted the term "regime". The definition of regimes I will use is composed of the most salient elements of the definitions used in several disciplines:[13]

> Regimes govern relations between diverse entities such as governments (and assimilated public bodies), enterprises (MNFs) and other economic or societal interests (NGOs) in a given area of (international) relations.

Their *form* is not fixed, they can be either:

- formal (e.g. the WTO regime for dispute settlement) or informal (such as the gold standard);

- explicit (e.g. written conventions) or implicit (i.e. understandings about the way the convention is to be interpreted);
- a well-structured organization (such as the WTO) or only an agreement (e.g. GATT) or a loose network or platform (the G8 or G20).

Their *purpose* is to stabilize international relationships through mutually beneficial agreements that reduce the uncertainty about the expected behaviour of interested parties, which contributes to the solving of problems of coordination about specific investments of participants and to the lowering of the transaction costs of obtaining specific goals. They include:[14]

- norms (general injunctions or definitions of legitimacy);
- principles (stating purposes and basic rules of the game);
- rules (specific rights and obligations);
- procedures and mechanisms (formal indications of instruments to meet objectives, for instance on decision-making, compliance and dispute settlement).

2.7.2 International aspects

Regimes cover a *given area of international relations*. Each of the two essential component terms can be defined in different ways.

Area

The fundamental aspect of specificity to one functional field is a consequence of the logic of collective action (as we have seen in the previous chapter). Some regimes cover a fairly broad area (such as trade), others are much more narrowly delimited (e.g. air transport). There is no unique way to define functions or policy areas; they may relate to a spectrum of policy areas such as trade (Chapter 5), finance (Chapter 6) or the environment (Chapter 8).

International

This book deals notably with regimes that have a global coverage. However, where useful we will also refer to international regimes with a more limited coverage, mainly regional arrangements.

Regimes at the international level are comparable to those at the national level in the sense that they both specify norms, principles and rules. However, there is a big difference between international and national regimes with respect to the way compliance is achieved. In the absence of a central authority at the world level, international regimes cannot be based on classical forms of coercion (such as police or military force). So, compliance with international regimes is often based on aspects such as benefits – for instance, the growth bonus due to specialization based on trade liberalization.

Another factor that stimulates compliance is reputation: abiding by international agreements means that you are a reliable partner, which will be a basis for more mutually beneficial arrangements in future. NGOs play an important role in compliance for reputation reasons. They target both companies and countries that do not comply with a regime, for instance in matters of labour and environmental standards.

2.7.3 Private or public?

Private forms may be tried out before public (intergovernmental) cooperation is envisaged. The motives of private actors to come to collective action are different for the two sides of the market:

- *Suppliers.* A field in which private regime-setting is quite common is the setting of technical standards. Sometimes this is left to competition in the market (e.g. in the case of videotapes), sometimes a small number of major firms come together (e.g. in the case of compact discs), sometimes there are industry-wide organizations that set standards (e.g. in electricity generation and distribution). However, where safety aspects for a wider public are involved, standard-setting organizations tend to become public (e.g. in matters concerning the safety of electric appliances).
- *Users* (consumers). In some cases the regime comes about because of strong needs on the part of a particular set of users. A very good example on the international level is the Internet (see Chapter 10 for more details).

A third category of (semi-)private actors pressing for regime-setting consists of those who feel the negative (external) effects of the activities of suppliers and/or users. They are often represented by NGOs. NGOs rarely direct their actions towards the development of private regimes; they tend to claim a strong say in public regimes.

There are considerable *problems* involved in the setting up of private-sector regimes. We mention the four most important ones:

- *Creation.* The negotiating costs quickly become prohibitive for many participants, so collective action will be difficult;
- *Development.* There is a risk that the regime will be hijacked by a small interest group that will not take into account the interests of a wider number of stakeholders. Private-sector regimes may quickly develop into cartels that restrict competition, which damages the interest of consumers. Such situations will trigger action by the public authorities. In order to avoid anti-trust charges, private actors will be reluctant to take initiatives.
- *Operation.* Self-organization leads to a lack of consistency between the various segments that cater for themselves. The partial solutions to sectoral problems may not be adequate in an international situation, and even less so in an intersectoral situation.

- *Legitimacy and compliance.* The effectiveness of a regime depends on the quality of its compliance mechanisms. Compliance issues often cannot be solved without the involvement of the public sector. As the public sector is likely to have its own views on the way a regime should best be set up, it is likely that it will take the leading role itself.

So, we come to the conclusion that private actions aimed at international regime formation are not common and that in most cases national governments are the key actors. They will take into account the economic and societal interests as voiced by business and civil society.

2.7.4 How are regimes created and, once created, how are they changed?

Regimes come about in many different ways.[15] A schematized view of the sequence of events that tends to determine the articulation of the *demand* for a regime is as follows:

- *Awareness.* The awareness that there is a real problem often comes only after major disasters that have a strong effect on the mass public. Recent examples are nuclear safety and the environment (Fukushima), or the financial crisis that began around 2008.
- *Knowledge.* The changes in values and positions that lead to regime formation and regime change are often based on scientific evidence. The more clearly and unequivocally the problem can be defined, the easier it will be to find a cooperative solution. If, on the contrary, countries have a different understanding of the problem and of the best way to solve it (or have different sets of values), regime formation will be very difficult.
- *Attitudes.* Changes in ideas about major issues (such as care for the environment due to an increase in wealth levels) or changes in political trends (such as the end of the Cold War) lead to changes in positions in internal political structures that change the attitude of governments;
- *Rising levels of interdependence.* Interdependence decreases the ability of states to realize their goals autonomously, so they will be inclined to cooperate. They realize that the cost of non-coordinated policies can be very high. Interdependence changes the power of internal coalitions, giving more weight to those interested in cooperation.
- *Interest.* Regime formation is more likely the stronger the interest of the parties involved. Interest increases with benefits and benefits increase with the intensity of transactions between participants. It also increases with the importance of the market failures an international regime can take away. The factor interest is generally confirmed by empirical studies as the most important.

2.7.5 Conditions for success and further development

Collective actions aimed at the setting up of regimes are more likely to succeed when certain conditions are fulfilled, as follows.

Effectiveness and efficiency

The regime has to show that it actually can deliver the public good in a way that is cost-effective. In other words, it has to show that it lowers transaction costs to participants or that it reduces risks. If the benefit:cost ratio is low, then at best a simple regime will result. However, if this regime is successful it will provide experience that lowers the barriers (transaction cost) to a stronger regime in the same area or to a new regime in another area. As the number and importance of interdependent policy areas increase, the cost of extending existing regimes will tend to be lower than that of the setting up of new regimes. Once established, regimes may lack the degree of efficiency that was planned for. Such a situation may persist for quite some time – actually, as long as the nuisance it creates for members is less than the cost of collective action to change it.

Power

Cooperation (or the organization of international negotiations to bring about a regime) is costly, and different participants will make personal cost/benefit calculations in order to decide whether they will move or not. The cost of collective action can be much reduced if there is a dominant power that has an important interest in common action and is prepared to take the leadership. However, theoretical and empirical studies do not provide support for the proposition that success in regime formation depends on a single dominant party. On the contrary; a rather symmetrical power distribution seems to be more conducive to regime growth (e.g. Drezner 2007).

Equity or fairness

Cooperation will not achieve results unless participants believe they can reach a fair deal (see Box 2.1). In general, this means that the benefits and costs have to be distributed among participants according to some criterion of fairness (equal access to resources, to pollution rights, etc.).

Repeated cooperative games

The ability of states to make agreements can be thwarted by externalities, uncertainties, informational asymmetries and opportunistic behaviour (see Chapter 1). If cooperative games are played, regimes can develop; if dilemma-type games or antagonist games are played, regime formation is unlikely. Integrative bargaining

---

BOX 2.1 THE DISTRIBUTIONAL ISSUE IN INTERNATIONAL REGIME FORMATION

The provision of global public goods is very much dependent on the cooperation of a large number of countries. The degree to which such cooperation will come about is in turn very dependent on the distribution over countries of the cost and benefits of such goods. Many distributional conflicts occur between countries at different levels of development.

Developed countries have a low tolerance level for the non-provision of certain public goods. Indeed, as welfare levels increase, a higher value is attributed to immaterial things. These may include fairly concrete notions such as clean air, but also more abstract notions such as long-term sustainability (e.g. in relation to biodiversity).

Developing countries often consider their contribution to the provision of a global public good as an unfair constraint on their growth potential. They see the developed countries as the cause of the public bad and think that these countries should bear the burden of coping with it while providing room for LDCs too to use a fair share of the world's resources. A case in point is pollution: the most significant polluters are the developed countries. They should not try to limit the expansion of pollution by newcomers, but rather restrict their own emissions.

---

permits parties to reach package deals, which are often easier to conclude than more focused ones. Of course, the negotiation and the reaching of an agreement will be the easier the more experience there is with the process, so the existence of previous agreements is a facilitator to new agreements.

Effective compliance mechanisms

The risk of opportunism and cheating of subscribers to a regime makes negotiators hesitant to conclude deals unless compliance can be guaranteed. So, cooperation is more likely the better the chances of compliance. These in turn depend on several factors. First, the greater the advantages countries gain from the regime, the more the regime will be self-policing. Second, the longer the transition time accorded, the more room countries will have to adapt their internal structures. Third, the speedier the detection of and the higher the penalty for infringement, the lower will be the inclination not to comply. Finally, the higher the flexibility with respect to ways and means, the greater the degree of compliance.

The possibility of de-seating free riders

Even in the clear case that it is in the interest of everybody to cooperate, a country may prefer to stay out of a regime. It will postpone the taking of action (in environmental regime-building, for instance, by subsidizing the changing of technical installations in order to reduce emissions). It will let others bear the cost of actions, while sharing in the benefits (for instance of clean air, a global public good because non-excludability and non-rivalry prevail).

Particularly important with respect to the factors "effectiveness", "power" and "equity" is the distribution of costs and benefits among incumbents and new-comers. The group of countries that have created a regime to suit their interests will after some time become incumbents. Those who stayed out because the set-up did not suit their needs may end up with a difficult choice: they either have to set up an alternative regime or accommodate to the existing one. The first alternative is very difficult, given the cost of collective action (see Chapter 1), and, if realized, it may prove ineffective (compare, for instance, GATT and UNCTAD in Chapter 5). So, if a particular group of countries feel they are not getting a positive reward for their participation in a regime and are unable to change it, they will try to obtain waivers of certain rules, long transition periods or compensation (e.g. financial help).

2.7.6 Do international regimes matter?[16]

Compliance with regimes influences national governments in three main ways, as follows.

Enhancing capabilities

A regime is a source of influence on states whose policies are consistent with that regime (in particular, its rules and decision-making procedures). Take an example of a strong state and a weak state. A strong, rich state that has been able to shape a regime to suit its ideas will see these ideas put into effect by the other countries that have adhered to the regime (compare Chapter 6 on the USA and IMF). A weak state may use a regime as a device for the reduction of its vulnerability to outside influences. A good illustration of this case is the country that has adhered to an exchange rate stabilization regime and finds that the regime wards off most attempts at speculation against its currency, which enhances its capacity to pursue its domestic policies.

Shifting interests

Regimes may alter their calculations of interest by assigning property rights and altering patterns of transaction costs. A good illustration of this case is the introduction of tradable emission permits by the climate protection regime (see

Chapter 8). Regimes also alter conceptions of self-interest by the exchange of information, by mutual persuasion and by the accumulation of scientific knowledge. Evidence of this happening is available for the trade rules of the WTO (Chapter 5), and the measures to avoid global warming (Chapter 8).

Altering governance

Regimes may alter the balance and workings of domestic policies and can have effects on states' action by:

- altering bureaucratic practices and rules (or habits);
- promoting learning about cause–effect relationships;
- altering ideas about legitimacy and effectiveness of practices;
- enhancing the political or administrative capacity of governmental or non-governmental organizations within countries.

2.8 Summary and conclusions

- The international economy has seen profound changes over the past centuries. These have largely been a response to fundamental changes that have occurred in matters of transport and energy technology. Together, these developments have produced a long-term increase in *global economic interchange*.
- Globalization has limited the capacity of national governments to effectively intervene in the economy to safeguard the provision of public goods. The answer to the challenge has been in two parts:
  1 a recasting of national institutions (and policies) aiming at the improvement of international competitiveness;
  2 a strengthening of the international (global) institutions so as to improve their capacity to deal with a set of high-priority global problems.
- Economic problems on the global level can often be defined as the underprovision of global public goods. Public goods are goods that are both non-rivalrous and non-excludable. Because of increased global interrelations, the number of such public goods with a global dimension has increased.
- The provision of global public goods calls for collective action on the part of national governments. Such collective action is not simple. It involves clarity about which actors will participate (who?), the definition of the public good (why?) and the choice of the instruments (how?).
- Therefore, what commonly occurs is the emergence of separate collective action for specific global public goods (regime formation). Something else that happens is the emergence of clubs: groups of countries of a limited number for which the definition of the benefits is easier and the cost of collective action lower (regional integration).
- Actions for the provision of public goods are conditioned by institutions. Institutions exist at different levels of specificity. At the top level we find values

and ideology; next, we find basic principles, followed at the third level by aspects of governance and on the fourth level by aspects of allocation. High-level institutions to a large extent determine the character of the institutions at a lower level.

- Regimes are defined as special sets of contracts that govern the relations in a given area of international relations. They are important as they set the rules of the game.
- International economic institutions evolve only gradually under external influences and tend to:
    - supply answers only to the most pressing needs; interest is the most important motive for action;
    - be organized on a functional basis as an answer to a sectoral problem;
    - become facilitated by unity of values, by the effectiveness of pre-existent structures, by the equity of outcomes and finally by the strength of the mechanisms that are put in place to enhance compliance with objectives;
    - be positioned at some distance from optimality, given the diversity of the interested parties; the risks of cheating and opportunism, etc.
- Once created, regimes matter: they create conditions and set the rules, and thereby influence the behaviour of actors in such a way that it becomes conducive to the reaching of objectives.

3

INTERNATIONAL ORGANIZATIONS

3.1 Introduction

International institutions can take different forms. In the previous chapter I defined regimes. In this chapter I deal with the most visible and tangible form of institution: the organization. The chapter is structured as follows:

In the first main section I define organizations as formal legal entities with clear instruments to reach a stated purpose. I define their rationale, the various forms they may take and the way they change under the influence of changes in preferences for public goods.

In the previous chapter I indicated that collective action problems lead to two types of solutions to international problems. We deal in separate sections with the organizational forms that these solutions have taken. The first is dealing with arrangements on a global scale. I recall that it leads to public-good-specific solutions. The danger is that these solutions will become inconsistent among each other. So there is a need for an organization on the world level with a very broad remit. This role is given to the United Nations. In the second main section I describe the general architecture of the international organizations (IOs) that are part of or connected to the United Nations Organization (UNO).

A second solution to collective action problems is to form clubs. These clubs have less than world coverage in terms of membership but often deal with a range of problems. We will describe two of them. The most important institution in this category is the G8 or G20, although its organizational form is very weak. The second is the Organisation for Economic Co-operation and Development (OECD), a regular intergovernmental organization.

A specific form of club is the *regional* one. The choice of this option is advantageous because many externalities that demand international action occur on the regional level rather than on the global level. So, to put the global organizations in perspective I devote the fourth main section to regional cooperation schemes, such as the European Union or MERCOSUR.

There follows a discussion of the representation of private interests – that is, of business and non-governmental organizations (NGOs). In that section we will see how these "private" organizations influence the activities of international "public" or intergovernmental organizations.

The chapter ends with a short summary of the basic findings.

3.2 Basic characteristics

3.2.1 Definitions

The term "organization" is used in a whole series of disciplines. I will not look at all the various definitions that are available, but just present the following mainstream definition:

> Organizations are more or less durable, formal legal entities to pool resources and deploy instruments in order to pursue one or several stated purposes.

Organizations create a hierarchical order that permits them to coordinate the actions of their various members and agents according to specific rules about decision-making and control. These rules have to be consistent with the objectives of the organization.

Organizations mobilize resources and deploy these resources according to certain governance methods (carrots and sticks).

There is a relation between regimes and organizations. The notion "purpose" in the definition of "organizations" often matches the notion "specific area of international relations" in the definition of "regimes". The compliance aspect of regimes is often given substance in organizations. However, as we will see in the upcoming chapters, there is no one-to-one relation between regimes and organizations. A multitude of forms coexist.

3.2.2 The rationale of organizations

Organizations are formed for good economic reasons. Economic interaction would be problematic without them. This may be illustrated with an example from the private sector and one from one of the public sectors.

A *private firm* is formed because it is an efficient way of producing goods. Imagine a person wanting to engage in the production of a good. He (or she) might want to limit risk and bring together the various production factors on a daily basis. He would then have to decide every day what amount of capital he needed and would have to discuss with his banker the financing arrangement on a short-term basis. He would also need to negotiate with people whose labour he wanted to hire; he would have to acquire information about their professional qualities and their personal integrity. Because he would not be sure about their qualities, he would have to monitor production closely. It is clear that all this involves extremely high information, transaction and monitoring costs. Making a permanent organizational arrangement in the form of a firm can do away with most of these costs (Coase [1937] 1952). Durable relational contracts within such organizations enhance the value of property rights for the various partners: labour can show what its productivity is and be remunerated accordingly. Capital prices can be set on the basis of the trust that a firm has built up with the banker by paying back its loans on time. Inventors will see their rewards improved, as sales of the product developed on the basis of their ideas by a well-established firm will be much higher than those sold by a one-day offshoot.

In the *public field* we again find the need for organizations. The provision of a public good (e.g. the setting up of an efficient financial system) is needed to avoid a situation whereby economic agents have to decide each day about how they are going to settle their contracts (barter). So, a country will establish a national currency. In order to facilitate exchange it will issue banknotes and set up a good system for electronic financial transactions. A central bank will then be created as an organizational form to cope efficiently with problems such as trust in paper money and in the quality of the prudential control of the financial institutions.

3.2.3 International organizations

Because the modern economy has increasingly taken on a global character (see Chapter 2), it need not come as a surprise that organizations also take on an international dimension. For the provision of private goods by private firms, this means the formation of multinational firms (MNFs). For public good provision it implies the setting up of international organizations (IOs). In line with the general definition of "organization", I define international organizations as *purposive entities, with bureaucratic structures and leadership permitting them to employ their resources to deliver a public good and to respond to events*. IOs are mostly forms of cooperation between national governments. Much in the same way as the public organizations described in the previous section are efficient solutions to a national coordination problem, international organizations are an efficient institutional solution to an international coordination or cooperation problem.

International organizations provide their participants with the following:

- information on developments relevant to the attainment of objectives;
- platforms for consultation and negotiation;
- rules for coming to decisions (voting procedures);
- fixing of contributions and access to resources;
- legal forms of agreements;
- monitoring of compliance of members;
- rules for dispute settlement;
- minimal mechanisms for enforcement;

- some provision for accountability and liability for actions;
- operational activities.

Different international organizations tend to vary in the way each of these elements is specified. Important elements that are common to all international organizations are:

- *Lack of coercion.* All international organizations rely on national governments to comply (see Chapter 4 for details). This difference in institutional strength strongly influences the capacity of IOs to provide a public good effectively.
- *Indirect accountability.* Within a democratic state the government is accountable for its actions to the parliament. On an international scale this is not the case, and the actions of the international organization have to be made accountable via the national governments and their elected body.

3.2.4 Membership

International organizations can be divided into three categories according to how restrictive in their membership they are:

1. *Restricted.* Most organizations tend to deliver advantages to members only and thereby discriminate against outsiders. Some do this for reasons of effectiveness. A case in point is the G8/20; a larger group would not be able to work effectively.
2. *Conditionally open.* These organizations have a predefined set of conditions for membership but are in principle open to all those that are prepared to commit themselves to observing these rules. They are designed to foster collaboration of like-minded countries and to cope with the problem of free riders by exclusion. They can be compared to clubs: a price must be paid to get access to the organization (in other words, access to the advantages of an excludable club good). States that do not want to pay this price (in other words, that do not follow the rules) are excluded from these advantages. A clear illustration can be found in the case of a regional organization, for instance the EU (see Molle 2011).
3. *Open.* Open organizations are mainly for information exchange and consultation; they are less good at actions. They have often a limited resource base. They arise where the options of "restricted" and "conditionally open" are not feasible. Here, any autonomous state can apply. A case in point is the United Nations, which has fairly minimal conditions and excludes only pariah states.

3.2.5 Factors for change

Organizations change under the influence of external and internal factors.[1] Change depends very much on the type of organization.

Private organizations such as firms, including MNFs, operate in a competitive environment, so they will be constantly looking for the best way to provide consumers with their products and services. Moreover, they will be constantly searching for ways to improve the efficiency of their production and marketing, and will adapt their governance structures accordingly. They will also increasingly take into account the views of civil society, as consumers and investors check critically on the values that the company applies. Illustrative in this respect is the fact that many firms have started to report on their contribution to sustainable production and consumption.

Public-sector organizations have a different rationale. They respond to political criteria; if a national government find it necessary to create certain agencies or departments, or to change their governance, the state's power will be used to make these changes. Lack of efficiency is less of a driver for change here than in the private sector, notably because efficiency is difficult to measure. On the other hand, lack of effectiveness will quickly lead to complaints about the waste of resources and to political action to force government to make the necessary organizational changes.

International organizations are in general created to provide a public good. Given the cost of collective action it is likely that only one organization for each good will be created. In principle IOs are thus not subject to competitive forces, as they are the sole provider of that good. So, the factors that trigger change in the private sector are absent here. The factors that bring change in the public sector on the national level do not operate very well on the international level either. The political and bureaucratic processes in IOs have to operate in the absence of a clear political authority that can show leadership and force change. Change is thus dependent on major changes in the environment of IOs. On the one hand, a change in values and/or principles can cause the redesign of governance structures of international organizations. On the other hand, the emergence of new public goods can lead to such change. Examples will be given in Chapters 5 to 10.

International organizations are dependent for their *effectiveness* on the compliance of the national member states with the principles, rules and decisions of the IO. The range and quality of the instruments IOs can deploy is the subject of the next chapter.

3.3 The UN system

3.3.1 Emergence

This book focuses on socio-economic international organizations. These are a segment of a much larger group that covers additional aspects such as security and health. In order to achieve a good understanding of the functioning of the organizations we are directly interested in, we have to look at this wider picture. The United Nations has a dominant place in this picture.

The forerunner of the United Nations was the *League of Nations*, founded by the Allies shortly after the First World War. The scope of its activities and the effectiveness of its efforts were very limited.[2]

The United Nations was created shortly after the Second World War to serve two purposes: first, it had to deal with security issues; and second, to oversee many multilateral agreements that had developed over the past outside a coherent institutional set-up. To make the new organization more effective than its unfortunate predecessor (the League of Nations), membership was enlarged and relations with other organizations strengthened.

3.3.2 Objectives and policy areas

The United Nations is comprehensive in the sense that it can cover all functional areas within the realm of an international organization. In this respect it can be compared to a national government, which is also comprehensive in its functional coverage. The major aims of the UN are the maintenance of peace and security, and the encouragement of economic and social progress, human rights and international law. As this book limits itself to socio-economic issues, I will restrict myself here to describing the most important competences of the United Nations in these fields.[3]

Trade

The General Agreement on Tariffs and Trade (GATT), later recast as the World Trade Organization (WTO), is not a UN agency. It is only loosely related to the United Nations. Its major task was to promote the liberalization of international trade. As a result of major rounds of negotiation on liberalization of trade the tariffs on manufactured goods have been reduced to a very low level. GATT, and later the WTO, has had somewhat less success with non-tariff matters. Membership, which initially was restricted to developed nations, has increased over the years and now encompasses virtually all the world's economies.

Financial stability

The IMF was set up to pursue two main objectives: first, the creation of a multilateral payments system based on convertibility of the currencies of all trading nations; and second, the introduction of an international competence in orderly adaptation of exchange rates. The Fund was given the task of helping member countries to restore balance of payments equilibrium and to realize exchange rate stability. In the course of the past quarter-century its task has shifted and become more complex. It now has to cope with flexible exchange rates and with high capital mobility, which can have a huge impact on the balance of payments, with the risks of currency runs. The Fund tries to carry out its objectives by providing loans to member countries in difficulties and by regular surveillance of the situation on international financial markets.

Development

The issue of development is covered by quite a few organizations within the UN family. Paramount among them is the International Bank for Reconstruction and Development, colloquially called the World Bank. Another main player is the United Nations Development Programme (UNDP). A specific role about the interface between development and trade and investment is played by UNCTAD.

The environment

In the post war era the United Nations increasingly took on the responsibility of addressing environmental concerns worldwide. A whole series of international conferences have been held under its auspices (Rio de Janeiro, Johannesburg, Kyoto; see Chapter 8), some of which created organizations with competences in specific environmental matters. One of the more active ones is UNEP, the United Nations Environment Programme, launched in 1972. It coordinates the existing institutions, sets a plan for action and adopts general principles to guide such action. Legal instruments were developed to enforce conservation of natural resources and environmental protection. In the last decade of the past century, new impetus was given by UNCED, the United Nations Conference on Environment and Development. It broadened the scope of the United Nations' activities and developed methods to ensure effective compliance.

Labour

The International Labour Organization (ILO) was created in 1919 at the end of the First World War. The initial motivations were mainly humanitarian (to enhance conditions of labour), political (to avoid revolutions) and economic (to ensure fair competition conditions). However, a leading idea was also that lasting peace cannot be obtained without social justice. The organization became part of the United Nations after the Second World War. The ILO has adopted a set of international labour conventions dealing with a diversity of aspects, such as hours of work, night work for women and young persons, and maternity protection.

3.3.3 Membership and internal structure

Membership has been expanding from an initial fifty-one to a quasi-complete coverage of the globe now. The UN system gives one vote to each member, irrespective of the size of the country. For economic matters this is considered to lead to unbalanced results, which is the reason why the strong economic powers tend to avoid using the UN platform. With respect to power distribution, there is a notable difference between most of the UN organizations, where the rule is "one country, one vote" and the two related finance organizations (the IMF and World Bank), whose rules are often characterized as "one dollar, one vote".

The United Nations is a complicated organization (see Table 3.1). Its essential constituent elements are of the following types:

- *Central organs*. The General Assembly makes recommendations on all UN matters. A limited number of members sit on the Security Council. Next one can mention the Economic and Social Council and the International Court of Justice. The daily work is done by a secretariat headed by the Secretary-General. The Economic and Social Council forms the coordinating machinery for the specialized agencies and the programmes and funds.
- *Specialized agencies*. These are autonomous organizations working under the auspices of the United Nations. Of particular note are the World Bank Group, the IMF and the ILO.
- *Diverse substructures*. These are created for the management of Programmes and Funds, such as UNEP (the United Nations Environment Programme) and UNCTAD (the United Nations Conference on Trade and Development).
- *Related organizations*. These are not formally part of the UN architecture but liaise with the UN (General Assembly). The most important is the WTO (World Trade Organization).

Compliance

The UN system comprises the International Court of Justice. However, the Court can only handle cases that both parties (member and non-member states) refer to it. It also has an advisory function to the various organs of the United Nations in matters of international law. The Court handles relatively few cases. Most of the compliance of the member countries with UN decisions is based on aspects such as self-interest and reputation.

The UN system is very complicated. On the one hand, there are many organizations that deal with the same subject, such as development aid (the UNDP, UNCTAD, the World Bank, etc.) or the environment (the United Nations Framework Convention on Climate Change (UNCCC), UNEP, etc.). On the other hand, there are cases where one organization deals with different public goods (see Box 3.1 on UNCTAD, which deals with both trade and development). This situation is the result of a long historical development in which different agencies have been created as a response to specific needs in a specific power constellation.

3.4 Other important organizations and regimes

3.4.1 The G8/G20[4]

Emergence

The G8 summits of the heads of government of the most important economic powers started off as single free-standing events. They were intended to cope with

TABLE 3.1 The UN system

Programmes and funds	Commissions	Specialized agencies (a selection)
UNCTAD (United Nations Conference on Trade and Development)	*Functional commissions* Social Development Human Rights Narcotic Drugs	IMF (International Monetary Fund)
UNDP (United Nations Development Programme)	Crime Prevention and Criminal Justice Science and Technology for Development	IBRD (World Bank Group)
UNEP (United Nations Environment Programme)	Sustainable Development The Status of Women Population and Development	ILO (International Labour Organization)
UNDCP (United Nations Drug Control Programme)	*Regional economic commissions* Africa (ECA)	ICAO (International Civil Aviation Organization)
UNFPA (United Nations Population Fund)	Europe (ECE) Latin America and the Caribbean (ECLAC) Asia and the Pacific (ESCAP)	IMO (International Maritime Organization)
UNCHR (Office of the United Nations High Commissioner for Refugees)	Western Asia (ESCWA)	ITU (International Telecommunication Union)
UNCHR (Office of the United Nations High Commissioner for Refugees)	*Other* Sessional and Standing Committees expert, *ad hoc* and related bodies	FAO (Food and Agriculture Organization of the United Nations)
UNICEF (United Nations Children's Fund)		UNESCO (United Nations Educational, Scientific and Cultural Organization)
WFP (World Food Programme)		WHO (World Health Organization)
		WIPO (World Intellectual Property Organization)
		UNIDO (United Nations Industrial Development Organization)

Source: www.un.org.

BOX 3.1 THE UNITED NATIONS CONFERENCE ON TRADE AND DEVELOPMENT (UNCTAD)

Emergence

In the post-Second World War period a group of developing countries became convinced that the major powers that dominated the international institutions (notably GATT/WTO and the IMF/World Bank Group) were using this dominance to their own advantage. As a consequence, these LDCs experienced adverse developments to their trade and their terms of trade. They felt they could not follow their own preferences in matters of economic growth and societal choices. So, they urged the creation of a negotiating platform where their interests would take centre stage. This discussion was set in the framework of the need for a "new international economic order". One of the constituting ideas was the creation of regimes that would make it possible to positively discriminate in favour of development. In 1964 UNCTAD was set up.

Objectives and tasks

The main objective of UNCTAD is to improve the development process of the LDCs and their integration into the world economy. To that end, it tries to bring about improved access of LDC products to the markets of developed countries and to improve the conditions for investment in LDCs. In the past it also tried to stabilize the market prices of the main commodities, but doing so proved very difficult.

Membership

All member states of the United Nations are members of UNCTAD. There are several groups; two of them cover regional groupings of developing countries; one groups together the most developed countries (more or less coinciding with the OECD). As UNCTAD follows UN principles, each member country has one vote. The numerical majority of the LDCs gives them much more voice in UNCTAD than in other international organizations, such as the IMF and World Bank.

Compliance

UNCTAD uses all three governance methods: it sets rules and codes of conduct (e.g. for the control of restrictive business practices), it finances programmes (e.g. for technical assistance to member countries about the way they can handle e-commerce) and it acts as a forum for deliberation and negotiation (e.g. on the most effective domestic policies for growth).

Effectiveness

UNCTAD has had some impact in terms of putting issues to the international agenda and in terms of stabilization of primary product prices. However, in trade matters UNCTAD has faded at the benefit of the WTO; it deals most with foreign direct investment.

Sources: www.unctad.org and Taylor and Smith (2007).

---

important specific problems that had been too difficult nuts to crack at the other levels of bilateral and multilateral decision-making. However, the summits soon became an annual series.

The G8 has often been criticized as being a club of the rich and powerful and as such not being capable of acting in the interests of the developing world. To solve that problem, a new forum, the G20, has been created (www.g20.org). In addition to the G8 countries, it includes ten of the major developing and emerging market countries.

Objectives and tasks

The leaders of the G8 countries have set guidelines for action that provide other international organizations with the necessary impulses to come to solutions (Stoehl 2007). However, they have not dealt with all the subjects discussed in the various chapters of this book to the same degree. In practice they have devoted most of their attention to questions of macroeconomic governance and finance. They now deal increasingly also with LDC problems such as sustainable development, employment creation, poverty reduction and debt relief.

Membership

The G8 consists of the United States and Canada in the Americas; Germany, France, Italy and the United Kingdom in Europe; Japan in Asia; and, since its transition, also Russia. China is a potential member. Given the transfer of many economic responsibilities from European nations to the European Union, the presidency and the Commission of the Union are present at many activities of the G8. The G20 consists of the G8 and the major emerging and developing countries (e.g. China and India in Asia; Brazil and Mexico in Latin America and the republic of South Africa). The EU is also a member. The IMF, World Bank and OECD are associated to the work of the G20. The G20 accounts for some 85 per cent of world GDP and includes 65 per cent of the world's population.

Internal structure

Both the G8 and the G20 are forums rather than organizations; they operate along similar lines:

- There is *no formal organization*, no headquarters and no written constitution or procedures. This has its advantages, such as flexibility, but also its drawbacks, such as the pressure it puts on the apparatus of the host country. It is thus not surprising to see growing pressure to develop an organization downwards, beginning with a permanent secretariat.

Meetings are at the level of *heads of government*. It has been deliberately set up like this to bring commitments among partners at the highest level of authority.[5]

- *Ministerial groups* are mostly composed of finance ministers. Personal representatives of these ministers meet to prepare meetings on the higher levels. The ministers do not meet solely in this framework; they often meet in the margins of meetings of the IMF and World Bank. With the broadening of the scope of subjects treated by the G8, other stand-alone and regular ministerial meetings have been introduced as well (such as meetings dealing with the environment or crime).

Compliance

The governance method applied by the G8 and G20 is a form of coordination. Summits usually are concluded with declarations. These are not legally binding. Neither the G8 nor the G20 has a formal enforcement mechanism. Yet the compliance of international organizations and national governments with summit commitments has in general been very high. A large part of the explanation is to be found in the existence of strong national procedures for compliance with decisions of prime ministers and treasury ministries.

3.4.2 The Organisation for Economic Co-operation and Development (OECD)[6]

Emergence

The OECD developed out of the former OEEC, the Organisation for European Economic Co-operation, created after the Second World War to administer the US aid to European recovery. Its objectives were to stimulate trade and to coordinate a number of national policies. After the creation of the European Union (or, more precisely, its forerunner, the European Economic Community), the OEEC extended its membership and redefined its role. It was relaunched in 1961 under its new name.

Objectives and tasks

The objectives of the OECD are of a very general nature (see www.oecd.org): the promotion of policies that will improve the economic and social well-being of people around the world. The OECD provides a forum in which the governments of member countries can work together to share experiences and seek solutions to common problems. To that end, the OECD measures and analyses data on a variety of subjects, such as productivity, growth, employment, living standards, financial stability, the environment, trade, investment, macroeconomic balance, government budgets and taxation.

Membership

With the recasting of 1961, the number of members was increased in such a way that the organization regrouped the world's most developed countries. It now covers Western and Central Europe (EU countries and most of the accession countries), North America (the United States, Canada and Mexico), the Antipodes (Australia and New Zealand), Asia (Japan and Korea) and recently South America (Chile). The Commission of the European Union takes part in the work via many working groups. Russia has been invited to become a member. As the OECD wants to be able to support the G20, it has concluded enhanced engagement agreements with Brazil, China, India, Indonesia and South Africa. The OECD liaises with representatives of employers (Business and Industry Advisory Committee) and with representatives of organized labour (Trade Union Advisory Committee) and NGOs.

Internal structure

The main authority is vested in the Council. All member states have one seat. The Council meets regularly at the ministerial level for important issues; meetings are prepared at the level of permanent representatives.

The secretariat is responsible for the preparation of the work of the Council and for the implementation of the decisions. The staff number approximately 2,500.

The actual work is done in numerous working groups and committees, often formed of experts from the administrations of the member states.

For very specific tasks the OECD has created Agencies (e.g. the International Energy Agency).

Compliance

The OECD mainly uses the governance method of coordination. However, its activities may lead to the adoption of codes and the setting of standards. Compliance with those codes is a matter for the members; the OECD will monitor compliance but has no ways to enforce them.

3.5 Regional organizations

3.5.1 A kaleidoscope of arrangements

Regional groups of countries tend to cover most of the international inter-wovenness of its members. So, the making of deals among a limited number of highly interrelated countries may solve a considerable part of the problems that emerge from the internationalization of economic activity. As we have seen, it is usually the case that the more similar the potential contracting partners are and the smaller their number, the easier it is to reach agreement. Now, agreements on a regional basis can be based on such similarity in cultures and governance structures and on the higher level of trust among members of a limited group. So, the second avenue for collective action by national governments – the forming of regional clubs – has been followed in many parts of the world. Most of the early schemes, based on the idea that they would help industrialization through import sub-stitution, had no success. Other schemes, basically open to the world market, have been more (or even very) successful (such as the European Union and more recent ventures in other continents: the North American Free Trade Agreement in North America and MERCOSUR in South America).

However, most of the latter arrangements are limited to some form of trade agreement. In a few cases, some further subjects have been addressed (such as investments), but only in one case has a regional grouping gone far beyond these issues. That is the European Union, to which I devote a separate section. All others have the form of an international agreement with limited ambitions as to objectives and with very modest organizational structures (generally only a small secretariat). The most important of these organizations are the following.

The *North American Free Trade Agreement* (NAFTA) came into effect in 1994. Members are the United States, Canada and Mexico. The objective is to create free trade; there is as yet no common external tariff; neither is there a common external policy (www.nafta-sec-alena.org). NAFTA covers manufacturing and most com-mercial services. Moreover, it has provisions for investment, for competition and for intellectual property. There are side agreements on labour and environment. Compliance is monitored by the members. Rules about dispute settlement have been agreed upon.

In South America the *MERCOSUR* treaty came into effect in 1991, with Brazil, Argentina, Uruguay and Paraguay as members. Recently Venezuela has acceded. Moreover, Mercosur has concluded cooperation agreements with the other major countries in South America. The primary objective is to create a common market. This has not been easy, as the whole process has suffered very heavily from monetary unrest and the Argentinian crisis. MERCOSUR also envisages the coordination of major economic policies. However, not much has been realized in these matters as yet. The governance structure of MERCOSUR is simple (see www.mercosur.int). Apart from MERCOSUR there are a number of other regional cooperation schemes in Latin America such as CARICOM (in the Caribbean) and the Andean

Pact. We will not go further into them, given the limited size of the economies and/or the limited objectives and results of the agreements.

The major organization in Asia[7] is the *Association of Southeast Asian Nations* (ASEAN). It groups the major countries in the region, among them Indonesia, Malaysia, the Philippines, Singapore and Thailand. The initial objective was relatively modest; in the 1990s, ambitions were stepped up to include the creation of a free trade area (AFTA: the ASEAN Free Trade Area) and even a customs union; including rules for foreign direct investment (FDI).[8] Initially AFTA has had limited progress, owing to important ideological differences and the fear that unequal benefits will accrue (with more going to the rich and less to the poor) – a factor that we found to be important in explaining regime change (see section 2.7). Recently these factors have carried less weight and significant progress has been made. Moreover, the other countries in the region have joined and a free trade arrangement between China and ASEAN has become effective. Plans exist to extend ASEAN cooperation into the ASEAN Community, based on three pillars: an economic, a socio-cultural and a security community. The governance structure of ASEAN is essentially based on intergovernmentalism.

In addition to ASEAN there is the *South Asian Association for Regional Cooperation* (SAARC). It covers countries on and around the Indian subcontinent. It is not a real economic integration area, in the sense that its objectives even fall short of a preferential trade area (www.saarc-sec.org). The history of the region has shown many conflicts between the major member countries, precluding any major progress.

The African continent has seen a large number of regional integration initiatives in recent decades. Many of these overlap, owing to the multiplicity of objectives and the lack of coordination between member states. Most were short-lived; many others that did survive failed to produce any material results. Of the ones that are functioning at the moment, I shall mention but two. The *Southern African Development Community* (SADC) was created in 1992 and has now fifteen member states (www.sadc.int). Its main objectives are equitable and sustainable growth and development, based on democratic principles. To that end, it wants to develop a free trade area. The *Economic Community of West African States* (ECOWAS), established in 1975, also has fifteen members. The treaty sets as its objective the creation of a common market and a monetary union (www.ecowas.int). Some progress has been made on the trade front and some of the members are part of a monetary union. Progress is difficult, however, owing to differences between member countries in power, in culture (language), administrative practices; political turmoil and security risks, participation in other integration schemes (e.g. the CFA franc zone), economic structure, transport, etc.

As this overview makes clear, none of these organizations has developed to the extent that it needs a separate representation in global international institutions. In these integration schemes the risk of inconsistencies must be removed by co-ordination between the secretariat of the international organization concerned and the relevant member states.

3.5.2 Europe

The *European Union* (EU) (Molle 2006, 2011) started off in 1958 with only six Western European countries as members. In several rounds of enlargement of its membership it has integrated almost all countries in Western Europe first and in Central Europe next. The European Union differs from the other regional organizations in two main respects.

First, its aims go far beyond the integration of markets right up to full economic integration and even political integration. These aims have largely been attained. After the creation of a common market for all goods, services, labour and capital, a full-fledged economic union has been realized. This implies that common policies have been elaborated and implemented for such diverse areas as competition, transport, external trade, environment, occupational health and safety, etc. Finally, a monetary union has been realized, which implies a common currency.

Second, the Union has set up an original governance system that is called supranational. It goes far beyond the structure of the classical international organization, but falls short of a federal structure. One of its main features is that much EU law is directly applicable in member states. Another important feature is that the EU Commission (rather than a Secretary-General) has the right of initiative for new legislation and has considerable executive powers (e.g. in trade matters). A final important feature is the role of the European Parliament, an institution that has no counterpart in the decision-making machineries of practically all other international organizations and provides democratic legitimacy.

These very special features mean that on a number of points the Union as such plays a role in international organizations alongside its member states. This is particularly so in matters where the EU treaty removes all competences from the member states and hands them over to the EU. An example is trade; so the Commission negotiates directly in the WTO. In the G20 the European Union is represented by both the Commission and the Council. In other organizations (such as the IMF) there is as yet no formal role for the Union, and all sorts of practical arrangements are made to accommodate its growing role.

3.6 Representation of civil society and business

3.6.1 The role of third parties in intergovernmental organizations

The previous sections have made it clear that international organizations are constructs in which national governments work together. This comes about because they have:

- the task of providing certain public goods and can only do that by organizing collectively what they can no longer do effectively individually (see Chapter 2);
- the legitimacy to regulate and the power to make actors comply with the rules (see Chapter 4).

The positions that governments take in the process of the creation of organizations (systemic) and in the work of those organizations (operational) are motivated by a multitude of private actors. Most of them act on a national level. So, much of the actual dealing is organized on the national level, and governments tend to take these dealings into account while going to negotiate in international institutions. Sometimes this includes the taking account of the views of experts and of interest groups by associating them to national government delegations.[9] Only in one case (that of the ILO) has this logic been pursued to its final consequence by providing for a formal tripartite constitution of national delegations (employers and trade unions alongside government officials).

This traditional mode of international cooperation is rapidly changing. The cost of communication and organization has decreased dramatically in recent years, so the capacity of non-governmental organizations to articulate such wishes directly on the international scale has grown considerably. For that reason I shall give some details of the operations of the two most important categories of actors influencing international institutions.

3.6.2 Business representation

According to the theory of collective action (see Chapter 2), the inclination of businesses to get organized and to defend their interest collectively is lower the more diffuse the gain to be obtained and the higher the cost of organization. This translates itself into different situations depending on the geographical extent of the institution.

Within *national states* the various business interests are well organized by branch. Moreover, many corporations themselves have direct access to government.

The competences of the *EU* in matters of markets, investments and other aspects relevant for business (such as emissions trading, or competition) are so extensive that the representation of business to the European Commission now more or less resembles the situation that prevails in individual member states. At the EU level there is an umbrella organization (UNICE) and a very wide spectrum of branch organizations. There are also informal groups such as the Round Table of Industrialists.

On the level of the *industrialized world* (the OECD) the regulatory powers are much less developed than on the national or regional level. However, it is an important platform for international regime development as it has built up credibility with a number of codes for economic issues. An important example of this sort of work is the Guidelines for Multinational Enterprises (see Box 3.2). In cases where there is little chance that a worldwide solution can be found, business tends to opt for such a second-best solution. At the level of the OECD there functions the *Business and Industry Advisory Committee.*

BOX 3.2 THE OECD GUIDELINES FOR MULTINATIONAL ENTERPRISES

The guidelines are *recommendations* for responsible business conduct, addressed by governments to multinational enterprises operating in or from adhering countries. They are endorsed by forty-three countries, together accounting for 85 per cent of all foreign direct investment.

The guidelines provide *voluntary principles* covering a broad range of issues in business ethics, including information disclosure, employment and industrial relations, the environment, corruption, consumer interest, competition and taxation. They are designed to prevent misunderstandings and build an atmosphere of confidence and predictability between business, labour, governments and society as a whole.

They have a strong status: countries are committed to applying them. Nevertheless, observance by business is voluntary and not legally enforceable. Some matters may, however, become the subject of national law.

Source: OECD (2011a).

On the *world level* the representation of business is not very institutionalized.[10] The most influential institutions are a private one and a semi-public one. The latter is the International Chamber of Commerce (see www.iccwbo.org), an organization that mainly represents large multinationals.[11] It has a consultative status with the United Nations and other important international organizations, such as the WTO and the G8. The private one is the World Economic Forum (see www.weforum.org and Pigman 2007), which aims to improve the state of the world by engaging business, political, academic and other leaders of society to shape global agendas.

So, most of the work is still done in a two-tier system. National governments try to be aware of the opinion of their business community regarding the stand they can best take in international negotiations. In many cases, representatives of the business community are actually members of the official delegation; this is the case with the WTO, for instance. This means that there is national arbitration in a multinational negotiation. For the IMF and World Bank this is not the case; here the financial sector tends to meet on the margins of the meetings of the institutions. It does not have the structure of an organization that is involved in the articulation of positions and in lobbying, but rather is a loose network for passing information.

3.6.3 NGO representation

Non-governmental organizations have no clear *definition*. However one can detail a number of characteristics such as legal constitution, objectives and staff.

The *legal status* of NGOs is much diversified, ranging from charities to not for profit companies. Non-governmental means not being a formal part of the government. This does not mean that governments may not have a strong influence; many NGOs are heavily dependent on government subsidies. NGOs organize interests without aspiring to be representative of all those who are supposed to share this interest. They play an increasingly important role due to the limits of inter-governmental and formal governmental organizations (in either legal, financial, diplomatic, effectiveness terms).

The *objectives* of NGOs are in general limited to a single issue (in line with the collective action problem discussed in Chapter 2). A vast field of work concerns development; many NGOs that are active in this area are not only activists for a certain cause but are involved in realizing practical projects to stimulate the welfare of LDCs (Lewis and Kanji 2009). Another area in which NGOs play a very important role is environmental protection. Environmental NGOs are often of the activist type; mostly dealing with issues that are likely to attract much attention from the media (e.g. Greenpeace). They tend to leave many of the technical issues aside. A third subject is the protection of human rights and labour standards. In the former category we find such organizations as Amnesty International; in the second category trade unions.

The *staff* of NGOs is mostly composed of a hard core of permanent professionals and a ring of volunteers. NGO bureaucracies are a cause of major concern as the cost of overhead risks getting out of proportion with the direct cost of programmes.

NGOs' *influence* comes mostly through their capacity to mobilize massive support for their issues by seeking coverage by the media. It is this public support that influences national governments both in their domestic and external policies. As far as NGOs are involved in practical projects their influence depends of course on their capacity to show that these projects are effective; in other words that they realize stated goals.

NGOs have increasingly organized themselves on the international level in order to influence directly the work of international (intergovernmental) organizations and the positions that governments take in these organizations (see, for example, Florini 2000; Stiles 2000; Doh and Teegen 2003; Sending and Neumann 2006). This input is appreciated by the international organizations as it allows vital experiences, expertise, information and perspectives from civil society to be brought into the process, to generate new insights and to test new approaches.[12] Many NGOs have obtained formal consultative status with the specialist international organization they are interested in. NGO activity on the international level has been greatly stimulated by the Internet, which has facilitated both networking and coalition-building among national and international groups by offering a low-cost means for exchanging information.

3.7 Consistency between national and international levels

3.7.1 The international level

During the Second World War a number of the foundations were laid for the setting up of new international organizations. In the economic field these concerned the creation of regimes for trade and capital relations. It was decided that specialist organizations would take care of different functions, thereby creating flexibility as to membership, rules, mode of operation and modalities of cooperation, etc.

Over the decades, these international regimes have undergone fundamental changes. There has been a general trend towards more liberalization of trade, investment and capital movements. Evidence of this tendency is to be found first of all in trade liberalization. The post-Second World War agreements concluded in the framework of GATT and later the WTO have resulted in a very considerable decrease in tariff protection (more than 40 per cent then, less than 4 per cent now). Moreover, many non-tariff barriers have been abolished. Second, evidence can be found on the score of liberalization of capital movements. Such liberalization got off the ground mainly after 1970; the IMF has stimulated many countries to move further on this path. Capital and trade liberalization have reinforced each other. They have permitted the development of international (financial) markets that have in turn led to new services and lower transaction costs.

3.7.2 The national level

Most national regimes have stayed consistent with these emerging international regimes. The tendency towards liberalization of international transactions has gone hand in hand with (and was reinforced by) a gradual liberalization of the internal markets of many countries, compelling business to improve competitiveness by doing away with rent-seeking and with many types of (unnecessary) transaction costs. Indeed, nationally most countries followed economic policies that stimulated technology change and productivity increases coupled with active macroeconomic stabilization.

This tendency has had different effects in the various categories of countries. In developed countries the major example is the completion of the internal market in the European Union in the 1990s. Since the fall of the Berlin Wall, most of the centrally planned (and often largely closed) systems have collapsed and these countries have gone through a transition stage to open, market-oriented regimes. In the same period, many developing countries abandoned their experiments with regimes based on import substitution. It is now generally recognized that an open internal and external trade system is most conducive to growth and development.

3.8 Summary and conclusions

- Organizations are more or less durable, formal arrangements to pool resources in order to pursue one or several stated purposes.
- International organizations are purposive entities, with bureaucratic structures and leadership, permitting them to employ their resources to deliver a global public good and to respond to events. IOs are mostly cooperation forms of national governments.
- Central on the world level is the United Nations. It groups in a fairly loose framework a patchwork of organizations that differ on a whole range of features, such as problem orientation, membership, scope, voting rules, governance structures, etc. There is considerable uncertainty as to the borderlines between these UN organizations.
- The most important global specialist organizations have been created by a bold and imaginative initiative in the post-Second World War period. Their scope has gradually been widened, while the structure of several regimes has also been strengthened.
- Next to the organizations with almost complete coverage of the 200-odd sovereign states in the world, there are a few organizations that group the main economies in the world. The most prominent and influential one is the G20. They tend to have very important tasks but weak organizational structures.
- Next to the organizations that operate on the global level, a number of organizations at the regional level exist. However, the degree to which they have developed differs greatly from one continent to another. Only in the case of the European Union does the functioning of the regional organization impact on the functioning of global organizations.
- Intergovernmental organizations are complemented by increasingly influential private organizations representing the interests of civil society and business. They tend to influence the actions of the intergovernmental organizations, but also influence developments by issuing their own codes.

4

GOVERNANCE AND COMPLIANCE

Methods and instruments

4.1 Introduction

In the previous chapters we have gone into the definition of the global problems and the type of solutions that may be brought to those problems by the creation of international organizations (by taking away the public bad they provide a public good). The present chapter presents the instruments that international organizations (IOs) have available to realize their objectives. As IOs have to rely on their members for putting policies into practice this means that we will study the way they make members comply with their obligations.[1]

The chapter is structured as follows. In the next section we discuss a few basic notions, subsequently dealing with the definitions of the main concepts, the presentation of the main governance methods and the type of instrument they generally apply.

Following that, I detail these instruments for each governance method. I present the main advantages and drawbacks of each of them in an international context. I will thereby also highlight the role of the various public-sector and private-sector actors.

Governance methods and their instruments are deployed to bring about a specified effect. So, it is important to see how effective they actually are. This will be the subject of the fourth section. We will discuss the different ways in which one can specify effects, and how they can be measured in the practical situation of international organizations.

The conditions under which instruments are deployed to a large extent determine their final effectiveness. So, one has to see what these conditions are, when assessing the possibilities to influence them. We will discuss three elements, among them the capacity of the main actors in charge of implementation to adapt to new circumstances.

Basically, IOs are dependent on national administrations for the putting into effect of their policies. So, one of the most important success factors is the quality of the national public sector. There are considerable differences in this indicator between parts of the globe and between individual countries. I will give some basic information about these differences.

As usual, the chapter concludes with a summary of the main findings.

4.2 Some basic notions

4.2.1 The policy cycle

The putting in place of an effective policy to cope with a problem can be presented as a circular process consisting of the following five stages:

1. *Definition and assessment of the problem.* This concerns usually a societal problem to which the market system cannot find a solution, so that government intervention is necessary.
2. *Setting of objectives.* These can be defined in general terms (e.g. to take away the public bad of global warming and create a public good, namely a stable climate). This stage can be elaborated further by defining specific targets, for instance a 20 per cent decrease of greenhouse gas emissions in order to limit the negative effects of climate change.
3. *Choice of the appropriate instruments.* This stage is particularly important because the specific type of problem and the socio-economic and institutional environments in which policies have to be executed differ considerably. In some instances, detailed regulation may be the best option; in other situations, soft methods such as coordination may be preferred.
4. *Implementation.* If rules have been set, it is necessary that the economic actors to which these rules apply do comply with them. Compliance can be stimulated by positive signals such as financial incentives or by negative actions such as sanctions.
5. *Evaluation of performance and making of proposals for policy adaptation.*

The first two stages are described in Chapter 2. We found there that intergovernmental negotiations lead to the conclusion of international agreements to solve problems that can no longer be attacked in an effective way on the national level. Here, in this chapter, we concentrate on the last three stages of the policy cycle. This covers what we have termed in Chapter 2 as the governance part of the institutional hierarchy.

4.2.2 Definitions

The word "governance" is used in the academic and the policy literature in a bewildering number of meanings (see, for example, Rhodes 2000; Kooiman 2003;

Treib *et al.* 2007). I have distilled from all these sources the following practical definition:[2]

> Governance is the exercise of political and administrative authority (including the allocation of institutional and financial resources) to implement effectively sound policies so as to realize stated objectives.

Note that the term "governance" differs in all instances from the term "government". The latter refers to a hierarchical set of public administrations that pursue policies for the solving of societal problems. So, government is about political leadership to societal goals, whereas governance is more about the deployment of instruments in implementing policies.

4.2.3 Different methods and instruments of governance

Once national governments have arrived at international agreements, they want to make them effective. This means ensuring that member states comply with them. To that end, different governance methods[3] can be applied. I distinguish between three methods. For each method, more or less intrusive instruments can be used. These are given in Table 4.1 and will be discussed in detail in the following sections.

The choice of instruments should in principle be made on the basis of their relative effectiveness: which instrument works best to reach the objectives of the policy. But effectiveness in terms of goal attainment itself depends on a series of factors, such as institutions, preferences, actor constellation, sector of activity, side effects, visibility, acceptability by target groups and perceived fairness. So, in practice the instrument choice is rather dependent on a trade-off between political preferences of national governments with respect to all these factors. There is, though, one general tendency to be noted: member states of IOs will prefer the instruments that make the least inroads into their sovereignty.

TABLE 4.1 Governance instruments by method

Regulation	Financial (budget)	Coordination
International law	Incentives: loans, grants, subsidies	Inform, consult, monitor, persuade
Self-regulation: conventions, protocols, contracts	Disincentives: user charges, taxes, excises, levies; but also fines and penalties	Guidelines, targets, strategies
Standards, codes		

4.3 Instruments for compliance by method

4.3.1 Regulation[4]

The main aim of the regulatory method is to normalize the behaviour of social actors by imposing obligations. To that end, instruments that set very binding rules and prescribe standards (e.g. in matters of child labour) can be used. More flexibility is given if the international level sets only objectives and frameworks, and leaves it to national governments to translate these into national law. Next to such substantive rules exist procedural rules that govern the way in which the game has to be played (e.g. how to put rules into practice; who should be involved, and when). The regulatory method is one of the main methods used by IOs.

Rules bring predictability in behaviour, efficiency in contracting, and conformity with social values. This is valid on all levels of authority and applies both to the private and to the public domain. But there are differences between the international and national regulatory systems. National systems have a central authority to establish the law and organizations to detect breaches, judge cases and punish violators. In international systems, law-making comes from several sources and institutions, monitoring depends on the institutional arrangements in place for specific issues, courts have no compulsory jurisdiction and it is in general impossible to force compliance on states. Admittedly, some embryonic elements of these national authority schemes do exist in several IOs. For instance, the detecting of breaches of the WTO's rules is done by the Trade Policy Review mechanism. Judging of cases is done by the Dispute Settlement Procedure. However, in most IOs such mechanisms are weak or absent, while means of punishing violators are almost completely absent (see Chapter 11).

International rules can take several forms (e.g. Brownlie 2008; UN n.d.). The most common ones that will be used later in this book are agreements, treaties and protocols. These are also called "hard law". However, several softer forms of regulation exist, ones that create moral obligations rather than legal requirements.

The key form of regulation is the *treaty*. In many cases, treaties are called conventions; in legal terms there is no difference between the two designations. To be considered a treaty, an agreement between sovereign states must fulfil three criteria:

1. It has to be a binding instrument, which means that the contracting parties intend to create legal rights and duties.
2. The instrument has been concluded by states, or international organizations with treaty-making power.
3. It is governed by the principles of international public law.

The next form is the *protocol*. This is a legal instrument that is subsidiary to a treaty in the sense that it deals with ancillary matters (interpretation of clauses; additional rights and obligations; measures to reach the objectives of the treaty, etc.).[5]

Finally, there are *agreements*. This term is used in the event that one or two criteria for a treaty are not fulfilled – for instance, because the agreement does not create binding rules for the future conduct of parties in terms of legal propositions, but rather refers to general norms and principles. Limiting a treaty to the mere reference *to principles* is often done in cases where there is much variation in the understanding of the workings of the system and the effectiveness of alternative instruments. Such agreements are nevertheless very important, as the voluntary acceptance of moral obligations is often the beginning of an endogenous process in which sovereign states change their behaviour over time and end up by accepting binding rules. They often lead to framework conventions (see Box 4.1).

BOX 4.1 THE WHY AND HOW OF FRAMEWORK CONVENTIONS

The chain of events that leads to the conclusion of a framework agreement and subsequent protocols consists of several links that can be explained using examples taken from matters relating to the environment:

- NGOs voice their concern and gain political support in one or more key states.
- A key state with a technology lead in abatement asks for a global regime.
- Negotiations lead to a weak global regime that is gradually put in place.
- Disaster leads to an increase in global concern and a change in the cost–benefit relation.
- The regime is strengthened as regards detail of commitment, instruments and coverage.

The main characteristics of a framework convention are:

- recognition by the signatories that there is global public good to be safe-guarded;
- creation of a set of soft obligations to foster the realization of that public good;
- attribution of a high status to the agreement but initial acceptance of a low content in order to maximize support;
- acceptance of ambiguities in text and a differentiated interpretation of them;
- agreement on the need to deal with detailed matters of content in separate protocols.

There are several ways in which international agreements *can be made effective*. Binding rules become effective for all parties to the agreement as soon as the treaty or protocol has come into force; mostly when it is ratified by the minimum number of countries required (a case in point is the Kyoto protocol discussed in Chapter 9). In other agreements the standards set become effective only to the member countries that have accepted to ratify the treaty (a case in point are ILO conventions discussed in Chapter 10).

There are several other forms that should briefly be mentioned. One such form is the code. Codes are in general stating norms that parties accept to observe in their behaviour. At a minimum they give recommendations or guidelines that do not produce binding rules (parties comply or explain). However, in their strictest form they provide also clear obligations both on countries (for instance on the national treatment of foreign investors) and firms (for instance on the observance of good governance).[6]

4.3.2 Finances

The main aim of the financial method is to induce actors to change their behaviour in the preferred sense. This can be done by both carrots and sticks; the first come in the form of financial inducements (subsidies) for policy-consistent behaviour and the second in the form of financial charges for behaviour that is not consistent with agreed policy. The financial method is very important in national policy environments. Taxes and excise duties penalize the consumption of certain goods (e.g. tobacco; energy); subsidies on the other hand stimulate consumption (e.g. culture, health). The financial method is used differently by international organizations, for several reasons.

Incentive schemes in the field of international public goods are not uncommon. An example is support programmes for countries that want to comply with international objectives but lack the resources to do so. A case in point is the support that the World Bank Group may give in terms of debt relief to developing countries that are willing to comply with environmental programmes. Moreover, there are technical assistance programmes for countries that would like to comply with labour standards but have difficulty in implementing the necessary regulation and in organizing enforcement.

Disincentives such as sanctions, penalties or fines are much used in national situations. The option is not very common in the framework of IOs, however. In general the tax instrument cannot be used, as governments do not want to give up part of their sovereignty in this highly sensitive matter. The instrument of fines (penalties) is not common in global institutions, as member states will shy away from it. Only in the rare cases where integration has gone a long way and there is a large amount of solidarity between partners are they used. An example can be found in the European Growth and Stability Pact, where a member country of the European Union may be obliged to pay a fine to the Union if it does not fulfil its obligation to ensure a balanced budget, thereby jeopardizing the macroeconomic stability of the Union as a whole.

4.3.3 Coordination

The main aim of the coordination method is to persuade interdependent actors to bend their behaviour in the preferred direction. This method operates mainly by making an appeal to norms, values and beliefs, and tries to change problem perception by partners. At higher stages of coordination there are attempts to reach agreements. Two categories can be distinguished. On the flexible side we find forms where member states commit themselves only to common objectives and decline to specify further how they will make sure those objectives are reached. On the rigid side are forms that are much more intrusive, where the objectives are translated into specific national targets and where recommendations can be issued by the IO on the type of policy instruments through which such targets are to be reached.

Coordination can best take place in the framework of an existing organization with known and stable governance practices.[7] The method of coordination suffers from a lack of commitment that can jeopardize its effectiveness. Effectiveness can be improved by the introduction of stronger instruments of coordination. Examples are the introduction of concrete frameworks for cooperation, formal obligations to participate, peer pressure and incentives to follow up recommendations. These various forms of coordination can be divided into three categories depending on the degree to which the partners accept inroads into their independence in order to pursue mutual benefits.[8]

Group 1: Avoiding surprise and conflict

1. *Informing partners.* This implies that partners communicate to each other the issues they are concerned about, the targets they set and the action they have in mind. It is a rather passive means of coordination, in which it is hoped that partners will adapt their behaviour on the basis of better knowledge of mutual motivations and interests. In the end, however, decisions are taken in an autonomous way.
2. *Consulting partners.* This implies feedback from partners. Active consultation is sought and arguments are exchanged so as to bring both partners to the conclusion that concerted action is in their common interest. "Convincing" or "persuading" involves elements of monitoring of developments, the exchange of best practices and the deliberate willingness to be open to new ways of doing things (in simple terms: arguing).
3. *Avoiding conflicts.* This involves mechanisms to avoid open divergences between partners and the introduction of soft forms of resolution such as arbitrage.

Group 2: Searching for synergy

1. *Seeking consensus.* The lowest form here is to seek a common denominator on which all partners can agree. The highest version is where partners agree on common objectives and on concerted action to reach such objectives. The form

in which this can be done is often through joint committees, working groups, project teams, consulting studies, etc.

2. *Setting parameters.* Constraints on the discretionary margins of each partner delimit the competences of all partners. These can take the form of setting quantitative limits to their margins of manoeuvre (e.g. on budget deficits in macroeconomic policy or emission standards in environmental policy).

3. *Establish common priorities.* This high-level coordination capacity presupposes in-depth analysis of problems, considerable agreement on the hierarchy of objectives and instruments, and a very high degree of agreement on the way subordinate objectives are formulated and policies implemented.

Group 3: Active promotion of consistency and synergy

1. *Adopting a common strategy.* This case refers to a situation in which the individual partners integrate their policies into one framework with consistent assessment of issues, definition of objectives, choice of instruments, procedures for implementation and evaluation of the results.

2. *Adopting strong measures for compliance.* The Achilles heel of the method is that partners can participate formally but fail to comply in practice. In cases when results for all depend on the efforts of each individual country, harder forms will be needed. If partners' preferences concerning a specific project are very different, they may be ready to change their preference in exchange for something they value more. This leads to situations where a partner is compensated for the (perceived) loss, forgone benefit or lack of opportunities (in somewhat negative terms, that partner is "bribed" into agreement).

4.3.4 Some comments on alternative options

IOs rely mostly on mutual commitments, on monitoring and on soft methods of coordination. Only in rare cases are stronger instruments used.

One such strong instrument to make actors comply is *coercion*. This can be used by national administrations, where the central authority is empowered to give orders, or in a situation of dependency, where the power of hegemony is used to force compliance (in colloquial terms: arm-twisting). IOs cannot use military or police force to make members comply. Another strong instrument used by national administrations is to withdraw committed financial resources from a local authority. This form of compliance can only in rare cases be observed in IOs. A case in point is the IMF; if a country does not comply with the conditions, the IMF can withdraw its support. As alternative financial help will be hard to find, the country will in general comply.

Another strong instrument is the sanction of *expelling a member from the organization*. This implies the exclusion of the non-complying partner from the benefits of membership (a club good). However, in many cases the exclusion of a country from an IO not only excludes that country from the benefits of the club good but also reduces the advantages of the club good for the remaining members. So, this measure is only used in extreme cases. In any case, many problems of non-compliance will be too small to justify such a drastic measure.

Non-compliance should not be left unpunished. It would incite others to go along the same path, with the risk of erosion of the whole deal. Fortunately, there are some forces at work that tend to stimulate compliance. These occur notably in repetitive games. The reason is that defection delivers short-term gains but these come at the cost of the loss of long-term cooperation, as partners will no longer trust the partner that has defected. So, compliance signals to the international community that you are part of a respectable set, which leads to benefits such as lower cost of capital or greater inward investment. Defection on a contract means forgoing your good reputation and with it the advantages it produced. Loss of reputation is therefore an important threat against defection. The effectiveness of the threat can be enhanced by making deviation public.

So, as the members of the international organization (or signatories to an agreement) are sovereign states, the most important way in which they can be made to comply is by convincing them of the interest they have in the agreement and in its application (so, persuasion in the stages both of negotiation and of implementation). Of course, disputes will always occur, hence the importance of strong institutional devices for dispute settlement.

4.3.5 Network governance: basic characteristics[9]

I have defined governance as a task for public-sector actors that meet in formal structures. However, for effective policy-making and policy implementation other actors need to be involved as well – in particular, representatives of the target groups of the policy, of scientific experts and of specific interests. Integrating them gives the formal networks of public actors a new dimension. Moreover, in cases where uncertainties exist as to the necessity to address problems and the best way to attack them, formal structures either will not yet exist or will not be adequate for finding solutions. So, there is a case for informal arrangements that permit experimentation and flexibility. Such network governance can best be defined in comparison with the characteristics of IOs and of the various governance methods, as follows:[10]

- *Membership* is in principle fluid. This stems from the dynamic character of networks, where relations intensify or weaken as opportunities and challenges change. It also comes from the fact that networks are task-focused, not structure-fixated. The authority is divided over the partners. The organizational form is flat; they illustrate that cooperation is essentially between equal partners with different backgrounds.
- The *status* of the results of the cooperation is in the form of commitments that have to be translated by each of the partners into decisions and actions within their proper competence and domain. These have, however, the advantage of

a large degree of consistency with the interest of others and thereby are likely to be welfare-improving.

- *Management* is facilitative rather than regulatory. Coordination is rather informal. It is oriented towards the identification of common values and interests, the mediation of conflicts, the definition of common actions, the management of the process, the convergence of fluid goals and the integration of opportunities. Very often the groups can be made operational only if some organization provides financial support for the running costs (secretarial and the organization of conferences).
- *Effectiveness* hinges on mutual trust and loyalty to partners, trust and loyalty that build up during successful common (inter)actions; this is the basis for further cooperation.

4.4 Effectiveness by governance method

4.4.1 Different approaches

Methods and instruments are deployed to realize an effect, for instance to stimulate the economic development of LDCs (Chapter 7) or to reduce the emission of greenhouse gases (Chapter 8). They sometimes involve the input of considerable resources (funds for development programmes – Chapter 7); investment in abatement technology – Chapter 8). It is thus of the utmost importance to check how far these resources are well spent – in other words, to check the effectiveness of the efforts. Numerous methods have been developed to evaluate policies. Here I will distil the most important ones, grouped by governance method.

As the starkest differences exist between regulation and coordination (the former being a top-down process, the latter a bottom-up one), we will for the time being limit our discussion to these two (see the rows in Table 4.2). We shall distinguish, moreover, between output and outcome (columns in Table 4.2). The difference between the two may be explained with an example from development policy (see Chapter 7). The final objective of the policy is the catching up of developing countries. This may be defined in *outcome* terms as a sustained higher GDP growth than the world's average GDP growth. In order to realize this, programmes will be executed – for instance, for agricultural development in a specific country financed in part by the World Bank. The *output* can be defined as the number of

TABLE 4.2 Effectiveness and governance methods

		Output	*Outcome*
Regulation	Top-down	1	2
Coordination	Bottom-up	3	4

Source: Inspired by Knill and Liefferink (2007: 151–154).

hectares of agricultural land that have been created with the support of the World Bank.

For *regulation* (top-down: cases 1 and 2), the degree of goal attainment (either in terms of output or outcome) serves as an indicator for the effectiveness of the implementation. The same would apply to the financial method.

For *coordination* (bottom-up: cases 3 and 4), effectiveness is more elusive. It can be defined as the degree to which the perceived outcomes correspond with the preferences of the actors involved in the implementation process.[11]

4.4.2 Effectiveness measurement by output (cases 1 and 3 of Table 4.2)

In the *top-down approach* the most common way of achieving effectiveness is by comparing an easily identifiable target variable with an equally easily identifiable output variable (case 1). Effectiveness in terms of output of the regulatory method is accepted if two conditions are fulfilled: the legal transposition of international law into national law, and the practical application by addressees according to the requirements defined by the international law. A case in labour protection regulation in the framework of the ILO (see Chapter 9) may explain this. Ratification of ILO conventions setting standards on child labour would fulfil the first criterion. Compliance with such standards by individual businesses in countries like India would fulfil the second criterion.

In the *bottom-up perspective* (case 3) there is no real measure of effectiveness; actually, the process itself is the output. The very fact that member countries participate in the coordination exercise is supposed to have a positive effect on the objectives of this common policy by decreasing conflicting behaviour and persuasion of the hesitant members to make their policies conform to common objectives. Of course, the monitoring of member states' behaviour can indicate how much progress has been made.

4.4.3 Effectiveness measurement by outcome (cases 2 and 4 of Table 4.2)

In the *top-down approach*, performance measurement in terms of outcomes (case 2) is difficult to put into practice. The main reason is that there is seldom a direct causal link between policy instruments and their effects. Moreover, many external factors may influence the impact. To give an example of environmental policy: air quality may have improved as a result of international legislation, but also as the consequence of other factors, such as reduced emissions resulting from the decline of very polluting sectors of activity.

In the *bottom-up approach*, the measurement of performance is even more difficult. One can distinguish between on the one hand a situation where targets have been set and on the other hand a case where this has not been done. In the former case it would be possible to take the basic quantified objectives (e.g.

stopping the increase in the average temperature in the world). Another way would be to use intermediate objectives as outcome measurement (e.g. a decrease in emissions of CO_2 to combat climate change) and check how far the actual situation corresponds to the targets set. If no concrete final outcome targets have been set and reference has been made only to very general objectives such as sustainability, outcome is very difficult to measure. Indeed, it is very difficult to establish a causal link between the policy objectives of IOs and the national and local processes of learning and problem-solving in environmental matters.

4.5 Factors influencing effectiveness[12]

4.5.1 Outcome predictability

In many cases the choice of governance method will depend on the sense of obligation on the part of decision-makers to reach targets. This works out as follows for the three governance methods:

1. *Regulation* scores high on outcome predictability in a national environment, as the force of law and the instrument of adjudication (by courts) can be used. Indeed, regulation by setting standards can completely specify outcomes. However, on the global scale this method does not work well, owing to the lack of institutional adaptation to IO requirements, with the consequence that implementation failures occur.
2. *Budget.* The mechanisms for steering tend to be fairly strong with the budgetary method. They comprise systematic output control, evaluation of outcomes at three stages of the cycle, etc. All this does not, however, lead to full outcome predictability. For instance, the stepping up of aid money is not certain to translate into higher growth in LDCs, and into convergence of wealth levels (see Chapter 7).
3. *Coordination.* Given the weakness of the incentives and the diversity of the environments of implementation, the soft forms of coordination tend to score low on output predictability. Indeed, there is a danger that the room for manoeuvre will be used by national authorities in such a way that the original objectives set on the IO level tend to get lost. While obligation is lacking, implementation rests solely on the willingness of the implementer to comply with policy objectives. This will happen only in cases where there is a broad consensus on the policy objectives and on political priorities. In other cases, hard forms of coordination are required. For that reason, we see that over time the concern for effectiveness leads to the complementing of soft forms of governance with steering and monitoring systems using adequate sets of stimuli and sanctions.

So, in view of the need for outcome predictability the methods of regulation and budget will be preferred over coordination.

4.5.2 Adjustment flexibility

Effectiveness is also dependent on the capacity to adjust to changing circumstances. High flexibility allows for swift redesign of the regime in the light of technological innovations and the taking into account of new scientific evidence, or of the results of the evaluation of experience with former approaches. Now, the different governance methods perform very differently on this criterion:

- *Regulation* scores low, owing to the fact that any change involves the making a new act of international legislation (treaty). This is a cumbersome process as it involves many public-sector actors and, on top of that, many stakeholders that represent a large diversity of interest. If none of these have been involved in the implementation process, they do not know from experience the types of problems that have to be resolved. So, negotiators have to judge on the basis of evaluation reports, and it may take some time for them to familiarize themselves with the issue – hence much institutional inertia.
- *Coordination* scores high. The partners involved take care of the whole policy cycle; they take responsibility for the setting of objectives, for the practical implementation and for the evaluation. Moreover, they permit non-governmental partners to take part in networks. So, the participative and iterative character gives continuous feedback from the implementers to the IO level.
- The *budgetary method* occupies a middle position. Here, the stages of preparation and adoption are mainly dependent on an annual process in a multi-annual framework. For the broad orientation, long-term decisions are needed, which have a negative aspect because they are very inflexible. However, this coin has not only a dark side but also a bright one, because the stability in allowances means that partners can plan for the years ahead, which has a positive influence on the size and speed of investments. Moreover, inflexibility in the long term is compensated to some extent in the short term as there is considerable flexibility as to specific projects within the allocations to broad categories.

So, in cases when environments change and require frequent adjustments, the coordination method will be preferred over both the budgetary and the regulatory methods.

4.5.3 Level of discretion and participation

It is often assumed that the *level of discretion of the implementer* is relevant for effectiveness. However, the studies that have been made of the relation between discretion and effectiveness are not conclusive. On the one hand, studies show the advantage of hierarchy: clear objectives and requirements help addressees to orient their effort to achieving targets. On the other hand, studies show the advantages of discretion: it makes it possible to adapt the measures to the social, political and administrative conditions of the member states and their regions.

In a similar manner, one might assume that the *participation of stakeholders* (implementers, beneficiaries and civil society) in the process does improve effectiveness. It is in this sense that networks can show their usefulness (see section 4.3.5). Indeed, the "buying in" to the process of different actors decreases possible barriers and increases support. To increase long-term learning effects, it is advisable to promote the inclusion of stakeholders in several stages of the policy cycle, including in the final evaluation stage. Evaluation processes are thus turned into interactive exercises involving consultation with (and arbitrage between) the persons in the public sector that are directly responsible for the setting up of the programmes and with the major stakeholders and other interested organizations.

4.6 Administrative conditions

4.6.1 The interface between IOs and national administrations

Checks on compliance are based on regular monitoring – that is, the degree to which the behaviour of the members of an organization corresponds to the rules and objectives set. In many cases this leads to regular consultations between officials of the international organization and officials of the country involved.

National bureaucracies have in the past developed in different institutional settings and have been geared to widely diverging socio-economic models. If member states jealously defend their areas of sovereignty, their bureaucracies equally jealously defend their prerogatives, ways of operating and autonomy. So, the implementation of IOs' policies and the compliance with their objectives, targets and standards needs to take account of this diversity and to allow much flexibility.

The compliance of national civil servants with international obligations is likely to be much enhanced if they have been part of the elaboration of such rules. For that reason, the committees of national experts that precede the international conferences of ministers are extremely important. The latter give the main orientation to the work; the former work out the agreements in technical terms. Moreover, many expert committees of national civil servants meet at regular intervals to discuss the various aspects of implementation of agreements and propose amendments to the political level. Now, the members of such committees coming from the national administrations have different allegiances. On the one hand, they have to defend the interests of their home state. On the other hand, they have to defend the common good. For the system to work smoothly and to preserve consistency, the individual participants have to find compromises between these (potentially conflicting) interests.

4.6.2 Quality of national administrations

IOs are completely dependent on national administrations to put their policies into effect. All three governance methods make quite significant demands on national administrations. Under the regulatory method international standards need to be transposed into national law to take effect. A similar situation obtains for the budgetary method: many development programmes are co-financed by IOs but managed in practice by the member states. The coordination method completely depends for its effectiveness on the willingness of national civil servants to translate the commitments taken in the IO into national programmes, projects and actions.

So, effective implementation of IO policies is dependent on the quality of the national administrations. The WB has made regular estimates of the quality of government of all its member countries according to four dimensions (see Box 4.2). The figures show that there is a fair amount of correlation between the four indicators. Let us analyze briefly both the geographical and time dimension.

BOX 4.2 GOVERNANCE QUALITY INDICATORS

Governance quality is defined as the capacity of a government to effectively implement sound policies. It depends on the respect of citizens and the state for the institutions that govern economic and social interactions. Governance quality can be measured according to the following dimensions:

- *rule of law*, capturing perceptions of the extent to which agents have confidence in and abide by the rules of society, in particular the quality of contract enforcement, property rights, the police and the courts, as well as the likelihood of crime and violence;
- *government effectiveness*, capturing perceptions of the quality of public services, the quality of the civil service and the degree of its independence from political pressures, the quality of policy formulation and implementation, and the credibility of the government's commitment to such policies;
- *regulatory quality*, capturing perceptions of the ability of the government to formulate and implement sound policies and regulations that permit and promote private-sector development;
- *control of corruption*, capturing perceptions of the extent to which public power is exercised for private gain, including both petty and grand forms of corruption, as well as "capture" of the state by elites and private interests.

Source: Almost direct citation from Kaufmann *et al.* (2009: 5–6).

Geographical. There are huge differences between countries. Some of them, in particular countries in North Western Europe have very high scores. On the other hand many of the least developed countries have very low scores.

Time. Although one can observe cases where clear improvements have been made, for many countries the problems seem to be very persistent.

The persistent low quality of government puts a break on compliance with IOs' commitments and hence on the effectiveness of IOs. Moreover, it reveals a more general development problem as there is much evidence of the beneficial impact of good governance on growth (e.g. Kaufmann *et al.* 1999a,b; Rodrik *et al.* 2004).

4.7 Summary and conclusions

Governance is the exercise of political and administrative authority (including the allocation of institutional and financial resources) to implement effectively sound policies so as to realize stated objectives. The main governance methods are regulation, finance and coordination.

- For each method, different *instruments* can be deployed by IOs. For regulation, the main one is the treaty or convention. For the financial method, the main one is the co-financing of programmes. For coordination, a hierarchy of instruments can be used, starting with the simple sharing of information with partners to the adoption of common strategic frameworks.
- Governance methods and their instruments are deployed to obtain a specified *effect*. These can be defined in terms of direct effects of programmes (output) and final effects (outcome) on a target variable. The effectiveness of actions of IOs is often difficult to measure, owing to a lack of specification of objectives and a lack of a clear relation between causes and effects.
- The *choice of method and instrument* depends to a large extent on factors such as the need for outcome predictability (favouring regulation) and for flexibility in adjustment to new circumstances (favouring coordination).
- IOs are dependent on *national administrations* to put their policies into effect. So, one of the most important success factors is thus the quality of the national public sector. Now, there are considerable differences in this indicator between different parts of the globe and between individual countries. These differences tend to be persistent over time.

PART II

Implementing the solutions (practice)

5

TRADE

5.1 Introduction

International specialization and trade permit countries to benefit from economies of scale and from innovation. But trade cannot thrive in the absence of a proper regime setting the rules of the game and enhancing the benefits of specialization.[1]

The *objective* of the present chapter is to expose the rationale, the main features and the effectiveness of the international regime that has been elaborated over the past half-century to liberalize trade and foster fair trade.

The *structure* of the chapter is as follows. First, I will describe the problem that has arisen in matters of international trade: the occurrence of much protection. In the next section I will show that it is in the interest of everyone to do away with protection; indeed, the realization of a regime that provides for free (fair) trade is a public good. I pursue the demonstration by describing the organizations that provide that collective good and the instruments they use to safeguard it. In a separate section I deal in particular with the governance aspects, as given form in the most important organization, the WTO. Finally, I will round off the discussion of this chapter by evaluating the present regime, assessing the future challenges and putting forward a set of propositions for improvement.

5.2 The main problems

5.2.1 Obstacles to trade in goods: reasons for such obstacles

All governments have been subject to pressures for protection, mostly from domestic producers seeking shelter against foreign competition. Most governments have given in to such pressures, so in the course of time, obstacles to trade in international production have become introduced. Protection against third countries is mostly done by means of *import restrictions*. From the extensive literature I have distilled the following arguments for such measures:

- *Nurturing so-called infant industries.* The idea is that young companies and sectors which are not yet competitive should be sheltered in infancy in order for them to develop into "adult" companies holding their own in international competition.
- *Defence against dumping.* The healthy industrial structure of an economy may be spoiled when foreign goods are dumped on the market at prices below the cost in the country of origin. Even if the action is temporary, the economy may be weakened beyond its capacity to recover.
- *Defence against social dumping.* If wages in the exporting country do not match productivity, labour is supposed to be exploited; importation from such a country is held by some to uphold such practices and is therefore not permissible.
- *Boosting employment.* If the production factors in a country are not fully occupied, protection can turn local demand towards domestic goods, so that more labour is put to work and social costs are avoided.
- *Diversification of the economic structure.* Countries specializing in one or a few products tend to be very vulnerable; problems of marketing such products lead to instant loss of virtually all income from abroad. This argument applies to small developing countries rather than to large industrialized states.
- *Easing balance-of-payments problems.* Import restrictions reduce the amount to be paid abroad, which helps to avoid adjustments of the industrial structure and accompanying social costs and societal friction (caused by wage reduction, restrictive policies and so on).

National governments are sovereign in their setting of the rules for international trade. Some of the motives for protectionist measures cited here have some basis in economics, such as that of protecting an infant industry. However, in general, obstacles will go against the interests of the economy, as they are introduced to protect less efficient industries or to permit rent-seeking by powerful national producers.

5.2.2 Obstacles to trade in goods: categories

Obstacles, or trade-impeding factors, fall into two categories: tariffs and so called "non-tariff barriers". They can be described as follows:

- Tariffs, or customs duties or import duties, are sums levied on imports of goods, making the goods more expensive on the internal market. Such levies may be based on value or quantity. Levies of similar effect are import levies disguised as administrative costs, storage costs or test costs imposed by the customs.

- Quantitative restrictions are ceilings put on the volume of imports of a certain good allowed into a country in a certain period (quota), sometimes expressed in money values.
- Currency restrictions mean that no foreign currency is made available to enable importers to pay for goods bought abroad.
- Other non-tariff impediments are all those measures or situations (such as fiscal treatment, legal regulations, safety norms or public tenders) that ensure a country's own products' preferential treatment over foreign products on the domestic market.

5.2.3 Obstacles to trade in services: reasons for such obstacles

Traditionally, national markets for services are much segmented. Obstacles to free trade in services are in general justified by either consumer or producer interests.

Most of the obstacles are supposedly drawn up to *protect consumers*. A few examples from different sectors may illustrate this:

- In banking and insurance, regulation serves to limit the risk of insolvency through surveillance of private operators by (semi-)public organizations (e.g. central banks). Since foreign suppliers are hard to control, access to the national market is barred to them.
- In air transport, the safety of the passenger is the main concern. Standards are accompanied by mutual import controls in the form of landing rights.
- In medical services, the interests of the patient are protected by the enforcement of standards for the qualifications of personnel (e.g. medical doctors).

Although the arguments for consumer protection are valid, they do not necessarily have to lead to trade protection; indeed, other policy measures can be devised with the same effect for the safety and health of consumers while leaving international competition free. However, even if consumer protection is the official reason for this protectionist regulation, in practice the reason is often that domestic firms want to be sheltered from international competition.

Another set of motives for measures against foreign competition in services concern the *protection of national producers*:

- control of macroeconomic policy (through the banking system);
- enhancing national prestige (civil aviation);
- control of key technologies (telecommunication);
- safeguarding cultural values (movies, television).

5.2.4 Obstacles to trade in services: categories

Many of the obstacles to trade in services are fairly comparable to those that hinder goods trade. However, there are also big differences. As the value of a border-crossing service is harder to control than that of a good, tariffs are seldom imposed, and restrictions on the trade in services are mostly of the non-tariff type. Moreover, because the provision of some types of service across the border involves direct investments, a set of restrictions to entry of markets by firms via investment is relevant too.

Trade in services can be hampered by the following instruments:

- Quantitative restriction on domestic consumption (for instance, shares of markets reserved for home producers of movies).
- Subsidies (e.g. in construction).
- Government procurement (e.g. in construction, data processing).
- Currency controls on transfers to foreign countries for services provided.
- Restrictions on the qualifications required to perform certain services (legal, medical).
- Restrictions on foreign firms to set up or take over subsidiary companies.

5.3 The main public goods

5.3.1 Objectives

The theory of international trade is very clear about the choice of the best regimes: it shows that protection has important negative effects on prosperity, and that the best way to avoid these negative effects is for all countries to adopt free trade.[2] Free trade stimulates a better allocation of production factors: capital and labour are used for those activities where they have the highest output. Moreover, free trade permits producers to use scale economies to the greatest extent, while the keener competition it engenders leads to cost reductions and innovations. So, the *objective* should be to liberalize trade all over the world. Progress in reaching this objective can be measured by the decrease in obstacles over time and of course by the ensuing increase in trade volumes.

Once a tangle of protectionist measures is in place, a changeover to free trade is not something that is going to happen by itself. On the contrary, one can show with a simple example of a two-country game that it is likely that a stalemate situation of all countries maintaining protection will come into being (see Box 5.1). If all governments give in to pressures from groups asking for protection, the group as a whole suffers collectively, as the benefits of free trade are forgone for everybody. Thus, in trade matters the public good of free trade can be provided only by collective action to install a regime that commits as many countries as possible to foster liberalization and to maintain fair trade. This will permit investors to have trust that individual protectionist actions by governments will not undo the conditions they assumed to exist while making their decisions.

The notion of public good as applied to trade can be made more precise in several aspects. The first is the aspect "public". To some, free trade is better called a *collective* good, as it may have more the character of a club good than of a public

BOX 5.1 A TRADE GAME LEADS TO GENERALIZATION OF PROTECTIONISM

The standard theoretical model that best characterizes the international trade game is based on the following *assumptions*:

- There are two actors, states A and B, which are unitary rational state actors that seek to maximize national income.
- Each state has one of two acts available to it: C, cooperate, or D, defect. To cooperate means to contribute to the public good by not imposing a tariff. To defect means not to contribute, and to impose tariffs.
- The game is non-cooperative, which means that binding agreements are not allowed. Moreover, each player selects only one act and the two players choose simultaneously.

Now, four different *outcomes* can theoretically result:

- CC: generalized free trade;
- DD: generalized protection;
- CD: country A being exploited by country B;
- DC: country B being exploited by A.

We assume that both players order their preferences for the outcome of the game in the same way. For country A, this is DC>CC>DD>CD. This is consistent with the fact that each country individually has an interest in having high tariffs on its imports while benefiting from the low tariffs on the partner country's imports (DC for A). It is also consistent with international trade theory, which prefers free trade (CC) to protectionism (DD).

By choosing C, a country runs the risk of ending up in the situation of CD. In order to avoid that risk, both countries will choose D. So, the rational behaviour of individuals tends to lead to a situation where the public good is not provided.

Source: Adapted from Carlson (2000).

good (see Chapter 2). Indeed, there exists quite some potential for exclusion, of producers from third countries to the markets of a group, so the formation of clubs is feasible. This expresses itself mostly as regional free trade arrangements. However, as most benefits can be obtained by a wide-ranging worldwide liberalization, I will henceforth speak of public good. The second aspect is about content. Free trade is in itself not enough to increase the efficiency sought for. It needs to be complemented by measures that make sure that the system works well. That means that certain principles about fairness have to be applied, that there is transparency about regulation and its application, etc.

The next question to answer is *how to arrive at a regime* that can provide the public good of free trade. Critical in this respect is the transition of protection to free trade. Given the situation that has evolved historically, all governments will consider their tariffs as bargaining chips that can be traded against similar chips of other countries. Liberalization can be achieved if the various governments involved can be convinced of the priority they should give to the long-term general interest over the immediate sectoral or individual interest. Now, each change in trade regime has redistributive effects: it benefits some while hurting others. The best way to bring forward a change in such a situation is to mobilize the most important beneficiaries of the opening up. Schematizing, one may say that this can be done by exchanging access of foreign producers to the home market for access of home exporters to the markets of the partner country. Each government will thereby have to overcome the opposition of import-competing activities, but it will be able to build on the interest of potential exporters. If everybody behaves in this way the allocation of production factors improves, and welfare increases for everybody (static gains). Moreover, the change in competition will drive towards further innovation and technological progress, which leads to dynamic gains for the participating economies. Once a certain level of free trade is established, the maintenance of the rules of the system and the further reinforcement of the deals can be worked on.

The liberalization of trade is only an intermediate objective. The ultimate objective is growth: it is expected that the changes in the economic structure that will be brought about by trade will enhance the economic development of the participating countries. Some go even further and would set the objective of ensuring that trade actually does support the alleviation of poverty and hence a better income distribution in the participating countries.

5.3.2 Principles

The parties involved in trade liberalization are confronted with the problem of how to achieve mutual advantages. The solution can be found in the application of the principle of *non-discrimination between different trade partners*, also called *the most favoured nation principle*. The relevance of this principle can be explained as follows.

Imagine that the first round of discussions is between two countries that assume they have something valuable to offer to one another. Country A has an advantage in the production of good X, country B in the production of good Y. Imagine further that both are of about equal importance and that both countries see further specialization along their comparative advantage as a net benefit. The first option that comes to mind is that both countries agree on a tariff cut of both good X and good Y originating from the partner country of, say, 15 per cent. This is not, however, a viable solution if there are third countries that produce goods X and

Y. Suppose country A, after having negotiated the deal with B, offers to country C a tariff cut of 20 per cent for good Y in exchange for a tariff cut of 15 per cent on its part for good X. It means that the benefits of the concession given to country B have become eroded for country B, as it will be outcompeted on the market of A by producers from C. On the other hand, the access of A producers to the market of B for good Y remains intact.

The mutual award of most favoured nation (MFN) status implies that countries A and B promise each other that they will not give better deals to any other partner.

5.3.3 International responsibilities: multilateral liberalization

The putting into effect of the MFN option in bilateral deals is beset with problems. These come about because in general there are many suppliers of many different goods. Trade negotiators are confronted with considerable uncertainty about the intentions of all other actors. In such situations, governments have an interest in pursuing *multilateral trade negotiations* (MTNs) (McCalman 2002), for two reasons:

1. *Hindrance of previous deals*. If, after the game described in Box 5.1, country A wants to reach a deal with country E on goods Z, there does not seem to be a conflict. However, if countries A and E also involve either good X or good Y in their deals, a problem arises. If A and E want to strive for a very significant liberalization, they are limited by earlier agreements, which implies that tariffs between A and E cannot be reduced below the level agreed on between A and B initially. The more deals country A has already entered into, the less it can offer in terms of access to its markets to new trade partners.
2. *Package deals*. Possibilities for trade-offs between different negotiation items and issue linkage increase with the increase in the number of participants.

In order to make the commitments negotiated in the MTN credible, a number of mechanisms have been devised. They are intended to make individual countries comply with the rules of the mutual international agreement they have subscribed to. This is important in the sense that each country will be tempted to breach the rules in individual cases while still benefiting from the general liberalization. In the absence of an international authority with coercive powers, the solution to this problem is simply punishment by members. In terms of tariff cuts the situation may arise that country A, which had agreed to cut its tariffs (just like all its partners) by 20 per cent, does not do so. Then, country B can immediately respond by not giving the promised tariff cut to country A either. And if all countries do that, country A will be virtually excluded from the advantages of liberalization.

Before the negotiation starts, every country will establish its objective function. In other words, it makes its *calculations about the possible benefits and costs of the results*. Countries that have much to win from liberalization will try to obtain considerable tariff cuts over a wide range of products. Countries that consider that they have little to win or much to lose on certain specific products will ask for lower tariff cuts and for exceptions for these specific products. The outcome of this game is determined by the objective function of the partner that has the lowest gains from trade.

The countries that have a strong interest in pushing liberalization will also have an interest in limiting the group of negotiating partners to those that are keen to safeguard similar interests. However, the restriction of participants runs counter to the results of the previous section, where we saw that countries had an interest in making the agreement as comprehensive as possible. So, a balance has to be struck between these two elements. A likely outcome is that countries that have a strong interest will form a core group of negotiators and then see how many others will be inclined to join the proposed deal.

5.3.4 National responsibilities

National governments have to make sure that they comply with the rules of the relevant international organizations they have entered into. To that end, they have to adapt their regulatory and administrative system (e.g. on custom duties). They have to make sure that national producers and consumers comply with these rules. In the past many governments have accepted international obligations to lock in nationally certain reforms that they thought were necessary for economic reasons but were difficult to realize politically. International commitments limit the risk that these reforms are undone by subsequent governments.

Trade liberalization is in the end a means for increasing wealth. However, in itself it does not lead to *higher growth*; other determinants of competitiveness on international markets have to be improved as well. The essential task of national governments is to provide the best conditions for competitiveness, such as a responsive industrial structure, an adaptive labour market, innovation, good support to FDI and stable institutions. Bear in mind that growth is sometimes also dependent on the equitable distribution of the benefits of trade and growth; so governments should put in place devices that attenuate the inequalities that may be entailed by increased trade openness.

5.4 Organizations involved in the provision of the public good

5.4.1 Major players

In matters of international trade, private firms are the most important actors. However, the public authorities set the conditions and the rules. Next to these two principal actors there is civil society, which has a stake in the outcome of the process. The roles of the various groups of players can be described in somewhat more detail as follows.

Multinational corporations (MNCs)

Multinational corporations account for a very large share of international trade. To MNCs, the conditions under which international trade is handled are of vital importance; these conditions determine to a large extent the possibilities for specialization and hence the profitability of their individual operations. Only the most important MNCs can hope to influence international negotiations directly; others have to engage in collective action to have their voice heard. So, many specialist groups of interested private-sector players have developed. Cases in point are farmers in developed areas such as the European Union or the United States (against imports), or producers of primary products in developing countries (in favour of exports). Often the interests of these different sub-groups are conflicting, but they all try to influence trade rules in their favour by means of very active lobbying. The more encompassing the lobby groups are, the more they tend to support the application of a limited set of clear, transparent rules (e.g. International Chamber of Commerce).

National governments

Since time immemorial, governments have influenced international trade, mainly for tax, security and industrial policy reasons. Under the influence of local beneficiaries, such measures have tended to become ever more detailed, specific and complicated. Moreover, they have tended to discriminate among various trade partners. The effect of this tendency has been that over the years a whole tangle of trade protection has evolved, consisting of elaborate sets of instruments (see section 5.2). Some countries have even nationalized part or the whole of their international trade. At present many of the barriers have been taken way and there are very few countries left that have state-controlled trade, but all governments retain a keen interest in international trade matters and it is they that are the players in inter-national negotiations on trade matters.

Non-governmental organizations (NGOs)

In general, non-governmental organizations are entities with voluntary member-ship that defend causes that are not directly economic, such as labour standards, environmental protection, food safety, and consumer protection. Often they are single-issue groups, such as environmentalist groups. They have become very powerful in mobilizing public opinion and on that basis have been able to raise considerable funds to make their views heard by decision-makers. Many groups with different claims have bundled their activities in an anti-globalization (or socio-globalization) movement (Murphy 2010).

5.4.2 Main international organizations

The institutional set-up that has to deal with these problems cited in section 5.2 consists essentially of *intergovernmental* organizations. So, the other stakeholders mentioned in the previous subsection, notably firms and NGOs, have no direct say in the dealings of these organizations. They have to turn to national governments or to the permanent instances of these international organizations to have their interests represented. The following international organizations deal with trade:[3]

- The *World Trade Organization*[4] (formerly GATT) plays the central role in trade liberalization. Its emergence can be explained as the result of awareness, as the crisis of the 1930s had taught the lesson that an international regime for trade was needed in order to avoid a rebirth of the problems that had led to the Second World War. We will go in much detail into the workings of the WTO in the following sections of this chapter.
- The *G8* and *G20* analyse problems, make suggestions and bring these to the agenda of the relevant international organizations. In recent years they have not been able to provide much leadership in trade matters, as members could not agree on basic issues.
- The *OECD* has played a limited but important role. The organization has always been helpful in making analyses of important trends and in coordinating the positions of the industrialized countries.
- *UNCTAD* was created because of conflicts between rich and poor countries over the organization of trade. UNCTAD has tried in many ways to put into practice more interventionist approaches to improve the trade position of LDCs. Notably, it has dealt with a set of commodity agreements. Its successes have been limited, and now its role is rather in information and analysis of the relation between trade and foreign direct investment.
- There are *specialist organizations*, for instance in the fields of transport and telecommunications. Such organizations are older than GATT and the WTO. Under the influence of technological change they have been forced to reassess their roles (see Box 5.2).

Finally, we draw attention to *regional trade arrangements*. These cover only a limited number of countries and in general strive towards a free trade area or a customs union. Examples are the EU in Europe, NAFTA in North America, MERCOSUR in South America and ASEAN in Asia (see section 3.5). The issue of regionalism has for a long time been the subject of considerable controversy (see section 5.5.2). A hybrid version of regionalization has developed in the framework of the WTO, where regional groups (e.g. Africa) coordinate their positions.

5.4.3 The WTO

The origins of the WTO can be traced back to the Second World War when the UN tried to set up a specialized organization for trade (the International

Trade Organization; ITO). As the negotiations dragged on a number of countries decided to move ahead outside this UN framework. They signed in 1947 the General Agreement on Tariffs and Trade (GATT). Over time the limits to the (still provisional) GATT set–up became visible and the need for stronger legal basis and for a real international organization became apparent. The WTO was created in 1995. The *contracting parties* to the General *Agreement* became *members* of the World Trade *Organization*. The WTO remained a freestanding organization however, loosely related to the UN system. Compared to GATT the tasks of the WTO were broadened to cover not only trade in (manufactured) goods but also in services and related aspects such as intellectual property rights (TRIPs) (see Box 5.3).

BOX 5.2 SHIFTS IN INSTITUTIONS DUE TO TECHNOLOGICAL CHANGE

In the telecommunications sector, technology to a large extent has determined the emergence and tasks of international organizations. The International Telecommunication Union (ITU), established in 1932, merged the activities of other, much older bodies that had regulated specific technologies, the most important example of them being the International Telegraph Union, set up in 1865 (there were others covering telephony and radio). In 1947 the ITU became a specialized agency of the United Nations (see Chapter 3). The ITU's main task is the setting of technical standards relating to equipment and use. Its member governments controlled very closely the activities of national monopolist telecom providers (often even publicly owned ones).

In the last half of the twentieth century, technological innovations (satellites) eroded the reasons for network monopolies, and the services of the telecommunications industry were liberalized. They became the subject of specialist trade negotiations in the framework of the WTO. In 1998 the agreement on basic telecommunication services came into effect (covering voice, fax and data). That means that the two basic rules of the WTO (see section 5.5.2) now apply to the telecom sector. Under the most favoured nation rule, concessions given to telecom suppliers in one WTO member country must be offered to suppliers from all WTO countries. Under national treatment, foreign telecom service suppliers established in a country must be treated identically to a supplier from the home country. Moreover, an agreement has been reached on regulatory principles, covering subjects such as competition safeguards, interconnection guarantees, transparent licensing processes and the independence of regulators. The latter elements are introduced to ensure that market access is not nullified by anti-competitive behaviour on the part of a (former monopolist) incumbent.

Recently, the Internet has revolutionized the telecom sector by permitting business and consumers to develop a whole new field of diversified Web-based services and activities. The Internet has grown up in a highly unregulated way. There is a big debate on whether and, if so, how the Web needs to be regulated to safeguard a series of public goods. (For further details, see Chapter 10.)

BOX 5.3 EVOLUTION OF COVERAGE OF THE WTO

Over time the members of the WTO have agreed to broaden its coverage on three scores:

- *Sectors.* For a long time, agriculture, textiles and clothing, and services were almost exempt from liberalization,[5] but in the 1990s all three sectors were brought under the working of the WTO rules. There are still a few exceptions, such as maritime and air transport, which remain (for historical reasons) outside the domain of the WTO. In order to prevent trade barriers emerging in new sectors, the WTO has agreed a moratorium in respect of e-commerce, implying that no customs duties or other barriers are to be imposed.
- *Areas.* GATT started with a limited number of signatories but over time it gradually increased its coverage. At the moment, most countries in the world are members of the WTO. Consequently, the principle of non-discrimination has gradually acquired universal application.
- *Instruments.* For a long time, exceptions as to quota and other non-tariff barriers pertained. The same was true for all sorts of safeguards against negative effects of specific trade measures. Most of these (such as the textile quota) have subsequently been dismantled.

The WTO pursues a *double objective*:

1. trade liberalization – in other words, the dismantling of protection in all its forms;
2. elimination of discrimination – in other words, equal treatment for producers, irrespective of the country of their location.

The *functions* of the WTO[6] concern:

- The setting of principles. The most favoured nation clause specifies that trade concessions given by a country to a third country immediately apply to all other members.

- Provision of a framework for multilateral negotiations on trade liberalizations (examples are the famous trade rounds; presently the Doha round).
- Surveillance of the system (e.g. through the Trade Policy Review Mechanism) and monitoring of the compliance of members with commitments.
- Settlement of trade disputes between nations that have a conflicting interpretation of the rules (a case in point is anti-dumping).

Membership is widespread: all major countries and almost all other countries in the world have acquired membership.[7] Membership of the United Nations does not qualify a country for WTO membership; it has to show that it is capable of enshrining all the rules of the WTO into national law. Because in the European Union external trade is a Union competence, the Union is a member of the WTO alongside the EU member countries. The contracting parties have in principle equal positions ("one country, one vote"). However, there is not much voting: parties sometimes negotiate in groups and try to reach consensus. Many informal groups are formed to press particular issues (for instance the Cairns group on agriculture).

The *internal organization* of the WTO is shown in Figure 5.1. It distinguishes:

- The Ministerial Conference – the highest authority in the WTO. It meets at least once every two years.
- The General Council, which is the top day-to-day decision-making body, meaning that it is responsible for the regular execution of the various tasks of the WTO. It has delegated much of this task to various bodies and councils: first, to the Trade Policy Review Body and the Dispute Settlement Body; and second, to the specialist Councils for (among others) Trade in Goods, Trade in Services, Intellectual Property Rights and Regional Trade Agreements.
- Committees and working groups prepare meetings and work out agreements on a multitude of detailed subjects.
- The Director-General (head of the staff, numbering some 600) has the task of preparing the meetings of the various conferences, councils, committees and working groups.

A specific aspect of the WTO is that it has *no executive body*. The Secretariat although professionally strong is politically weak. They are not allowed to take independent views, but have to align to the common positions of the members of the organization. Proposals for introducing such an executive body were never accepted, owing to lack of agreement on its composition and roles between major players (the European Union and the United States), and opposition by the LDCs. Apparently trade is too sensitive a matter for governments to let international civil servants influence decisions. So, notwithstanding its high profile the WTO is only a small organization (its total budget is comparable to the budget for travel expenses of the World Bank!).

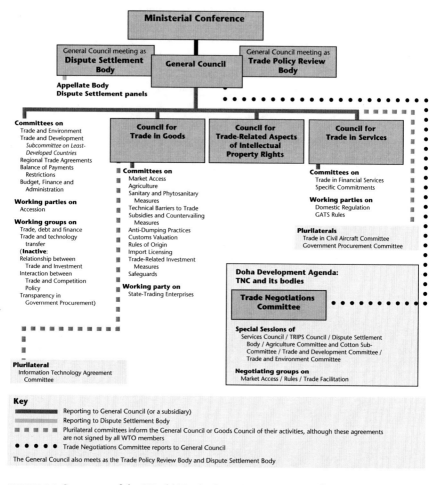

FIGURE 5.1 Structure of the World Trade Organization (WTO).[8]

Source: WTO website; www.wto.org.

5.5 WTO governance

5.5.1 General

Fundamental in the WTO is the recognition of the members that trade is a matter of common interest and that changes in national trade regimes according to international standards have to be made by negotiation with trade partners and have to be followed by the possibility of settling disputes.

So, the first role of the WTO is to serve as a permanent forum for negotiations. These concern in the first place the way in which the objectives of the organization should be reached – that is, to reduce hindrances to trade. Devising an effective formula for negotiations on trade liberalization has led to the *reciprocity rule*. This means that a country that is prepared to make concessions in matters of liberalizing its trade can make these conditional on similar cuts in protection from its partners.

The concessions can be in regard to the same issue (e.g. mutual liberalization of car trade), but may also be cross-issue (e.g. tariff reduction in cars by country A against reduction in subsidies to domestic agriculture by country B). This approach of *comprehensive bargaining* has an advantage in the sense that it opens up possibilities for coalitions that permit package deals that offer a better final outcome for everyone. Multi-industry bargaining permits the breaking of powerful special interests of industries that are seeking to maintain protection from imports; they can now be overturned by coalitions of parties with an interest in the broader deal of mutual liberalization. The approach also has a disadvantage as in negotiation terms this is difficult: it involves barter (exchanging something for something different). There is no common denominator that could facilitate the functioning of such a "market".

The objective of these negotiations is to come to an agreement on the mutual lowering of obstacles. This has been realized in several major multilateral trade negotiation rounds. After the first round (Geneva) in 1947, the Dillon and Kennedy rounds of the 1960s represented a big step forward and so did the Tokyo Round in the 1970s and the Uruguay Round in the late 1980s and early 1990s. The present Doha Round, which started in 2001, has failed to come to a conclusion and is still dragging on.

The WTO practice is that such an agreement includes all partial deals (this is called "Single Undertaking") and has to be agreed on by consensus of all its members. This is very constraining as it means that nothing is agreed until everything is agreed, and that all members have to subscribe to the whole package without the possibility of opting in or opting out.

Once the results of these negotiations is put down in a WTO legal act, the next task of the organization is to see that the agreements are observed. To that end, the WTO makes regular analyses of the trade policy of its members. Finally, the WTO has set up a way to deal with disputes among its members.

5.5.2 Regulation

WTO law concerns five areas. The first is directly derived from the fundamental principles of *non-discrimination* between:

- Different trade partners. This principle has been given its legal form in the Most Favoured Nation (MFN) clause.[9] This means that if you favour one member, you have to favour all. MFN is in principle unconditional and takes effect immediately (see further Horn and Mavroidis 2001).

- Imported and home products. This principle is laid down in the National Treatment Provision (article III of GATT) that requires like or directly competitive or substitutable foreign products not to be treated less favourably on the domestic market once they have been imported.

The other four areas of *WTO material law* concern (van den Bossche 2008):

- Market access; these comprise rules about tariffs and non-tariff trade protection measures.
- Unfair trade; these concern aspects such as protection against dumping and against distortions of competition due to government subsidies.
- Harmonization of national rules concerning, for instance, technical specifications and sanitary and phyto-sanitary measures (food safety).
- Conflicts between trade rules and societal values and interests, such as defence; internal security; action against economic crises, etc. In this vein also come exceptions to the application of the general principles, such as regional integration schemes (see Box 5.4), preferences to less developed countries (see Box 5.5) and exceptional circumstances (Box 5.6).

BOX 5.4 THE CONTROVERSY BETWEEN REGIONALISM AND MULTILATERALISM

Regional integration implies the abolition of trade barriers between partner countries. Important examples of regional schemes for trade liberalization are the European Union, NAFTA and MERCOSUR. Many other, less successful attempts have been made. Notably, initiatives based on import substitution have failed to develop. Trade liberalization on a regional basis has been a controversial issue for a long time.

Advocates (notably the European Union) put forward the argument that regionalism is an expedient way to liberalize trade. Geographically contiguous countries tend to have a higher propensity to trade with each other than countries that need to bridge important distances, so important trade flows tend to be liberalized. Under some conditions that are relatively easy to satisfy, such trade liberalization has positive welfare effects.[10] Moreover, groups of countries that have similar objectives in trade matters and tend to have similar levels of development are likely to reach effective deals for full free trade more easily than countries with different types of economies and cultures.

Opponents point to the fact that regionalism violates the basic principle of non-discrimination, and it is true that under regionalism, trade advantages are only given to partners in the scheme, not to everybody. Moreover, they consider that regionalism erodes the effectiveness of deals on a global level (notably Bhagwati 2008).

The theoretical debate about the effects of both strategies for liberalization has gone on for some time without reaching a clear conclusion. However, the WTO has accommodated regionalism (under article XXIV) under the pressure of regional schemes such as the European Union. Regionalism has thus been accepted as a sort of second-best option. However, this exception to the basic rule of most favoured nation can only be accepted on two conditions:

1. no increase in protection of the new group towards third parties;
2. no sectoralism; a free trade area should cover substantially all trade between members.

Recently, new forms have come up in which the regional trade agreements (RTAs) try to extend their reach by concluding preferential trade agreements (PTAs) with a third country. These are not confined to countries in the same region. In recent decades, RTAs and PTAs have been proliferating. In 2011 some 500 were notified to the WTO, of which some 300 were actually in force. The explanation for the dynamism is that RTA and PTAs provide a comfortable halfway house. As global deals become bogged down in a long, winding negotiation process, regional deals make it possible to move on[11] and include new issues such as national regulation and societal issues such as the conditions under which production takes place (labour and environmental standards). So, the new generation of PTAs are less concerned with trade liberalization and more with "disciplines that underpin the trade–investment–service nexus" (Baldwin 2011).

Many of the RTAs and PTAs partially overlap, which has created a sort of "spaghetti bowl" of arrangements. The average WTO member is a partner in sixteen PTAs. Although RTAs and PTAs in general have positive trade and welfare effects and are found in econometric studies to be building blocks for a global trade regime (Herz and Wagner 2011a), they have aspects that may become stumbling blocks (Lee *et al.* 2008). The WTO (2011a) has analyzed the points where the two can collide (in liberalization, regulation and litigation) and has formulated a work programme to improve coherence between its own actions and those of PTAs.

BOX 5.5 COPING WITH THE ASYMMETRY BETWEEN DEVELOPED AND LESS DEVELOPED COUNTRIES

The WTO membership is very diverse. On the one hand we find big countries that have very highly developed and diversified economies. On the other hand we find small countries that are among the poorest in the world and have little by way of human and other resources. The former are generally capable of adapting their production structures to new conditions without too much difficulty. The latter, on the contrary, are often caught in situations from which it is difficult to escape without external help.

Accelerated development of the LDCs is in everybody's interest. Trade is an effective way to foster growth in LDCs. So, LDCs should be given facilities for entering the markets of the developed countries without being obliged to offer the same advantages to developed countries on their markets (non-reciprocity). Several instruments have been put in place to that effect.[12] The instrument that has drawn most attention is the special and differential (S&D) treatment of LDCs (Hoekman and Ozden 2006).

S&D provisions within WTO agreements can be grouped into three categories allowing *developing countries*:

- greater flexibility with regard to rules and disciplines governing trade measures;
- longer transition periods for the implementation of WTO agreements;
- technical assistance to help in the implementation of commitments.

Moreover, there are S&D provisions that apply to *developed countries*. These particularly concern the preferential treatment of LDCs' exports to developed countries' markets. In essence this means applying a lower tariff to goods originating from LDCs than to goods originating from other countries. Although preferential treatment breaks the principle of non-discrimination, it has been accepted as a means of solving the conflict between objectives and means. Both the United States and the European Union have set up (unilaterally) a Generalized System of Preferences (GSP). Their putting it into operation has given rise to problems regarding the selection of countries and products, and the margin of preference for different categories of LDC according to their relative level of poverty. In the past, GSPs were of limited relevance as many of the products of LDCs were hurt by other measures (notably the agricultural policy of the most developed countries, such as the United States, the European Union and Japan). Recently the GSPs have lost relevance, as tariffs for many products have been considerably lowered so that the effective preference is in many cases no longer substantial.[13] However, notably in sensitive products (of considerable interest to LDCs), considerable protection remains.[14]

BOX 5.6 ACCEPTING EXCEPTIONS

The commitment to the regime that the WTO has installed is sometimes put under severe strain. Countries that are feeling the effects of strong external competition may be under such heavy pressure from internal forces that they will feel compelled to give in. This will notably be the case if they feel that the damage to their industry is being done by unfair trade practices of producers in other countries. Now, the dispute settlement procedure (described in Box 5.7) can be very long-winded, and as the outcome is uncertain, governments may want to return to protective measures. If the WTO did not provide for such a possibility, countries might be inclined to leave the organization altogether, forgoing the benefits but avoiding the immediate cost. This would weaken the world system and is therefore better avoided. In order to deal with such problems, the WTO has installed a system of *escape clauses*. These are temporary exceptions to the obligations of members that are accepted by the WTO for the sake of the long-term survival of the regime.

The *rule-making function* of the WTO has led to a series of legal acts. Examples include the General Agreement on Trade in Services (GATS) and the agreement on Trade-Related aspects of Intellectual Property (TRIP). The WTO rules have great advantages as they create predictability of conditions and reduce the asymmetry in power between large and small states, and between the rich (developed) and the poor countries (LDCs).

5.5.3 Dispute settlement

The situation of GATT and, later, the WTO in matters of compliance has evolved over time. When GATT began, no effective enforcement procedure was set up as nobody thought that the organization would be long-lived. However, over time a simple yet effective procedure has been worked out. It is based on the obligation for transparency of national trade measures so that breaches of WTO rules can be easily detected. In the event of violation there is a standard procedure to be followed. The workings of the WTO dispute settlement procedure are given in a schematized form in Box 5.7.

The WTO situation in matters of compliance is quite exceptional; no other international organization has developed so far a compliance system by dispute settlement. Most rely on less effective measures such as self-interest and reputation. The emergence of this specific feature of the world trade regime can be explained by a number of factors. First trade issues typically lead to conflicts of direct interests; this is much less the case for issues in other regimes. Moreover, all countries have a strong interest in a smoothly functioning trade system; and a compliance

BOX 5.7 THE WTO DISPUTE SETTLEMENT PROCEDURE (SCHEMATIZED)

Step 1: A dispute arises

A member believes that there is a problem because another member is infringing the rules or violating the result of negotiations. The parties concerned have to enter into bilateral talks in order to see whether they can solve the problem. The director-general of the WTO may be asked to act as an intermediary.

Step 2: The conflict persists: request for a panel

If no solution can be found, the complaining party may request that the WTO set up a panel. Such a panel typically consists of international experts in trade matters that are not party to the conflict. The terms of reference for the panel are set up.

Step 3: The panel at work

The panel examines the facts, meets with the interested parties, draws its conclusions and presents these to the interested parties and the Dispute Settlement Board.

Step 4: Decision-taking and/or appellate body

The Dispute Settlement Body reviews the panel report and makes a decision. In the past the report had to be accepted by the General Council, which gave the infringing country a veto over decisions. This is no longer the case; under WTO rules a decision is binding unless it is rejected by consensus. However, if a party cannot accept the decision, it may refer to the Appellate Body. This appeal may be based only on arguments related to law or legal interpretation, however. The decision of the Appellate Body is in practice final.[15]

Step 5: Implementation

The parties must implement the decision of the WTO within a reasonable time period. If the infringing party does not comply, the complaining party may ask permission to retaliate – that is, to use trade protection measures against products from the infringing party, not necessarily products in the same sector. In order to end the conflict, the offending party may also make proposals for advantages in other areas (compensation in trade) or even in financial terms.

mechanism is essential to such a system. Next countries know that they are in a repetitive game: even if an individual member may lose out in one case, it may benefit in the settlement of the next case. Finally there is the locking-in aspect. A national government can blame the "loss" of a case of a particular pressure group on international obligations.

The WTO's Dispute Settlement Procedure (DSP) has clear advantages but also considerable weaknesses. These can be listed as follows:

- *Government filter.* Business interests are taken up by governments, the only actors with legal status in the WTO. Because of issue-linking, governments may not bring up important cases even if they would have improved the efficiency of global allocation.
- *Delays.* In the past, a long time elapsed between the moment a matter was brought up by the complaining party and the implementation of the WTO's decisions by the infringing party. Recently the situation has been improved by the setting of a maximum duration for each of the stages of the DSP.
- *No coercion.* There is no other instrument than national retaliation and international opprobrium. The latter is generally not very effective, particularly if the infringing party has a strong national interest. Punitive action by third countries would be a very effective instrument but has been explicitly ruled out.
- *Retaliation hits the wrong groups.* The exporters of the infringing country have to bear the cost of the protection of the interest group that causes the infringement. Consumers of that good in the importing country will also be damaged as they have now less choice at a higher price. Often the country that retaliates also hits domestic groups, mostly the importers of the products that are subject to retaliation.
- *Asymmetry of country sizes.* The members of WTO are of very different size. If one of the major countries is responsible for an infringement, a small country has little power to respond effectively. This applies both to its capacity in institutional terms (diplomacy, legal counsel, etc.) and to the credibility of its retaliation. Moreover, small developing countries often fear that they will lose out on non-trade issues (financial aid).

The *conclusion* of this section may be that the WTO's Dispute Settlement Procedure, although imperfect, has the advantage of being operational. Even without coercion powers on the part of the WTO, members have almost always complied with decisions taken in the DSP. The main reasons for this phenomenon are likely to be the dynamics of repetitive games and reputation (see section 2.7.5).

5.6 Evaluation of the past and options for the future

5.6.1 Major achievements: trade and income effects

The primary objective of the WTO is to liberalize trade and maintain the results of previous liberalizations of trade. So the output variable of the policy is fewer obstacles to trade. Trade liberalization has been given substance in several major multilateral trade negotiation rounds. Together, these rounds have resulted in substantial *reductions in tariffs and quantitative restrictions*, and in improvements of the conditions for fair trade. At the moment the tariffs for industrial products in developed countries are very low, in many cases even zero. Moreover, the ban on non-tariff barriers has done away with many quotas, voluntary export restraints, etc.[16]

Moreover, the coverage of the WTO trade liberalization agreements has increased on two scores:

1. *Geography*. The number of countries taking part in the WTO has increased continuously, so the WTO rules cover an increasing share of all world trans-actions. However, developing countries still maintain considerable protection, some of which involves particularly high (practically prohibitive) tariffs on specific products.
2. *Products*. The initial accent was on manufacturing. Recently, some other sectors, such as telecoms (see Box 5.2) and financial services, have been integrated as well. Although considerable progress still needs to be made, significant segments of sectors such as services and agriculture are now subject to WTO rules.

The overall record on the trade liberalization issue is very impressive: recent estimates show that about 50 per cent of worldwide trade is now free of tariffs.

Another positive aspect that should be mentioned is *the creation of reinforced regimes* in terms of:

*   *Fair trade*. The WTO has set rules in order to take away distortions emanating from other sources, such as export subsidies, dumping, etc.
*   *Dispute settlement*. The device to cope with disputes has been working well on average and has permitted quite a few problems to be solved. Moreover, the system has prevented major new protectionist pressures due to the recent crisis from translating themselves into effective measures.

Have these changes in conditions *actually increased trade*? On the surface the answer seems clearly "yes", as the total volume of trade has increased considerably during the decades in which the WTO has been decreasing barriers. In the past two decades (1990–2010) global trade has even increased fourfold. Traditionally, most international trade has been between the rich countries. However, in the past two decades so-called North–North trade has decreased in relative terms (from

60 per cent to 45 per cent) in favour of both South–North trade and South–South trade (OECD 2010b; UNCTAD 2011).[17] Bear in mind that this shift in structure has much to do with the increasing weight of intermediate goods in total trade and with the increasing complexity of production networks.[18] However, if we dig deeper, the relation between decrease in trade barriers and increase in trade is not so obvious, as trade has also increased for countries that did not participate in the WTO. So, the evidence is mixed. Some empirical studies did not find any WTO effect (e.g. Rose 2004); others concluded that the WTO had had a clear net effect on the volume of trade flows around the world (e.g. Subramanian and Shang Jin 2007). Studies that put the WTO in the framework of many other relevant variables seem to corroborate the latter view (Herz and Wagner 2011b).

The ultimate rationale of the trade regime is not liberalization but enhanced growth and, if possible, a more equitable distribution of growth. So, in order to measure the *outcome performance* of the trade regime we have to look at the *income effects*. This relation also seems clearly positive at first sight, as many countries that have shown high growth have also opted for openness. On average a 1 per cent growth in trade led to an increase in GDP of some 0.2 per cent (Lewer and van den Berg 2003). However, if we look more closely at the intricate relationships, we see that much depends on the economic and institutional conditions in each country (Singh 2010). The overall positive relation thus masks both negative and positive influences (Kneller *et al.* 2008). Some believe that the positive effects can only be grasped by countries above a particular threshold of development; below that threshold the effect is negative (Kim and Lin 2009). There is some evidence that trade openness in developing countries can have more negative than positive effects (Thirlwall and Pacheco-López 2009; George 2010). To sum up; poor countries tend to gain less from openness than developed countries. This implies that across the board trade liberalization is not readily accepted by many poor developing countries.

The distribution of income over countries with different wealth levels has improved during the past decade (OECD 2011b: 38). This growth tends, however, to hide quite significant changes in the internal income distribution of trade partners. Indeed, in the past decade the income distribution of many countries has become much less equal. This applies both to certain developed and many developing countries. However, the link between income disparity and openness to trade is very weak (OECD 2011c). Other factors, such as technology, and public policies and institutions, carry a much heavier weight.[19]

After considerable success in the past century, progress in the past decade has been very slow. Part of this lack of progress is attributable to faults in the system, which is not geared to the needs of the twenty-first century. A large number of proposals have been made to improve the situation. Most of them are of a partial character and favour practical reforms on a specific subject. We will discuss them in the following sections, distinguishing the main elements of the remit of the WTO and the main characteristics of its governance.[20]

5.6.2 Trade

The first major task of the WTO is to continue work on its primary task, which is the further liberalization of trade. A particularly important point in this respect is the extension of the sectoral coverage of the WTO regimes; in particular, in agriculture and services there is much unfinished business. A somewhat more limited point is that the WTO should integrate the trade work of some specialist organizations, for instance those on air and sea transport.

However, for the time being progress on this agenda seems to be fairly difficult to achieve. The factors that have led to a stalemate in the Doha Round negotiations seem to be rather persistent (Bouet and Laborde 2010). These are (1) the sheer number of the participants in the negotiations, (2) the diversity of their interests, (3) uncertainty as to the effects of measures taken, and (4) the creation of changing coalitions. There are solutions to some of these factors (such as leaving out of the negotiations the smallest participants with the largest diversity of interests and compensating them for any negative result of the deals later). However, these are both institutionally (the WTO practice prescribes consensus) and politically (because of lack of trust between players) very difficult. A likely consequence is that in future the regional and bilateral route will be favoured over the multilateral one.

Moreover, as the general economic situation has deteriorated quickly in the years since the outbreak of the crisis in 2008, protectionist tendencies have reappeared. However, probably of more importance is the change in the distribution of economic power that has occurred during recent decades as a result of the increased growth of major segments of the world economy. That growth has engendered a heavy pressure on the demand for many raw materials and food products. Limiting access to such materials and export bans will become increasingly important. The challenge to the WTO is now to find new ways of promoting its objectives and standing firm on the rules it has established (WTO 2011b).

5.6.3 "Trade and"

The second major challenge is to come to grips with the so-called *"trade and" agenda* (see Hoekman and Kostecki 2009). Some of these concerns relate to subjects that are not yet agreed on in the framework of the WTO (WTO-Plus), such as differences in regulation on procedures for public procurement. Others concern issues that move beyond the competence of WTO into other fields (WTO-X). Many of the latter subjects have been brought forward by NGOs, such as environmental protection, direct investment, labour rights and fair competition. The following *proposals* have been made to address these issues:

- *Investment.* There is a very close relationship between trade and direct investment. Moreover, the method of integration that WTO has used in the past for trade issues could very well be applicable to this area as well.

- *Competition*. Here again there is a close relationship and a possibility that the WTO framework could accommodate this. However, in the immediate future it does not seem desirable to charge the WTO with this, for two reasons. First, many countries have no experience with this sort of policy nationally. Second, the international distributional effects (who gains and who loses) are highly uncertain.
- *The environment*. Trade and environmental issues are interlinked in many ways (see, for example, Batabyal and Beladi 2001). Yet in the past international organizations have developed in stand-alone negotiations. The WTO finds that the principles on which it is based have to prevail in cases where trade and environmental issues collide. It suggests that environmental agreements are so designed that they have as little impact as possible on trade.
- *Labour standards*. Some developed countries have proposed that all ILO standards may be enforced by trade measures against countries that do not observe them. LDCs particularly fear the possible misuse of such policies. The WTO governance mechanisms do not seem adequate for dealing with such issues.

Progress on these issues has been very limited. The 1996 Ministerial conference of Singapore has put four of the latter subjects on the agenda: investment; competition, public procurement and trade procedures.[21] The 2001 WTO ministerial conference of Doha has taken a very cautious route in matters of the extension of the role of WTO; it has demanded that working groups investigate the issue further and to clarify the principles and possibilities. Most of the proposals have actually been rejected after discussion. As conditions are unlikely to change in the immediate future, it is doubtful whether the WTO competence in these matters will be extended (Evenett 2007). We will come back to these issues in Chapters 10 and 11.

5.6.4 *Preferential trade*

Box 5.4 highlighted the proliferation of RTAs and the emergence of a new type of preferential trade agreement (PTA) that is practised notably by the United States and the European Union. These agreements not only cover the traditional trade aspects (and take the form of free trade agreements; FTAs) but increasingly cover *regulatory issues* as well. Some of these are presently covered by the WTO (e.g. intellectual property); many others are not (such as investment protection, competition policy, public procurement and environmental and labour standards). It reflects the wish of these main players to export their regulatory standards in the absence of a global agreement on such issues (Horn *et al.* 2010). Note that the latest of these agreements provide for dispute settlement also in cases when disputes involve aspects such as labour standards, and in some cases they may even lead to trade sanctions.

The WTO has assessed the pros and cons of RTA and PTAs (WTO 2011a), and has identified ways to come to grips with the challenge that the new forms of

RTAs provide to the global system. For the time being, these negative effects seem to be limited. They do not seem to lead to much trade diversion. There are no indications that alternative trade dispute rules create conflicting case law or an erosion of the WTO DSP system. However, regional and bilateral agreements have been shown to be an expedient way to integrate so called WTO X issues such as labour and environmental standards (Brown and Stern 2011).

The WTO has identified several avenues of action to improve the situation on the multilateral–regional interface. The first is to increase its critical examination of the present FTAs on aspects such as the net welfare effects on Third World (developing) countries. The second is to develop a set of legal principles that should be taken up in all approved RTAs so as to safeguard their conformity to WTO principles and dispute settlement procedures.[22] The final course of action is to check whether the standards set in RTAs for new WTO-X issues are capable of multilateralization: in other words, whether they tend to converge into a new set that in time could be adopted by the WTO and other international organizations. Mind that the first has hardly been implemented while the last two have not been implemented at all.

5.6.5 Development aspect of trade

The importance of the "development" dimension of trade issues is reinforced by the growing importance of emerging economies and of LDCs in the world trading system (including by the accession of China as a member). Their increased role has changed not only the power balance in the WTO but also the way the WTO functions.[23] Developing countries are disappointed by the limited positive effects for them of the previous rounds and by the lack of progress in the present Doha Round. LDCs are, moreover, very concerned about the burden that certain WTO agreements place on their administrative and financial resources, and the constraints on development they may constitute. This means that WTO rules and practices may lead to inferior outcomes for low-income countries and justify support from both the trade side (WTO) and the aid (World Bank) side.[24] A whole series of proposals have been made to improve this situation (Deere Birkbeck 2011).

The major challenge, then, is to increase the relevance of the Special and Differential Treatment. A number of specific proposals have been voiced.[25] These take into account the considerable differences that exist between large emerging economies such as Brazil and small, backward economies such as Burkina Faso. So, the new proposals try to go beyond the present arrangement of the unilateral GSPs, without granting rights to all developing countries to a standard S&D treatment. This differentiation involves the need to carry out a sound economic analysis of individual cases as a basis for agreements. Given the complications involved, this is likely to lead to confused situations. So, some authors go further and propose to create a separate body (along the lines of the structure of the DSP) to make independent assessments and resolve individual disputes.

5.6.6 Governance aspects

In the past decade the structure of international trade has changed profoundly, and it is poised to continue to change in the coming decades. First, the trade in intermediary goods has overtaken the trade in consumer and capital goods. Moreover, the trade among developing countries has increased much more rapidly than either the trade among developed countries or that between developed and developing countries. This leads first to increasing stakes for more diversified players in the trade game and to ever more complex situations as to the determination of the origin of a product, the interest of the trade partner and the effect of possible retaliation measures.

These trends have very serious consequences for the governance of the WTO, in terms both of negotiations for new trade rounds and of the division of roles within the organization while implementing existing rules. The main suggestions for improvement of the governance of the WTO address these problems; they focus on the following subjects:[26]

- Improve the *decision-making process*. With some 150 participants, the present situation based on consensus is no longer workable. A better system could result from the creation of a sort of Executive Board (compare the World Bank) and some sort of weighted voting system. However, this idea has been strongly opposed by LDCs, which fear that it would strengthen the dominance of the already powerful. Another proposal is to do away with the 'single undertaking' and let the WTO facilitate deals that are binding for a limited part of the membership only; this would make partial progress for a subset of countries possible.[27]
- Reinforce the role of the *secretariat*. At present this role is fairly limited both in the negotiation stage and in the implementation stage. In the negotiation stage the role of the secretariat could be enhanced by better exchange of information about the magnitude and characteristics of problems and about the pros and cons of solutions (including the likely distributional effects over partners), thereby bringing about a better basis for the definition of mutually beneficial options. In the implementation stage the secretariat could be given a stronger role in providing technical assistance.
- Give more *voice to NGOs*. Some advocate doing this by accepting them as partners in the negotiation process, even in the dispute settlement stage. However, the issue of accountability precludes acceptance of this option to the full; a better alternative is to associate NGOs more closely in preliminary stages such as fact-finding and proposal formulation. To that end the WTO has greatly improved the transparency of its operation.
- Reinforce the implementation of the decisions of the *Dispute Settlement Procedure*. Retaliation is not an efficient system: theoretically it would be better to introduce a fine system (see Pelzman and Shoham 2007).[28]

5.7 Summary and conclusions

- Under the influence of powerful interest groups, protection has tended to override the advantages of free trade and became widespread in the first half of the twentieth century.
- Economic theory indicates that protection is very costly, and so progressive trade liberalization has become recognized as a global public good.
- Over the past half-century, GATT and, later, the WTO have provided the organizational framework for negotiations on trade liberalization. The WTO has gradually increased its coverage as to number of member countries and subjects (not only industrial products, but also services).
- Trade negotiations are done in a multilateral way. Nothing is agreed until the package has been agreed. There is no flexibility as to opting in or out for certain provisions. Nevertheless, a large number of negotiations have resulted in a considerable decrease of protection.
- In the past decade this process seems to have come to a halt and some think that it is slightly moving backwards now. Due to the lack of progress along the multilateral route many of the major countries now favour the preferential route of regional agreements.
- The WTO has a relatively strong instrument to make its members comply with the commonly agreed rules: the Dispute Settlement Procedure. It may authorize offended partners to retaliate against the offender.
- The WTO is confronted with several main challenges. The most pressing one is to come to grips with a considerable "trade and" agenda (concerning subjects such as social and environmental sustainability). The second is to make sure that trade sustains economic development; to that end, the LDCs need to be given more voice and it is necessary to make sure that the trade regime will lead to a better sharing of its fruits. Finally, it should change its modes of governance to generate more flexibility and hence more effectiveness.

6

FINANCE

6.1 Introduction

The advantages of international specialization are enhanced if capital can move freely from one country to another. Yet capital movements – in particular, short-term capital movements – can also be highly disruptive. With increasingly liberalized global capital markets, most national actions to combat instability ("sudden stops") are not very effective. So, an international regime has to be developed that mobilizes the positive and avoids the negative effects of international capital.[1]

The *objective* of this chapter is to expose the rationale, the main features and the effectiveness of the international regime for stability in monetary and financial matters. The *structure* of the chapter is as follows. In the first main section I describe the essential features of the basic problem: the fact that the inherent instability of world capital markets tends to create major crises. These crises lead via a loss of confidence to a loss of investment opportunities and a loss of growth – in severe cases even to absolute losses of wealth. In the second section I indicate that the cost implied can be avoided by creating a regime that improves the conditions for financial and monetary stability. In order to be able to deliver effectively the public good in stability, such a regime must be based on certain principles and must consist of a combination of national and international actions. It must, moreover, consist of strong organizations that can use a set of adequate instruments. I describe in the third section the essential features of the main organizations involved, in particular of the IMF. Finally, I describe the instruments that the IMF deploys to put its policies into effect. I round off this chapter with an evaluation of the regime in place and some ideas for improvement of the weak points of the present system.

6.2 The main problems

6.2.1 Capital mobility and controls

In the period after the Second World War a system of fixed exchange rates prevailed. In that period, most transactions involving foreign exchange and/or short-term capital had a direct relation with the real sector of the economy. Restrictions on international capital movements were widespread. In the past decades, two major developments have changed that picture. The introduction of floating exchange rates has meant that many international capital flows are now reactions to real or expected changes in the external value of currencies. The restrictions on international capital movements have been gradually removed as a corollary to the liberalization of national capital markets. This tendency has been led by the most developed countries but these were quickly followed by other countries, including some developing countries.

There are several reasons for the liberalization of capital markets – in other words, for the abolition of capital controls. First, liberalization leads to a better allocation of resources. Second, modern means of telecommunication have increased the capacity of traders to circumvent controls. Third, capital controls proved rather ineffective in the long run anyway. Finally, they often seemed counter-productive in the sense that they slowed down the necessary adaptation of the economy.

6.2.2 Increased risk

As a consequence of liberalization, the international flows of capital have increased tremendously. Moreover, their composition has changed. A large segment of present-day transactions are portfolio investments instead of trade- or direct investment-related operations. In order to facilitate these flows, new financial intermediaries have emerged.

This new configuration has created a number of *extra risks to stability*. They have emerged from the increase in:

- *Volume*. Short-term portfolio flows have increased dramatically. A large portion of these flows goes to emerging economies that have a financial sector that functions under an inadequate regulatory and supervisory regime. Short-term financial flows tend to be very volatile, and large outflows may very quickly become a source of instability for both the private and the public sector, possibly even leading to a collapse of the national financial system (Griffith Jones *et al.* 2001).
- *Transmission*. In the modern world of financial integration the risks of contagion are much larger than they were in the past. Some of this contagion is regional (e.g. through trade channels); some is global and affects the lenders, which often come from the major developed countries.
- *Sophistication*. Financial markets have developed a very wide array of products that are adapted to the specific circumstances of particular groups of clients.

Some of these products became very popular in the short term and the regulators have had little time to get to grips with the systemic problems that the use of such products implied. Corporate chief financial officers have difficulty in seeing through the intricacies of such products. This problem exists at the level of major banks, as witness the collapse of some of them.

These extra risk factors make the supervision and control of financial operations much more difficult than before. Hence, the systemic risks have increased.

6.2.3 Considerable market imperfections

Markets do not always function well, for a variety of reasons:

- *Information and interpretation.* With the wide range of products now internationally available, there is a very great need to acquire good information so as to judge correctly the real facts and adjust accordingly. However, this is not always easy to do. Market intermediaries, which would help to provide this information, have difficulty in coping with the theoretical intricacies and cultural variety, and are not always neutral players. Moreover, similarities in situations are often taken as indicators of the same types of problems, which need not be the case.[2]
- *Moral hazard.* A debtor may accumulate excessive debt with the intention of forcing his (or her) creditors to accept that he cannot pay back on normal terms; in so doing, he may hope to get a more advantageous deal. Moreover, lenders may go along with such a strategy, as they may count on a bailout by public organizations and/or international institutions that will pay for the debtor in question. This may even lead to a coalition of lenders and borrowers at the cost of the public sector.
- *Adverse selection.* While most countries will want to have their finances in order and to adapt to market signals, a limited number of countries may be willing to borrow even in cases where interest rates go up drastically. That would mean that only bad borrowers would remain. As they need it so badly, they are willing to take the capital at almost any price. As good lenders refrain from lending at such high rates, only bad lenders would remain. In such a situation, lenders may shy away, so that capital supply dries up.
- *Multiple equilibria.* Asset prices are based, first, on the expectations of future returns and, second, on the presumption of the stability of the institutional system. Now if real estate prices are high, credit is adequate and economic activity sustains rents, there is a high-level equilibrium. However, a slackening in demand causing revenues from real estate to decrease may lead banks to review their lending. This may lead real estate investors to liquidate their assets more quickly than foreseen, causing a loss. Such a change can bring the whole system to a lower equilibrium of prices, credit and economic activity.

- *Herd behaviour* is a powerful factor to explain why equilibrium at one level may be replaced by another equilibrium at a different level. A good example here is the increasing public debt problem of a country like Greece. For a long time there was no increase in the risk premium on its bonds. Suddenly an external factor brought the fragility of the situation to light, and there was a very strong and massive reaction.

6.2.4 Latent problems: financial instability

The effective functioning of the market economy depends on a number of conditions. One of them is monetary and financial stability, which provides the environment for rational decision-making regarding savings and investments. It is often the opposite that attracts attention: the absence of financial stability. Financial instability can be defined as *a situation in which economic performance is potentially impaired by fluctuations in the price of financial assets or in the ability of financial intermediaries to meet their contractual obligations.*[3]

There are several *reasons* for the inherent instability of the international financial system:

- *Wrong fundamentals*. Governments are continuously tempted, for internal policy reasons, to carry an expansionary monetary and budgetary policy too far. Such excessive spending can lead to unsustainable public debts and to external borrowing beyond the financial capacity of the country.
- *International spill-overs*. As more and more trading takes place between actors in different countries, a dense international network of interlocking claims and liabilities has developed (Sell 2001). So, the degree of spill-over and hence the potential of contagion has increased too.
- *Market failures*. I mentioned in the previous subsection the lack of quality of information and the poor performance of financial intermediaries and related organizations (e.g. rating agencies). So, markets may react in erratic and maniacal ways. Moreover, often there is no gradual adaptation of the price of finance to changed circumstances. This means that there is a rather violent reaction once the retarded movement of adaptation starts.
- *Race to the bottom*. Banks and other financial service providers tend to go for high-margin market niches. This is part of the dynamics of the markets. However, high margins tend to go hand in hand with high risks. Consequently, there is a lack of transparency as to the size and character of the total exposure of major players. So, the sort of buffers needed, and their size, is not always clearly assessed.
- *Lack of insight with prudential control*. The control of public organizations over the exposure of market players has weaknesses as well. One is derived from the lack of basic information (see previous points). Another is the consequence of the increasing sophistication: the authorities (notably of countries with small resources) have great difficulty in coping with these intricacies. Even the

authorities of developed economies have difficulties with putting adequate structures and regulation in place for political reasons.

6.2.5 Acute problems: a three-stage model of financial crises

Financial instability can lead to negative effects on the economy as a whole. For that reason, it is considered as a public bad. The main problem of financial instability is that it may deteriorate into a financial crisis that in turn may end up in a deep economic crisis.

The *definition of a financial crisis* has two dimensions (see, for example, Mishkin 1992; Bordo *et al.* 2001):

1. *function default*: episodes of disruption of financial markets (they cease to function in a normal way) in which adverse selection and moral hazard problems become much worse, so that financial markets are unable to channel funds efficiently to those who have the most productive investment opportunities;
2. *effect on actors*: episodes of financial market volatility marked by significant problems of illiquidity and insolvency among financial market participants (incapacity of financial institutions to meet obligations) and/or by official intervention to contain their consequences.

Several *types of crisis* can be distinguished:

- banking crisis, characterized by financial distress resulting in the erosion of most or all of aggregate banking system capital;[4]
- currency crisis, characterized by a forced change in parity, abandonment of a pegged exchange rate and/or an international rescue operation;
- public-sector debt crisis; a deterioration of the balance of payments may lead to uncertainty about a country's ability to pay back its debt.

In many cases, several elements of the three types of crisis tend to interact and complicate the solution of the crisis (Dreher *et al.* 2006).

The *anatomy of international financial crises* is now fairly well understood. The process (see Figure 6.1) often starts in one segment of the economy and then spreads out to other parts. The major features of the latest global crisis are described in Box 6.1.

Stage 1: The origin

The origin of a crisis may be rather trivial. It can start with the emergence of some underlying weakness. This may have a variety of characteristics: a balance of payments problem, political unrest, etc. Clearly, these are very common problems and mostly their existence does not give rise to a real crisis. However, if for one reason or another a risk starts that is assumed to be potentially dangerous, such as

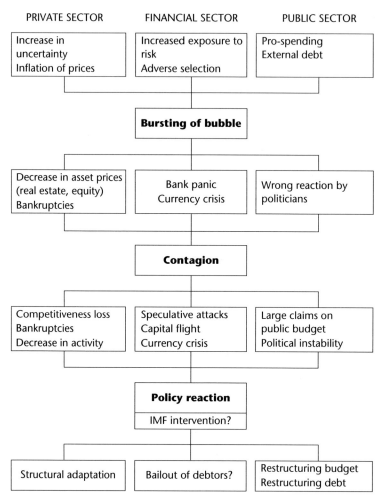

PRIVATE SECTOR   FINANCIAL SECTOR   PUBLIC SECTOR

Increase in uncertainty Inflation of prices	Increased exposure to risk Adverse selection	Pro-spending External debt

Bursting of bubble

Decrease in asset prices (real estate, equity) Bankruptcies	Bank panic Currency crisis	Wrong reaction by politicians

Contagion

Competitiveness loss Bankruptcies Decrease in activity	Speculative attacks Capital flight Currency crisis	Large claims on public budget Political instability

Policy reaction

IMF intervention?

Structural adaptation	Bailout of debtors?	Restructuring budget Restructuring debt

FIGURE 6.1 Anatomy of a financial crisis.

a bankruptcy, a small reaction by one party may actually spark off a crisis. This has happened with the currency crisis of Mexico in 1994, the real estate crisis of Thailand in 1997, the private-sector debt crisis in Korea in 1997 and the stock market crisis of the new economy in 2000.[5]

Many of these crises have originated because some favourable event led to the bidding up of asset prices. Price increases lead to further buying as more actors enter the market to take part in the bonanza. Paper profits induce speculators to engage in further operations, often financed with borrowed capital. This herd behaviour, based on expectations of other members of the herd, leads to deviation of asset prices from fundamentals. When an external event occurs that reveals that many assets are heavily overvalued, some asset holders will start to sell or will be obliged to sell. Then the bubble bursts: lack of demand leads to a sharp decrease in asset

BOX 6.1 MAIN FEATURES OF THE 2007–2012 CRISIS

The crisis that started in 2007 had its origin in the United States. Under political pressure mortgage lending even to poor citizens has been massively promoted. New packages of products had been developed on the basis of these (sub-prime) mortgages that were sold by intermediaries as very solid investments. When their lack of value became apparent, defaults of some major specialized banks sparked off a systemic banking crisis. It started in the United States, but soon contagion became apparent. This concerned in particular Western Europe, where financial institutions had invested massively in such American products. The first reaction of the public sector was a national one: both the USA and major EU countries had to rescue their major banks to avoid a meltdown of the financial system. The consequence of this bailout has been a considerable increase in their public debt. The second reaction was an international one; a coordinated effort has been made to strengthen the international institutions charged with the setting of standards, the surveillance of the financial and monetary system, and the provision of financial support to countries in difficulty.

Unfortunately, the fundamental problem was not only in the United States. In Europe, several countries on the periphery of the European Monetary Union, in particular Greece, showed a combination of a high public debt (compared to GDP) and a high deficit on the current account of the balance of payments. This created the risk of a country's defaulting on its sovereign debt. Credit rating agencies downgraded the bonds of these countries. Given the high exposure of many financial institutions in other EU countries to government bonds of the downgraded countries, a considerable loss of assets occurred. This added to financial instability, as many banks were severely damaged and consequently other banks became more prudent in their interbank operations. Given the commitments of the EU governments to rescue banks their public debt levels have greatly increased. Subsequently, rating agencies downgraded even major countries such as Italy and France.

The reaction of the European public authorities has been twofold. First, the European Union has created a new fund to rescue Greece and other countries from a sovereign default. The IMF has contributed to this rescue operation with considerable lending. Both the EU and the IMF loans have been contracted under strict conditions on two issues: considerable cuts in public-sector expenditure, and structural reforms in the labour and sectoral markets. Second, the European Union has urged all member states (whether with high or low debt) to put their public finances in order by fiscal consolidation so as to restore confidence of the financial markets in the sustainability of their debt.

Sources: IMF (2011b) and Blanchard (2009).

prices (real estate, equity, etc.). A country that finds itself in trouble will then often be subject to a bank and currency crisis. Speculation will set in: foreign and domestic depositors suddenly shift their funds into a foreign currency. This speculation will often oblige the country to devalue its currency.

Stage 2: The spreading out

The collapse of one segment of the market is likely to have a disastrous effect on those whose portfolios were financed with borrowed capital, including financial intermediaries such as banks. The incapacity of one organization to pay its debts provokes often the collapse of others that were its creditors, leading to waves of bankruptcies. If the public loses confidence in financial institutions that have become vulnerable because of substantial losses, they may be tempted to withdraw their deposits. They thus aggravate the situation, because in this way organizations that are in principle sound will risk falling victim to the crisis. The crisis in the financial sector will often lead to a slowdown of the real sector as it limits the capacity of many firms to obtain short-term credit for their daily operations and long-term credits for investments (e.g. by issuing bonds) in share capital. In the end the combined effect is a slowdown of growth and possibly even a fall in GDP.

Financial crises tend to spread rapidly from one country to another. This effect of *contagion*[6] is due to a combination of psychological factors and system characteristics. A specific aspect of the latter point is information. As foreign lenders are often in a poor position to judge the quality of their assets in faraway countries and the robustness of specific financial intermediaries, they tend to react on signals. Financial institutions in countries for which the fundamentals are good may thus come under attack because their situation with respect to exposure to shocks or institutional characteristics bears some resemblance to that in countries which have proved vulnerable. A problem in one segment of the system may then induce depositors to withdraw their funds from banks that are sound. These banks may get into difficulties because they cannot cope with such sudden explosions of withdrawals. So, the sound parts become infected as well. Bank cross-holding may oblige others to reinterpret their overall position and pull out as well.

Stage 3: The reaction of the public authorities

The public authorities will intervene in order to restore confidence and stability, and to cushion as far as possible the negative effects on the economy. If the crisis hits hard at the solidity of financial intermediaries, such as banks, there may be a risk of a "system default". Banks that have become too big to fail will have to be rescued by the public sector, worsening the public debt situation. Over time, this debt will have to be recovered by increased taxation or lower spending, reducing further the capacity of the country to recover from the crisis.

Policy reactions based on the interpretation of the crisis in terms of incorrect fundamentals will imply a contraction of budget and credit (much along the standard view). Markets will interpret this as meaning that there is indeed something wrong and will adapt accordingly. An additional problem that may occur in these cases is that countries for which the fundamentals are sound but nevertheless become the subject of such a crisis consider that they are unjustly under attack. As international help has mostly occurred only in fairly bad cases where the fundamentals were substantially wrong, accepting such international help would lead to a stigma. In order to avoid such a stigma, countries have been tempted to postpone asking for international help. So, there is a case for a soft procedure whereby international bodies gradually step up their involvement in the support to countries encountering this type of difficulty.

Now, the problem is that the capacity of governments to intervene is very unequal. What is worse, such differences in initial capacity tend to be magnified as a consequence of the crisis. Indeed, we see on the one hand that weak countries will have to go through a very costly and problematic adaptation process. Their budget situation does not permit them to spend more; on the contrary, the crisis will force them to cut public spending drastically, or increase taxation, thereby aggravating the slowdown of the economy and the doubts about the sustainability of their public debt. Moreover, markets and public pressure (regaining competitiveness) will often compel them to devaluate[7]. On the other hand, the stronger states tend to stay aloof and covered. The resilience of their systems tends to make them into a haven where risk-averse investors tend to seek shelter from the turbulence. This reinforces their position by decreasing the interest rates that both the private sector and the public sector have to pay for their borrowing.

As a reaction to a crisis, public authorities increase the surveillance of the financial sector in order to identify risks at an early stage and avoid a new crisis. Yet crises are a recurrent phenomenon. This is because the lessons of the previous crisis tend to be quickly forgotten. As many new players and new products come to the market, awareness of risks tends to decrease and major private and public players tend to be uncertain about the institutions and rules that have to be put in place to cope with possible risks under the new technological and market circumstances. This creates the conditions for a new crisis to develop (Reinhart and Rogoff 2009).

6.2.6 The cost of a crisis

The cost of financial crises can be very high. However, they are quite different for different players.

Many of the crises that occurred during the last half of the previous century originated in developing countries. The cost of most of these crises ranged between 6 per cent and 20 per cent of GDP of the country concerned. However, in some cases much higher losses were incurred, going up to 40 per cent of GDP (see, for example, Bordo *et al.* 2001; BIS 1997; World Bank 2000: 36). In many of these developing economies the crises not only involved a loss of income and jobs for workers in the export sectors but also caused a significant rise in the proportion of people living below the poverty line (see, for example, Chu and Hill 2001; Zlatko 2011).[8] The effect of the present crisis seems to touch mostly the developed world, with the effects on developing and emerging market economies seeming to be relatively limited. The latter have experienced some decrease in export possibilities owing to the slackening in demand in the developed world, but this seems to be largely compensated by a growth in demand coming from the emerging markets (IMF 2011a).

It is not very clear how much of the costs of the previous crises have ultimately been borne by the international community. The cost to the global taxpayer of the major bailouts of the past (where the IMF has given loans to countries in difficulty) has been very small, as almost all loans have been paid back over time (Jeanne and Zettelmeyer 2001). This leads to the conclusion that the real cost of the past crises has been fully borne by the countries that got deepest into difficulties, often emerging market countries but also poverty-ridden LDCs. The present crisis is different. A large part of the value losses are borne by the investors in EU banks and by the taxpayers of countries that had to rescue banks in difficulty (IMF 2011b).

6.3 The main public goods

6.3.1 Objectives

It is evident from the previous section that the lack of financial stability is a public bad. So, a stable financial system is a global public good. This implies that the *objective* of collective action should be the creation of a regime capable of preventing the occurrence of crises and of coping with financial crises (which happen in a capitalist system notwithstanding these preventive measures). This definition poses a problem in terms of the measurement of effectiveness, both for the outcome variables (in terms of overarching objectives) and on the concrete target variables (in terms of output of the policy efforts). For all practical purposes we will work with institutional indicators for the latter (for instance, have certain rules on bank capitalization been enacted, have certain institutions that have to check government deficits been put in place?). For the former we will adopt the ultimate goal of stability – that is, a higher growth rate for the economy of the different members of the regime. Remember that the countries most vulnerable to the negative effects of instability are the poor countries, so we will also pay attention to the effects on these countries, and in particular to the effects on poverty.

Creating the conditions for stability is more easily said than done, because our understanding of the causes of a crisis is imperfect and hence it is difficult to predict a crisis and to set up effective mechanisms of prevention.

In such circumstances any collective action to achieve results is difficult. Moreover, there is the important issue of the fair distribution of the cost and benefits. Many feel that the public sector has had to rescue the financial sector at a huge cost to society, so they want to recover that money. However, as long as there is uncertainty among many major actors as to the principles on which new regimes have to be built, on the influence that different types of countries need to have in the elaboration of regulation, and on the distribution of potential cost and benefits, it will be difficult to achieve results.

6.3.2 Principles

The issue of principles in matters of financial stability is largely unsettled. In the world of finance the liberal ideology is dominant. This ideology has been translated into a principle of free movement. However, the case for free capital movements is not as strong as that for trade in goods: economic theory shows that in the former case, protection can have beneficial effects. This is particularly the case for the disruptive effect of short-term capital flows. From economic theory one can borrow the notions that stability is dependent to a large extent on sound funda-mentals of national policy, a low public budget deficit, low government indebted-ness and a sustainable current account balance. Consequently, the global regime has to take into account a variety of different views as to the best arrangements.

This throws us back to the two basic elements for stability policy: prevention and cure of the disease. As the specialist finance literature is largely silent on the issue, I propose the following principles, based on a comparison with other regimes:

- *Precaution.* Where prevention is important (as in the case of the environmental regime), the principle of precaution is applicable. Although we do not know exactly why, when and how crises occur, we know that the chance of their occurrence decreases when certain conditions are met. These concern in particular standard-setting, prudential regulation and clarity about liability.
- *Solidarity.* When a crisis has occurred and should be cured, it is important that an international organization can draw on means (provided by all members) in order to rescue one of its member states.

The adoption of these principles implies that mechanisms have to be put in place at two levels, national and international.

6.3.3 National responsibilities

A condition that is a *sine qua non* for stability is the existence of adequate institutions and policies. The design of the national institutions and policies has thus to be carried out in such a way that they create the macro conditions for an optimal functioning of the economic process in general and of the financial sector in particular. These involve first the basics such as the effective enforcement of property rights, the legal obligation for shareholders to commit themselves, and bankruptcy laws which make sure that the burden of failure of individual firms will be borne in an equitable way by all those who have taken risks. Moreover, they involve the creation of macroeconomic conditions that are conducive to growth and stability, which implies sound public finances, an adequate exchange rate regime, a tax system that brings as few distortions as possible and a sustainable current account. Finally, they involve adequate institutional requirements in such diverse areas as labour and equity markets.

The primary objective of stability policies is *prevention*. The main instruments in this respect are regulation and coordination. They should create the conditions that minimize the risk of a crisis actually developing.

Market actors

The quality of the financial system depends critically on the quality of the major actors – that is, on the financial sector. The individual consumer of the services of financial institutions cannot judge whether they are trustworthy. He or she is unable to evaluate whether a bank will be able to pay back deposits, or whether an insurance company will be able to pay in a few decades from now the pension that it has promised to the subscriber to a life insurance policy. So, public authorities have to provide that trust. They do so in two ways: first, by limiting access to the trade to firms that meet the basic criteria for sound finances; and second, by prudential control of the financial intermediaries – that means, by constantly preventing financial firms from taking risks that might endanger their long-term viability. So, adequate rules for such prudential control will avoid the occurrence of failures in the system. However, such regulation also has a negative side in that it may hinder innovation. Innovation is needed to improve the performance of the system. An increase in sophistication of the products will increase the complexity and decrease the transparency of the system. So, in order to deal effectively with the risks of modern financial markets, ever more sophisticated forms of surveillance are necessary. The problem is thus to strike the right balance between rigorously applying the results of proven good practices and prudently experimenting with new forms.

Market functioning

The proper functioning of markets implies that both institutions and regulation require the various actors to be as transparent as possible. In many cases the information that actors provide is difficult to interpret, as firms use different terms for the same notion and vice versa. So, the setting of standards for accounting and the setting of minimum rules for reporting (with respect to content and frequency) all mean that actors can react adequately and in a timely fashion to market signals. The proper functioning of markets implies the free flow of international capital. This is rather uncontroversial for long-term capital flows that serve to improve the structure of the economy. However, the case for free short-term capital flows is less compelling, as they tend to create high volatility and thus increase the risk of a financial crisis. For that reason, many countries operate systems for monitoring and controlling capital movements in order to limit the occurrence of financial crises and to reinforce the country's capacity to cope with an emerging crisis. However, the effectiveness of controls on capital flows is limited, notably in the event that the fundamentals are seriously wrong. Moreover, they come at a cost, in terms of a loss of macroeconomic efficiency. Temporary controls of capital inflows to prevent overheating of the economy can be effective and have a positive welfare effect. These welfare gains may, however, disappear and even turn negative if controls are maintained (Reinhart and Smith 2002). Again the problem is to strike the right balance between liberalization and control.

All the previous measures may not be enough to prevent a crisis. In order to avoid the collapse of a bank and the ensuing contagion, governments and/or central banks (CBs) have to assume an active role. At this stage the previously discussed instruments of regulation and coordination will no longer be sufficient and the financial instrument will be deployed. If the problem is only one of illiquidity, the CB may act as a lender of last resort and provide the bank in difficulty with the necessary finances to see to its obligations. If the problem is one of insolvency, the CB, in cooperation with the government, will try to put a safety net into place, followed by an orderly takeover by another player belonging to the private sector. In this way, moral hazard problems are avoided and the consequences of the taking of undue risks will fall on the bank's shareholders. The crisis that started in 2007 has shown that governments can get into deep trouble as a result of these rescue operations, as they have to borrow to bail out banks, which can actually decrease their own solvency (as it may lead to higher interest payments). Unfortunately, some banks have reached such a size that the national authorities are no longer capable of effecting such a rescue operation.

6.3.4 International responsibilities

On the international level there is also a double objective: first, to create conditions that should prevent a crisis from occurring; and second, if a crisis has occurred, to manage it in such a way that it does as little harm as possible. The consequences of this objective for the design of an international regime can be specified as follows.

Prevention

Countries are autonomous in their policies. However, inadequate national policies increase the probability that a crisis will occur. So, there is a need for regulation – the setting of international norms and standards – and for coordination – continuous communication between the international organization and the national governments. A lot of work has gone into the elaboration of such standards, applicable to both developed and developing countries. Next, there is a need for international monitoring of the way individual countries perform. If information on what is going on shows up cases where the norms are not being complied with, action of course needs to follow. However, the possibilities for coercion are limited, so the system should at least provide the country concerned with the best practices available. The problem is, of course, that the norms are stricter the weaker the situation and the higher the risks. On the other hand, the capacity of the country to deal with the problems will be weaker the more risky the situation. So, adequate measures for technical and financial help in the early stages in which such national problems develop are required.

Adequate crisis management

Once a crisis has occurred, it needs to be managed effectively in order to limit its negative consequences. There are various stages to such management:

- *Diagnosis.* To develop an adequate policy reaction, it is necessary to know where the problem has arisen and how it is developing. Establishing these facts is much more difficult than many people think. First, there is often very large uncertainty as to the fundamentals. Moreover, instability is not always due to bad macro policies; actually, there is an unlimited variety of self-fulfilling elements. Finally, notwithstanding our increased knowledge of the anatomy of a crisis (see Figure 6.1), it is mostly unclear whether a problem will develop into a crisis situation or not.
- *Immediate response.* In view of the wide variety of developments and of the considerable uncertainties involved, those responsible for managing the crisis will have to make sure that they have a large amount of room for flexibility as to the way in which they handle it and the means they wish to adopt. However, there are a few lessons to be learned from earlier crises that seem to have general applicability. First, the country in question should take adequate fiscal and monetary policy measures. Second, the international community should make large-scale interventions possible at an early stage, so as to prevent the "too little, too late" problem. This implies the availability of very considerable funds to help countries get back on track. Third, there should be a credible programme to deal with the source of the crisis. Fourth, a consistent programme to restore equilibrium should be set up, specifying the objectives and means.
- *Containment of the problem.* Contagion can be contained by providing, so far as possible, adequate information about the character of the crisis and the way it is going to be handled. Here, concerted action by the international and national authorities is needed. A big issue here is the containment of moral hazard, as some of the concerted policy measures risk favouring economic actors whose irresponsible behaviour has been at the origin of the crisis.

6.4 The organizations involved in the provision of the public good

6.4.1 Major players

The previous sections have made it clear that a number of actors are critical both in the understanding of financial crises and in the efforts to get out of a crisis. I am referring in particular to the three-stage, three-actor model of Figure 6.1.

Paramount among those in the *private sector* are financial intermediaries (mostly banks and insurance companies, and their specialized branches). They have been created to avoid imperfections of the market. They attract savings and pay them an average price. They use this pool of savings in their borrowing operations. They limit adverse selection by the evaluation of risks and by price discrimination between different types of borrowers. They limit moral hazard problems with their clients by monitoring their performance and behaviour over time. Financial intermediaries have used their position to broaden their services. One of them is adapting the products to the time preferences of their depositors and creditors so as to increase liquidity in the market. As long as lenders and borrowers maintain their confidence in the capacity of the bank to meet its contractual obligations, it is unlikely that any problem will occur. However, as soon as doubts arise, a bank run may follow. This may have a chain effect as described on pp. 109–113.

The major *public players* are national governments and central banks. With respect to the relation with the private sector (a major source of instability), there is quite some variety in the division of responsibilities over the central bank (CB), government and other institutions (e.g. those charged with the prudential supervision of the pension system and pension funds). In many countries the CB has been given responsibility for the regulation and prudential supervision of the banking system; in other countries, separate regulatory bodies exist. In most countries the CB has the task of intervening if irregularities are observed (Brealey *et al.* 2001). This is true for both industrialized and developing countries. The smaller and less developed the country, the more extensive is the range of responsibilities of the CB.

With respect to the possible problems that may arise in the public sector (high indebtedness; a large budget deficit), there is of course only one actor: the national government itself. But let us not forget that the public sector acts very often under the influence of the private sector. Its systemic design has been formed as a result of intensive lobbying for lenient regulation by the major players of the financial sector, while the application of the rules by the public authorities is also subject to much interference by private sector actors.

6.4.2 *Main international organizations*

In matters of the stability of the international financial system a series of institutions play their role. They have evolved gradually under the influence of major technological and political changes (e.g. Eichengreen 2008). Among the *intergovernmental organizations* the IMF takes pride of place. Organizations such as the G8 and G20, the Bank of International Settlements and the OECD (see Chapter 3) also consider world financial stability a matter for their concern. None of these institutions assumes operational responsibility for coping with the problems of the financial sector. The only one to do that is the IMF (which we will discuss in more detail in the next subsection).

To improve the preventive part of the global financial system, an important role has been given to the *Financial Stability Board* (see www.financialstabilityboard.org).

The institution was created in 1998 in the aftermath of a crisis as the International Financial Stability Forum (FSF). At its 2009 meeting the G20 decided to transform the FSF into a Financial Stability Board (FSB) with a strengthened mandate including all G20 members and the EU Commission. Its mandate is to:

- assess vulnerabilities affecting the international financial system;
- identify and oversee regulatory, supervisory and related actions to address these vulnerabilities;
- improve coordination and information exchange among the authorities that are responsible for financial stability.

The FSB cooperates with the IMF on the creation of early warning systems. It brings together senior representatives of national financial authorities (e.g. central banks, treasuries and supervisory authorities), international institutions (such as the IMF, World Bank, OECD, and the Bank of International Settlements (BIS)) and international regulatory and supervisory groupings of the financial sector.[9] The FSB is serviced by a small secretariat housed in the Bank of International Settlements in Basel. The BIS is in charge of establishing rules and means for international financial operations. It is the venue of a gathering of representatives of the major central banks.[10] In order to keep the structure manageable, the number of participants is kept at a relatively restricted (some twenty-seven) level. The major product of the Basle institutions is international agreements on the standards for banking supervision to prevent banks from taking excessive risks and hence prevent new crises from occurring. At the end of 2010 a new agreement (called Basel III) on minimum requirements for banks' own capital was reached. Work is still in progress on the extension of regulatory oversight to all systemically important financial institutions, instruments and markets (including hedge funds and credit rating agencies).

Professional associations complement the work of the intergovernmental organizations. They work on the adoption of standards and good practices. The most relevant ones are the Basel committee on banking supervision, the International Organization of Securities Commission for stock trading and the International Accounting Standards Committee for accounting practices. The IMF refers to the standards adopted by these organizations.

On the *regional* level only a very few organizations deal with the stability problem. A case in point is the European Union, which has adopted a single currency and created a European Central Bank. Initiatives in other regions are fairly timid; only in Asia have they been developed to some extent (see Box 6.2).[11]

6.4.3 The IMF

The IMF grew out of the necessity to recast the global financial system and, notably, to reform the international monetary system in the light of the payment difficulties many countries experienced as a result of the ravages of the Second World War. The IMF has on several occasions been reformed so as to be able to

BOX 6.2 IS REGIONALISM A SOLUTION? THE CASE OF ASIA

It is not self-evident that regional initiatives in Asia will emerge. East Asian countries have a history of enmity, competition and uneven distribution of power. Most countries in the region see their integration into the world economy as their first priority. So, there was not really a strong impetus to engage in regional arrangements. Yet ASEAN has been created for trade integration and its coverage and institutional set-up have recently been strengthened.

East Asians have had two reasons for searching for a regional mechanism in matters of financial cooperation, too. The first was the major financial break-down following the 1997 crisis, which seriously affected a number of countries in the region. The second was the slow progress on the global level in matters of providing a mechanism adapted to Asian countries' needs.

The Chiang Mai Initiative initiated financial and monetary cooperation in the region. It now involves the ten members of ASEAN plus China, Japan and Korea. Initially it set up a simple regional credit support mechanism (based on bilateral agreements) for countries experiencing balance of payments problems. A multilateralization was agreed and a fund of some $120 billion was created. In 2012 the size of the fund was doubled. Its objective is to prevent an extreme crisis or systemic failure in a country and subsequent regional contagion. It creates time to work out other, more structural solutions in cooperation with the IMF.

The advantage of such a scheme is that it considerably reduces the need for individual countries to keep large amounts of currency reserves. Pooling of reserves and making them available under certain conditions permits the creation of effective lines of defence against emerging problems due to the instabilities of financial markets. Moreover, a number of participants have agreed to cross-holdings in public debt for very significant amounts. The reasons are twofold: to eliminate the risks of an excessively high concentration of their holdings and to make themselves less vulnerable to shocks in the financial markets.

Sources: Park and Wang (2000), Park (2002) and Grimes (2011).

deal with the new exigencies of rapidly changing global economic relations. The Fund's capital has been contributed by the members on the basis of a quota system.

The *objectives* of the IMF are wide-ranging. It aspires to:

- promote international monetary cooperation and the stability of the monetary system (exchange rate[12] and international payments);

- make its general resources (in the form of loans) temporarily available to those of its members experiencing balance of payments difficulties (under adequate safeguards);
- shorten the duration and lessen the degree of disequilibrium in the international balances of payments of its members.

Following the crisis that began in 2007, the IMF has clarified and updated its mandate to cover the full range of macroeconomic and financial issues that have a bearing on global stability. It has organized the responsibilities for the execution of its tasks in the following way:

- The *board of governors* (BoG) is the head of the organization; each member appoints one governor (usually the minister of finance or the president of the central bank). Each governor has one basic vote, but this vote is weighted according to the country's quota in the capital.
- The *executive board* (EB) is responsible for the operational aspects of the work of the IMF. Indeed, the BoG has delegated most of its powers to the EB. The EB consists of a number of directors (twenty-four), some of whom are appointed by the largest five member countries; the remaining nineteen are elected by constituencies[13] of the other countries.
- The *managing director* heads the staff (some 2,500 at the end of 2011, mostly based in Washington, DC) and is responsible for the day-to-day management of the organization. The work is organized according to Table 6.1.

The way the various organs work together has recently been changed to make the IMF more responsive to new global conditions (IMF 2008a, 2009). Notably, the EB's role of oversight was strengthened and a number of executive roles were devolved to management and staff.

The *membership* of the Fund has greatly increased over time. Since its modest beginnings with some thirty countries, the Fund now covers almost all sovereign states in the world (187 in 2011). These members do not, however, carry equal weight in the organization: representation is based on a quota system that takes account of both the financial commitment of each member state to the IMF and

TABLE 6.1 Departmental structure of the IMF

Geographical area	Functional area	Special service
Africa	Monetary and capital markets	Research
Asia and Pacific	Strategy, policy and review	IMF Institute
Europe	Fiscal affairs	Statistics
Middle East and Central Asia		Treasurer's
Western Hemisphere		Legal

Source: Adapted from IMF website information.

its voting power in the BoG and the EB. In the past the major Western countries (in particular the United States) made most of the contributions to the capital of the Fund, and as power is distributed on that basis, in practice they controlled the organization.[14] The IMF is in the process of bringing these shares more into line with the actual weight in economic or population terms; in 2010 it decided to shift quotas from the overrepresented countries to the new emerging market countries. The largest ten members are now the United States, Japan, Brazil, China, India, Russia and the four largest European countries (Germany, France, the United Kingdom and Italy). Moreover, it has decided to move to an all-elected EB.

Members have committed themselves to comply with the rules of the IMF and will:

- inform each other about the exchange rate and the arrangements determining it;
- refrain from restricting the convertibility of their currency;
- pursue economic, fiscal and monetary policies that will contribute in an orderly way to national and global wealth creation.

The IMF has no means of coercing member states to comply with their commitments other than the refusal to give more financial assistance. However, as alternatives are scarce, even the threat to use this instrument is very effective. So, compliance is induced by two mechanisms (see Chapter 4): finances (conditional loans) and persuasion (partly by IMF staff and partly by peer pressure from other members).

6.5 The IMF's governance

6.5.1 General

The IMF has several objectives that stem from its double role as a monetary and a financial international institution. The instruments it deploys are determined by the objectives but also by the fact that there is a division of tasks with other international organizations. The main instrument for the prevention of crises is monitoring, surveillance and consultation. We will go into that in the next subsection. The prevention of crises depends on a large number of institutional factors, some of which are in the realm of international authorities, others in the realm of national authorities (see sections 6.3.3 and 6.3.4). On both levels, legal and regulatory aspects are important. The IMF does not set formal rules for all these elements itself; this task is mostly entrusted to the Financial Stability Board (see section 6.4.2).[15] However, the IMF does help member states in understanding the legal aspects of stability measures, and supports the adoption of good practices (IMF 2008b).

The IMF in its second role (that of an international financial institution charged with coping with a crisis) mostly uses the loan instrument. We will deal with that in section 6.5.3. Now, the IMF does want its loans to be paid back at a later stage and for that reason it sets conditions. Note that these conditions go far beyond the more technical financial aspects of loans and concern national institutions, laws and policies. In so far as the IMF prescribes certain changes in these institutions that it deems necessary for the recovery of its member country, there is an aspect of imposing standards as well. We will deal with the aspects of conditionality in section 6.5.4.

6.5.2 Information, surveillance and consultations

The IMF's first objective is to improve *the stability of the international financial order* – in other words, to prevent crises. To accomplish that objective, the IMF has adopted a two-stage process:

1. Rendering the processes on international capital markets and the situations in member countries more transparent. The IMF does so by publishing regular and incidental reports (see, for example, Mathieson and Schinasi 2000). It provides regular assessments of global prospects in its *World Economic Outlook*; of financial markets in its *Global Financial Stability Report*; and of public finances in its *Fiscal Monitor*. This procedure is intended to show the weaknesses in the system.
2. Improving the consistency of national institutions and policies.

To pursue these objectives, the IMF has essentially two instruments. The main one is *surveillance*. Financial stability is the result of a series of good policies. So, the IMF evaluates the economic performance of each of its member states on a series of indicators. Traditionally these involve aspects such as macroeconomic equilibrium, balance of payments, exchange rate policies, financial markets and external reserves. IMF surveillance has been extended in the past to include an increasing number of subjects. One very important element is the surveillance of banking soundness through Financial Sector Assessment Programmes. Other elements are good governance and the observance of international standards, and codes of good practice; the IMF publishes Reports on the Observance of Standards and Codes. The assessment of the risks involved in member states' (macro) policies is done more candidly. The IMF concentrates attention on countries where economic disturbances are likely to spill over to the international community. This bolstering of the surveillance task has been decided in the wake of a number of major crises that have shown the variety of origins and channels of contagion. The IMF has made special precautionary arrangements, including enhanced surveillance of countries that need to bolster international confidence in their policies.

The second instrument is *consultation*. To improve consistency of policies, IMF staff meet regularly with representatives of the governments of each member country. These follow in general a standard procedure in which several stages can be distinguished. In a first stage the IMF staff members collect statistical data on a range of indicators such as trade, money in circulation, budget deficit, etc. Next there are discussions with high-ranking government officials to establish the effectiveness of the policies of the previous year and the perspectives for the next year. Finally, a summary report on the country's performance is written and submitted to the IMF's executive board and the government of the country in question. These reports often contain specific suggestions for the strengthening of weak points in the member state's policy.

This surveillance and consultation system is operated in a continuous and candid way on behalf of the credibility of the policies of the organization as a whole and the individual members. It covers all factors that may have an influence on exchange rates or are possible causes for a financial crisis, such as the functioning of the financial sector.

6.5.3 Financial assistance

The second objective is to *provide sufficient official liquidity to countries in crisis*. The main instrument that the IMF uses is loans to member countries with payments problems. These funds originate from the quota each member has paid to the Fund on its admission. The allocation of such aid has been very dependent on conformity with US foreign policy as well as the member state's immediate financial need, inflation, economic growth problems and such factors as democracy and administrative quality (e.g. Pop-Eleches 2009). By the late 1990s and early 2000s the IMF had lost much of its relevance; very few countries turned to it for a loan, mostly because they did not want to be subject to its severe conditions (see the next subsection). The global crisis that began in 2007 has changed the role of the IMF dramatically. First, the total amounts of loans surged to unprecedented heights (see Figure 6.2). Second, support no longer goes merely to low- and middle-income countries but also to high-income countries (e.g. Greece).

To cope with the challenges of the global crisis, a series of quite *fundamental reforms in the size and form of its lending activities* were made. These comprised, first of all, a very considerable increase in the total funding available and member countries' access to the IMF resources. Next it introduced several new forms of lending that make the IMF instruments more flexible and better adapted to specific country circumstances, including:

* A new flexible credit line for countries with robust policy frameworks and a strong track record in economic performance. Here the IMF has turned to *ex ante* conditionality (rigorous pre-qualification criteria) and no longer asks for traditional programme conditionality.
* A new Precautionary Credit Line for countries that have sound economic policies and sound fundamentals but are still faced with vulnerabilities. This model combines the *ex ante* conditionality of the former with a light form of *ex post* conditionality, in particular focused on the vulnerable side.

The last of these new objectives is to *enable countries that have got into severe long-term problems to work out their debts in an orderly way*. The pursuit of this objective is

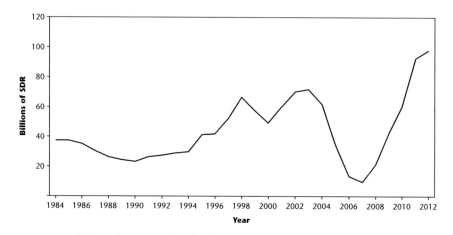

FIGURE 6.2 IMF credit outstanding for all members, 1984–2012 (in billions of SDR).

Source: IMF website. SDR stands for Special Drawing Right: the currency that is used by the IMF. In 2012 1 $ = 0.65 SDR; 1 euro = 0.83 SDR.

important because it will permit countries to make a new start and avoid a situation in which fragile countries become a threat to the system. The main instrument of the IMF has been the coordination of the willingness of creditors to write off part of their claims; however, the IMF has not been very effective in this role.

6.5.4 A major debate: how far should the IMF go in the conditionality of its interventions?

Before the IMF releases its loan it may request the member country to take a number of policy measures and sometimes even to embark upon in-depth reforms. The IMF will do this if it considers that these measures are necessary to solve the fundamental problems that led to the occurrence of the financial problem. The reason for applying this principle is that the IMF wants to make sure that the member country in question will be able to pay back the money in a reasonable time period of three to five years.

The borrowing country that has run into difficulty will have to make sure that the conditions will be created for sound finances. Along with its request for a loan, the potential borrower presents the IMF with a plan for reform. Such a plan includes macroeconomic variables under the control of the government, for which quantitative performance criteria are set, such as reductions in the budget deficit. Others deal with certain structural weaknesses – for instance, the privatization of inefficient public enterprises, the breakdown of monopolies, etc. Over the years the conditions have tended to become ever more detailed and cover ever more areas of the government activity. This has led to much controversy (see, for example, Killick 1995; Goldstein 2000; Jeanne and Zettelmeyer 2001; Evrensel 2002; Allegret and Dulbecco 2007; Mayer and Mourmouras 2008; Jeanne *et al.* 2008; Dreher 2009).

The *proponents of strict conditionality* argue that the IMF needs to go along this path of increased detail in order:

- To make sure that the adjustment programmes of the member countries do not stop halfway. The IMF considers that its long experience has shown that the basic condition for sustained growth is a consistent set of good policies and adequate institutions. It considers that countries are often not capable of implementing the necessary adaptations without IMF conditions, owing to opposition by the ruling elites.
- To avoid its bailouts being used to facilitate bad economic policies, thus creating moral hazard problems at the expense of the (international) taxpayer.

The *opponents of conditionality* (very often member countries that have to borrow from the IMF – in particular, LDCs) complain about these conditions. Their arguments are that the IMF conditions:

- Put an unnecessary strain on their operations. In some cases the conditions of the IMF are indeed so severe that they have caused very serious social unrest, leading to the disruption of economic activity and of national institutions essential for growth. Faced with such restrictive conditions, countries may actually refrain from calling on IMF aid altogether.
- Interfere in an unjustified way with the sovereignty of the borrowing country. LDCs complain about the fact that the IMF demands very thoroughgoing structural reforms that it would never dare to ask from major developed countries, thus infringing the principle of equal treatment.

Loud voices have also come from independent economists who consider that the IMF should be careful in getting involved in deep structural reforms because of its:

- *Poor competence*. The IMF strays from its core competence into a host of other areas for which it is ill-equipped. This leads to poor crisis management and a loss of credibility of the IMF in this area that spills over into its core competence areas.
- *Poor operationality*. The criteria for getting the macroeconomy right are fairly simple; by contrast, criteria by which to measure the progress of structural reform are many (say over fifty) and performance is sometimes difficult to assess (for example, on a total of 50, is a score of 25 good, 15 bad and 10 poor or a satisfactory performance?).

This controversy can best be arbitrated by evaluating the effects of the IMF conditionality in practice. The evidence is at best mixed.[16] So, the IMF has changed its policy quite drastically. It has made its conditionality more focused on the main objectives, more flexible as to the type of problem a country faces (see previous subsection) and coupled to a commitment by the government to strengthen the use of social safety nets. The main points of criticism have thereby been taken away.

6.6 Evaluation of the past and options for the future

6.6.1 Major achievements

The final objective of stability is improved wealth creation; the immediate target is the creation of institutions that are conducive to stability (see section 6.3.1). We will deal with the performance on both scores in reverse order.

Institutions have been indeed created and their functioning improved. In the recent past the G20 has on several occasions given guidance to changes in the global financial architecture. The IMF tool kit has been strengthened. Its regular consultations with national governments have contributed to the notion that governments need to maintain a stable economic environment. It has helped to create the conditions for stable saving and investment and it has helped to convey the right signals in terms of prices and policy measures. Moreover, the IMF surveillance mechanism (Lavigne and Schembri 2009) has been overhauled in depth to make it fit for crisis prevention. The new set-up implies the inclusion of all countries in the process (notably the United States), the further clarification and specification of the indicators to be taken into account and the strengthening of IMF advice ("speak truth to power"; Lücke 2009).

The financial support that the IMF has given to countries confronted with a sudden imbalance (shock) triggers very different judgements. IMF critics say that the whole period of the Washington consensus has been marked by the negative effects of a wrong ideology-based recipe of structural adjustment, pushing many countries that had become dependent on IMF support into a prolonged period of slack, aggravating poverty and increasing vulnerability to new shocks (see the next subsection). Since the turn of the century the IMF has changed its modes of operation and now its general record seems to be rather positive (e.g. Dreher and Walter 2012). Moreover, it has been able to adapt its mode of operation to the challenges of the latest crisis by boosting the size of its lending and by becoming more flexible as to the type of lending.

In the same way one can evaluate the other aspects of the IMF toolbox, such as its contribution to the setting of standards. Unfortunately, the latter are not always easy to implement by developing countries.

This brings us to the final question about *policy outcomes*: has the IMF a good track record in terms of wealth creation? Earlier in this chapter I indicated the sometimes enormous cost of the various crises that have struck the world. Although concrete estimates of the growth bonus by avoidance of crises are lacking, we can safely assume that they are substantial. Moreover, as the latest crisis has shown, the improved conditions in emerging and developing countries have meant that they have remained substantially aloof from the problems. It is notably the developed world that has been hardest hit. So, it would seem as if income distribution in the world has recently somewhat improved, unlike in the past, when crises tended to hit poor countries in particular. A shady side of the increased financial integration seems to be that the income distribution *within* countries has deteriorated, owing in part to the exceptionally high remunerations in the financial sector. However, empirical evidence for this effect is very weak (OECD 2011b, c).

6.6.2 Inadequacies and challenges

In the past the IMF has been severely criticized as in many cases it made the wrong diagnosis or prescribed the wrong therapy (see Box 6.3). There is indeed abundant case material in the literature relating to the way in which the IMF (mis)handled for instance the Asian, Argentinian and recent European crises.

BOX 6.3 AN ERA OF CONFLICT OVER THE FUNCTIONING OF THE IMF

For a long time the IMF was subject to severe criticisms. To a large extent, these misgivings were based on the following three elements.[17]

Ideology and principles

The actions of all international economic organizations are shaped by ideology (see Chapter 2). In the 1980s the dominant ideas in the Western, and notably in the Anglo-Saxon, world shifted to "market fundamentalism". In this view, government involvement in the economy does not provide a solution to a problem of externalities or of market failure. On the contrary, government involvement is seen as causing the problem in permitting rent-seeking, corruption and inefficiencies. More markets are seen as the solution to this problem. The IMF has aligned its operations according to this view.[18]

Instruments

Founded on a belief in the efficiency of markets, the IMF has pushed countries into the liberalization of exchange rates and long- and short-term capital operations. Such policies tended to fail to produce good solutions in many LDCs, whose economies and institutions are small and vulnerable.

Interests

The concerns of the Fund tend to be dominated by the treasury ministers of Western countries that in turn were tributary to the major actors on the international capital markets. Power was concentrated with a few Western countries; others had little voice. Part of the lending of the IMF seemed to have

---

been given more to bail out Western capital providers instead of to help LDCs' economic activity to return to higher levels. This encouraged the former to lend without regard to risk. So, many operations of the IMF did work out in an inequitable way and were at odds with the interests of the developing countries.

The IMF has listened to these criticisms. It is in the process of adapting its internal structure and the orientation of its operations[19] to meet the new challenges of the international economy, the new geopolitical reality and hence the legitimacy of its actions.[20]

6.6.3 Proposals for improvement

There are a few sweeping proposals for a *completely new set of organizations*. These involve the setting up of a World Central Bank or a World Monetary Authority. In view of the results of the theoretical discussion in Chapter 2, it is clear that such proposals have very little chance of being realized. So, most authors writing about adaptation of the present global structures[21] start from the assumption that it is better to think about *gradual reforms* that have a chance of being implemented in the medium term. Given the persistent limitations of other organizations (such as the G20[22]) proposals tend to focus on the IMF.

A first proposal (that has resurfaced again during the crisis) aims at a reduction of the chances that problems will occur and aims at placing the burden of a possible crisis on the private sector. Particularly hotly debated in this respect is the introduction of a tax on (foreign) capital movements, which should limit the volatility of capital flows and mobilize resources for a fund from which crisis measures can be financed.[23] The EU Commission has proposed introducing such a tax on all international transactions. The United States has up till now favoured an approach that is based on institutions (banks, etc.) rather than on transactions.

Other suggestions for improvements concern the remit of the IMF. Some of these tend to refocus the organization on its primary task and to strengthen its governance:

- The prevention of crises by the setting of *higher standards for the private sector* and better compliance with such standards. At present the responsibility is split over several organizations (see section 6.4.2) that are supposed to collaborate (e.g. the FSB). However, solutions that are worked out in these frameworks tend to take much time to implement; progress is often frustrated by the financial sector's influence in these organizations. Concentration of these various functions in the IMF would give the IMF a position on the global level similar to that of the central banks at the national level.
- The possibility that the IMF could deal with *major currency misalignments*, often related to prolonged current account imbalances, has been suggested. These are

sometimes the result of deliberate government policies. As they cause considerable negative spill-over effects in other countries, there is a case for a global public good-oriented intervention of international institutions (Frieden 2009). The G20 has asked the IMF to analyse the feasibility of an increased surveillance of this aspect, coupled with a mechanism for publication that one hopes would lead to pressure for adaptation. Although this is a political minefield, there are ideas to make such a system effective (e.g. Blanchard and Milesi-Ferretti 2011).

• To deal with crises in the most effective way would suppose that the IMF withdraws from some activities it has undertaken in the past. The Malan Report (2007) proposes in this respect that the IMF leave all long-term lending for development purposes to the World Bank and concentrate on medium-term lending to help countries with liquidity and solvency problems.

• Moreover, some propose to give the IMF a clear role in the working out of sovereign debt. This is necessary in cases when the government of a country runs the risk of defaulting on its loans. An orderly arrangement for restructuring the debt is then needed. Some have proposed to give the IMF a leading role, including the authority to declare a standstill on payments, to organize restructuring negotiations and, if a qualified majority accept the deal, to bind also the minority of creditors. Some (Eichengreen 2002) argue that a better option in this respect would be to include in loan agreements clauses for collective action and collective representation.

Finally, a number of proposals have been made that address the lack of representativeness and accountability of the IMF. To that end the *voting power* in the IMF has to be rebalanced so that it reflects more the present reality in economic power in the world. This should involve a single seat for the European Union, and a considerable increase in the votes for the emerging and LDC economies so as to represent their legitimate interests. This might actually take the form of a merger of the G20 meeting at ministerial level with the executive board of the IMF.

All these proposals concern the multilateral route. Indeed, notwithstanding increased trade integration and hence increased interdependence in macro-economic terms in many areas of the world, full-fledged regional monetary integration (Economic and Monetary Unions) is not on the cards for both economic and political reasons. One will however see many forms of cooperation in financial and monetary matters develop that offer gains of increased financial and monetary stability without too strong constraints[24.]

6.7 Summary and conclusions

• Under the influence of liberalization the size and complexity of global capital flows have increased very considerably. This in turn has led to financial instability and recurrent financial crises.

• The cost of these crises is very high. In the past they affected primarily the most vulnerable developing countries. The recent crisis has been very costly to the main developed economies too. So, prevention of crises is very important and financial stability is a global public good.

- The responsibility for the provision of this public good has been entrusted mainly to the IMF. Each of its member countries contributes part of the capital of the IMF. Voting rights are associated to the number of shares. The Western countries dominate the IMF, as they have the largest shares in the total. A shift in shares from the Western countries to the large emerging economies has been agreed.

- The IMF tries to prevent crises by creating the right conditions. Moreover, it tries to avoid the negative effects of crises by giving financial assistance to countries in difficulties. It attaches conditions to such aid; the inroads these make into national sovereignty is a source of much controversy. Recently the IMF has introduced much more flexibility into its lending, adapting the tool and attached conditions to specific country circumstances.

- The track record of the IMF is fairly mixed. On the one hand, it has not been able to prevent major crises and it has too often given patients the wrong medicine. On the other hand, it has helped to create the conditions for more stability and has indeed helped crisis-ridden countries to recover.

- The world financial system is confronted with three major challenges: first, to improve the macroeconomic management of the world economy; second, to regulate the financial sector to the extent that a financial crisis will no longer result in a public sector crisis with the ensuing losses to the tax payer; and finally, to adapt the internal rules of the IMF so as to render them more apt to contribute to the catch-up capacity of LDCs.

7

DEVELOPMENT AID

7.1 Introduction

The world is confronted with underdevelopment and poverty that affect large segments of the globe. This is morally unacceptable and economically inefficient, so there are good reasons to develop policies to enhance growth in the less developed areas. However, opinions diverge greatly on how to achieve this enhanced growth. To many, the main avenue is access to the markets of developed countries (Chapter 5) supported by good macro conditions (Chapter 6). However, many others think that this will not be sufficient to arrive at more balanced economic growth in the world and foster development aid.

The *objective* of this chapter is to expose the rationale, the main features and the effectiveness of the international regime for the improvement of the condition of developing countries through international development aid.

The *structure* of the chapter is as follows. First I describe the problem of underdevelopment and I argue that it is in the interest of everyone to do away with the considerable disparity in wealth levels; and that the way to do so is through development aid – this on both solidarity and economic efficiency arguments. In the next section I present the major aspects of the delivery of the global public good of solidarity through development aid, detailing the principles involved and the main national and international responsibilities. I pursue the demonstration by describing the main organizations that provide that collective good and the instruments they use to safeguard it. The international organizations dealing with development are not the only players; on the contrary, regional and national players have important roles as well. In a separate section I deal in particular with the governance aspects of the organization that is centre stage: the World Bank. Finally, I round off this chapter by evaluating the present regime, assessing the future challenges and putting forward a set of propositions for improvement.

7.2 The main problems

7.2.1 Inequitable wealth distribution

There are very large differences in wealth between the countries of the world. These are generally expressed in terms of GDP per head. Other indicators are also used, such as quality of life and financial assets.[1] They traditionally show a North–South divide: the North (mainly North America, Europe and Japan) is developed and rich, while the South (to name just large countries such as Brazil, Argentina, China, India, Indonesia, Nigeria and South Africa) is underdeveloped and poor. Some countries are particularly stricken by poverty, for instance Bangladesh. In Africa too, poverty is a widespread phenomenon, in particular in the Sahel zone. Table 7.1 shows very clearly the large wealth differences that exist between the different groups of countries.[2] If we group the basic data by population deciles, we find that the richest 20 per cent of the world population holds about 80 per cent of the total global wealth.

The existence of such large differences is considered morally unjust and eco-nomically inefficient. So, a major policy objective is to reduce such inequalities. Such a policy has been pursued for more than half a century, and the question is how far it has been successful. This can be studied with the help of indicators of convergence (less disparity over time) or divergence (more disparity over time).

In the past century, divergence prevailed.[3] In that period many LDCs have not been able to catch up with the most developed ones, and some have even lost ground. Around the turn of the century this trend was reversed. Table 7.1 shows that in the first decade of this century there was convergence: wealth increased faster the lower the starting position. This can be seen by comparing the ratio between the highest and the lowest category; it decreased from about 160 in 2000 to about 40 in 2010. This convergence is the net effect of two developments. On the one hand, growth has been enhanced in all regions outside the traditional developed world, and in particular in Asia, where some countries have shown double-digit growth over a prolonged period. On the other hand, growth has been modest in most of the highly developed countries.

The figures cited above hide huge differences that exist between different categories within a country. In many countries the income distribution has become

TABLE 7.1 Global wealth per capita by class[a] (€'000), 2000–2010

	High	Middle	Low
2000	90	5	0.5
2010	120	14	3

Source: Allianz (2011).

Note:
a These classes correspond to the ones the World Bank uses in its analyses.

less equal over time. This is partly due to technological development that improves the position of the highly qualified, but also partly due to government measures: less intervention in general improves the position of those that are best equipped to grasp the opportunities that are offered by the overall growth.[4] However, these national tendencies can sometimes hide the development of the global interpersonal income inequality over time. Notwithstanding many data difficulties, some studies show that in the past few decades the share of the world population below the poverty line significantly decreased.[5] The results are strongly influenced by the good performance of the two most populous countries: China and India. Their figures have dwarfed the bad results of the African countries.

7.2.2 Effects of openness on LDCs' growth and poverty

In Chapter 5 we saw how over the course of the past half century many countries have abandoned protectionism and adopted a policy of openness. This triggers a double question. First, whether a liberal trade policy does contribute to the enhanced growth of the developing countries and hence to an increase in equality of the income distribution in the world. Second, whether an open trade policy helps to decrease the poverty problem in LDCs.

Performance. Openness to trade does show a positive sign in growth equations (see WTO 1998; Dollar and Kraay 2001; World Bank 1997, 2002) and the general conclusion of a survey of the recent theoretical and empirical evidence (Winters 2004) shows that liberalization generally induces an increase in growth. However, part of the benefits of trade liberalization depends on other policies and institutions being supportive but there is evidence that openness actually induces improvements in this dimension.[6]

Poverty alleviation. Openness to trade tends to reduce poverty in the long run and on average.[7] However, changes in trade measures often have a distributional impact and these can have important short term negative effects on poverty. The ultimate outcome depends on many factors; the precise trade reform, who the poor are, how they sustain themselves, etc.

Moreover, in Chapter 6 we have dealt with aspects of openness of capital movements. In Chapter 11 we will deal with labor movements. These discussions trigger the question of how far openness of the markets for production factors, capital and labour influences development.

Openness to international capital movements is not always beneficial to the growth of the LDCs. A review of empirical studies (IMF 2004, 2012) finds a weak link between liberalization of capital and growth. Positive effects may come about when capital openness is linked with higher domestic private investment, positive spill-overs of foreign direct investment (see Box 7.1) and a boost to domestic financial depth (a measure for the quality of the domestic capital market). The positive effect is enhanced if the country also pursues an openness policy with respect to trade. However, capital inflows can also lead to financial instability, which has a negative influence on growth. Indeed, when liberalization occurs in tranquil times, capital

---

BOX 7.1 FDI OPENNESS AND DEVELOPMENT

For some time, many developing countries were hostile to FDI, believing that MNCs would exploit their human resources, deplete their natural resources and manipulate the local institutions. In recent decades the attitude towards FDI has changed considerably in view of the positive contribution that FDI can make to development, given certain conditions.[8]

For FDI policies to be effective, two types of actions need to be taken:

1.   Get the basics right by providing:
     - sound macro and monetary policies;
     - reliable and efficient institutions;
     - a strong commitment to openness.

2.   Link FDI policies into other policies for development aimed at:[9]
     - increasing domestic financial resources for development to supplement domestic savings and investment and, more basically, fostering enterprise development, as the creation of an efficient domestic supply capacity requires competitive economic agents;
     - enhancing the technology, skill and knowledge base, given that these intangible resources are increasingly at the heart of the development effort;
     - boosting trade competitiveness by broadening the demand base, as internationally competitive firms can contribute better to development by reaping the benefits of economies of specialization and scale;
     - maintaining competitive markets, to ensure that former statutory obstacles to investment and trade are not replaced by anti-competitive practices of firms; and
     - protecting the natural environment, to maintain the basis for future growth and development.

---

flows tend to increase and boost positive effects; the opposite is true in turbulent times. So, the net benefits depend very much on (1) the strength of the domestic macroeconomic policies, (2) the quality of the financial regime, and (3) good sequencing for liberalization.

The effect of *openness to labour movements* on development is very unclear. In practice this accounts mostly for the access of surplus labour of the developing countries to the markets of the developed economies. Some (e.g. Walmsley *et al.* 2011) find a general positive effect for both developed and developing countries. However, results differ according to the situation of the developing countries; some suffer as a consequence of the brain drain, others gain considerably from remittances.

7.3 Major public goods

7.3.1 Objectives

The previous sections have made it clear that the system does not automatically lead to a better distribution of wealth in the world. So, as regards development there is a case for its being a global public good (GPG). Indeed, the markets are not capable of providing capital to LDCs on terms that are sustainable. Moreover, the poverty of many developing countries has a negative effect on the world as a whole, as it limits growth and diminishes the support for other GPGs such as sustainability.

The international community decided it would put in place a policy with the objectives of stimulating development and fighting poverty. For a long time these objectives were not made more precise in terms of outcome, for instance in terms of a decrease in disparity. On the contrary, they were defined in terms of policy inputs (quantity of development aid). As early as the 1960s, several national and international organizations adopted the target that Official Development Assistance (ODA; see section 7.5.1) should amount to 0.7 per cent of the GNI of the developed countries. Important international players such as the European Union and other members of the OECD have adopted that target.

More interesting than input targets are of course *output* or *outcome targets*. Fairly general objectives have been set in the Millennium Development Declaration, solemnly adopted in 2000 by the United Nations and all its member states. They have also been embraced by the most important international organizations that have a stake in development policy. These objectives have been worked out in the Millennium Development Goals. They specify some goals of a socio-economic character, one with an environmental character and many that have more of a human development character. The aim is to achieve them by 2015. Each of these goals has been worked out in the form of concrete *targets* that are defined in terms of the improvement of the wealth of the LDC.

7.3.2 Principles

Development aid is based on the principle of solidarity. It implies that those who are rich have to care for those who are not. This principle is based on two considerations: that leaving other human beings in poverty is morally unjust and that developing the poor is beneficial to all countries in the world.

The basic principle of solidarity has not been elaborated in terms similar to, for instance, the principles adopted in environmental policy. However, it has been elaborated in major paradigms that have shifted considerably over time. There are several explications concerning such shifts. One is changes in the ideologies of the dominant donors that also influence the policies of major international organizations. But in practice this evolution of norms is much more intricate and also involves the interests of the IO bureaucracy and the interests of recipients (Park and Vetterlein 2010). Box 7.2 gives an overview of the development over time of the main paradigms.

BOX 7.2 PARADIGM SHIFTS

Financial push, 1950–1960

In the 1950s the development problem was seen as a problem of production factors. In developing countries labour was abundant but capital scarce. So, a policy of support for investment in enterprise, infrastructure and education was thought to be essential. Often this went hand in hand with technical assistance.

Socio-economic conditions, 1960–1980

The policies of the 1950s and 1960s led to growth but also to some new problems. One was the high degree of indebtedness of many developing countries. Another problem that became more acute was the inequality that had resulted from the process of industrialization. So, a more complete role for the state was advocated, one that should ensure that wealth was more equally (re)distributed, that investments in health and education were made and that rural and agricultural development could improve the food situation. However, in many cases the administrations of the development countries were unable to cope with the increasing responsibilities, and inefficiencies became widespread.

"Washington", 1980–2000

The neo-liberal view came to dominate the US government, and through its influence on the major international financial institutions such as the IMF and the World Bank (both located in Washington, DC) this view was also exported to the developing world. In this view, markets can take care of much of development, and governments are rather part of the problem, owing to rent-seeking, inefficiencies and corruption. So, the solution was supposed to lie in open regimes for trade and capital flows and in deregulation and privatization.

State capacity, 2000–2010

By the end of the century it became clear that the neo-liberal approach to development had not worked and that development could not be realized without strong governments executing good policies (among them the creation of the right conditions for private-sector development). This realization has been elaborated in the principles of the Comprehensive Development Framework, such as competitiveness, poverty reduction, country ownership and results orientation. A new emphasis was given to the support to administrative (or institutional) capacity building.

Sources: Hermes and Lensink (2001) and Kremer *et al.* (2009: 16–18).

7.3.3 International responsibilities[10]

Development is dependent on a large number of factors, many of them internal to the country in question, many others relating to the actions of partner countries and the conditions created by international organizations. The main instrument that is used is financial: loans or grants. Apart from this, aid is often given in the form of technical support and capacity-building. Moreover, coordination of aid programmes with other policies is important, given the interlinkages of these policies with growth policies.

Multilateral *financial aid* is preferable in principle to bilateral aid for several reasons. First, the former is less likely to become subject to changing political forces in the donor country that might impact on the relations with the recipient country. Second, multilaterals are in a better position than bilaterals to judge the quality of the investment environment. Third, multilaterals are likely to be better aware of the real development needs of the recipient countries, and more predictable as to the continuity of aid flows. Finally, they will attach conditions related to the development purpose, while bilaterals may tie aid to completely different issues (commercial; security).

Moreover, *coordination* is important. In order to realize the Millennium Development Goals (see pp. 148–149) of the United Nations, many developed countries have adopted the "*Policy Coherence for Development*" (PCD) approach. This aims at the harnessing of other policies with a potential positive effect on global balanced development. Many international organizations have provided input into the formulation of such an integrated approach to development.[11]

The most obvious example of such a policy is *trade*: permitting the access of the less developed countries (LDCs) to the markets of developed countries. The World Trade Organization (WTO) has set very strict rules concerning the way in which trade has to be conducted. One basic principle is non-discrimination. However, in view of the barriers for LDCs in matters of market access, the WTO has integrated the development agenda within trade negotiations (WTO 2011a; see also Chapter 5). Market access is not sufficient for developing trade, however; another set of conditions have to be fulfilled, among them knowledge about export markets, commercial skills, etc. The WTO has set up a special multi-donor programme, the Enhanced Integrated Framework (EIF), aimed at removing supply-side barriers to trade integration. Many donors have oriented their aid towards the building up of such capacities through targeted programmes (e.g. De Lombarde and Puri 2009; OECD 2010a: 55–84).

Another example concerns the global *monetary and financial institutions* (see also Chapter 6). In principle the IMF improves the stability of currencies and in so doing improves the macroeconomic environment, which is generally conducive to growth. However, in practice the actions of the Fund do not always work out in such a positive way. In order to be able to benefit from financial support by the IMF, the latter gives detailed prescriptions as to the policy packages and institutional set-up of LDCs. To many observers such conditions run counter to the long-term convergence of these countries. The IMF and the World Bank have been induced to change their policies in the framework of the Monterrey Consensus on development finance, adopted in 2002.

A third example is in the field of the *environment* (see also Chapter 8). The global policy measures taken to limit the negative effects of greenhouse gases on climate change (the Kyoto Protocol and Copenhagen conference) have adopted the principle of common but differentiated responsibilities. It implies that no targets have been set for the reduction of emissions by less developed countries. This is understandable from the point of view of their low contribution to overall pollution levels and their limited financial capacity to contribute to investments that are needed for abatement.

The policy examples given here show clearly how widely their effects on world cohesion differ. Coordination of these policies remains a very difficult exercise, however, given the fragmented structure of the global organizations (see Chapter 11).

7.3.4 National responsibilities

On the *donor* side the main obligation is to assure an effective and efficient contribution to the objective of development. This is done in several forms: contribution to the financial resources of multilateral organizations, and bilateral aid. The allocation of bilateral financial aid from major donors to the various developing countries is to a large extent determined as much by the commercial and geopolitical interests of the donor as by the developmental interests of the recipient. For instance, EU aid is traditionally very much oriented towards the former colonies of its major member states (Berthélemy 2006). This often does not represent an efficient use of the aid volumes. In order to increase the effectiveness for the developing country, many pleas have been made for the untying of aid (see Box 7.3).

BOX 7.3 UNTYING AID

When aid is tied, funds intended to foster development and alleviate poverty have to be spent on suppliers from the donor country. Tying aid raises the cost to developing countries of many goods and services by 15–30 per cent on average, and by as much as 40 per cent or more for food aid. In fact the real cost may be higher, as these figures do not incorporate the significant indirect costs of tying, such as higher transaction costs for partner countries. Another problem with tied aid is that it is at least partly guided by commercial considerations, which do not necessarily match developing countries' needs and priorities. When aid is tied, it also makes it difficult for developing countries to feel a sense of ownership of the projects concerned.

Source: OECD (2010a: 23).

The *recipient* countries are confronted with a multitude of proposals for support to individual projects. Yet they have in general limited capacity to programme and to administer aid. In order to be effective they have to make clear what their priorities are and where the inflowing aid is to be directed. A national development programme coupled with close budgetary control is therefore essential. To optimize results donors should orient their support to these plans in a coordinated way.

7.4 Organizations involved in the provision of the public good

7.4.1 Major players

The main donors are the national governments of the rich countries. Moreover, there are a host of private organizations that foster projects in developing countries. Many of these have a humanitarian objective; others have also a more direct economic objective. An example of the latter is the Bill and Melinda Gates Foundation. As a consequence the donor side of aid is very fragmented.

Official Development Aid (ODA) is defined as financial flows that are provided by official agencies (mostly from sovereign states) to developing countries and to multilateral institutions that aim at the promotion of economic development and welfare in the developing countries.[12] They are often in the form of loans with a grant (concession) part. Concessionality is achieved either through interest rates below market rates, by long grace periods or by a combination of the two. In order to qualify for ODA status a loan has to have a grant element of at least 25 per cent.[13]

The ODA consists of different types. We make distinctions on the basis of two criteria: the type of instrument and the degree of internationalization.

In the *grant category* we find international aid agencies that provide funds that do not need to be reimbursed. Among them we find on the world level the agencies of the United Nations such as the United Nations Development Programme; on the regional level the European Development Fund (EDF) and on the national level USAID.

In the *loan* category we find specialized banks that provide loans at low rates to developing countries. Prominent among them is the World Bank; others are regional banks like the Asian Development Bank (ADB) and the Inter-American Development Bank (IADB). On the national level a large variety of structures exist; an example is the FMO of the Netherlands, which provides loans for private-sector developments in developing countries.

The various categories of organizations have very different weights in the total of ODA (see Table 7.2). The table shows clearly that grants are the largest category; three times bigger than loans.

In the *grants category* the largest segment is the bilateral one. The detailed OECD data shows that the ten biggest donors (among them the United States, Germany, the United Kingdom, France, Japan and the Netherlands) provided about three-quarters of total ODA. The combined effort of the European Union (multilateral)

TABLE 7.2 ODA by instrument and donor/lender[a] (billion $)

Category	Grants		Loans	
Donor/lender	1990	2010	1990	2010
Bilateral	83	88	19	20
Multilateral	10	29	10	20
of which:				
EU	5	13	–	–
Dev. banks and funds	–	–	3	4
IDA	–	4	–	–
IBRD	–	–	6	12
UN	5	4	–	–
IMF	–	–	1	2
Total	**93**	**117**	**29**	**40**

Sources: www.OECD.org; DAC database.

Note:

a Development banks and funds include: African Development Bank, African Development Fund, Asian Development Bank, Asian Development Fund, Caribbean Development Bank, Arab Agencies. UN institutions include: UNAIDS, UNDP, UNECE, UNFPA, UNHCR, UNICEF, UNRWA, UNTA, WHO and WFP.

and its member countries (taken up under bilateral) constituted by far the greatest donor effort (some 2.5 times that of the United States). After these large bilateral donors comes a whole list of much smaller ones; together, the next twenty bilateral agencies accounted for less than 10 per cent of the total effort. We mention also the multilateral aid; the amount of aid channelled through both the IDA and the UN organizations is about of the same magnitude as that of countries like France or Germany. So, the total effort is extremely fragmented. The situation is actually worse, for two reasons. First, many countries have split their effort over several agencies. Second, the aid of each agency is divided over a multitude of projects in a range of sectors in a large number of beneficiary countries. Finally there is also an increasingly important category of private organizations and NGOs that often use aid in kind, such as food, medicines, medical care and education. The conclusion is that this leads to diseconomies of scale and high overhead costs on both the donor and the beneficiary side.

The *loan category* presents a different picture; here the bilateral and multilateral channels are of equal importance. The loan instrument is very differently used by the various countries. Japan is very active in this segment and to a lesser extent also France and Germany. Among the multinationals the World Bank (IBRD) takes pride of place.

7.4.2 Main international organizations

On the global level the main organizations that are responsible for development issues are all part of the UN system (see Box 7.4).

BOX 7.4 UN-RELATED DEVELOPMENT AGENCIES

Two groups can be distinguished: specialized agencies and programmes and funds (see also Figure 3.1).

Specialized agencies

The specialized agencies are (legally) independent of the central United Nations, even though their work is formally coordinated by the Economic and Social Council of the United Nations. They have considerable autonomy and have their own governing bodies and their own budget frameworks. Their boards or councils are constituted by representatives of the member states (in particular, of those that fund them). Paramount among them is the World Bank group that consists of a number of different agencies. Four of them play a significant role in the development of poor countries: the International Bank for Reconstruction and Development (IBRD), the International Development Association (IDA), the International Finance Corporation (IFC) and the Multilateral Investment Guarantee Agency (MIGA). They use the grant and loan instruments. Other specialized UN agencies involved in official development aid are the International Labour Office (ILO), the Food and Agriculture Organization (FAO), the United Nations Industrial Development Organization (UNIDO), the World Health Organization (WHO) and the United Nations Educational, Scientific and Cultural Organization (UNESCO). These specialized agencies provide technical assistance and advice in their respective fields.

Programmes and funds

Unlike the specialized agencies, the various programmes and funds do not have independent boards and they fall directly under the General Assembly. The most important among them in matters of socio-economic development is the United Nations Development Programme, which is present in some 160 countries. It used to channel much of its funds to the various specialized agencies, but since a major reform in the 1990s it now concentrates on the coordination of all UN activities in a specific host country and gears them to the needs and strategies of the host country.

Source: Riddell (2007: 81–85).

Apart from these UN-related organizations there are several others. The *Organisation for Economic Co-operation and Development* (OECD) has taken a particular interest in development issues and its Development Assistance Committee (DAC) develops strategies, monitors aid flows and proposes systemic improvements.[14] We mentioned already in the previous section the important role of *Regional Development Organizations*, both for loans and for grants. Finally, the role of many *non-governmental organizations* (NGOs) which are organized on a multilateral basis needs to be mentioned (Aldashev and Verdier 2009). They take care of a sometimes significant share in the actual development aid effort (see, for example, Lewis and Kanji 2009).

7.4.3 The World Bank

Emergence

One of the main problems facing the world economy in the 1940s was the reconstruction of the economies devastated by the Second World War. It was felt that the provision of a sound financial system with balance of payments aid would not be sufficient to bring accelerated growth to these countries; long-term finance would also be required. This would reinforce the capacity of countries to stand up to competition, which would in turn help the gradual liberalization of trade. This was to be provided by a newly created institution: the International Bank for Reconstruction and Development (IBRD), colloquially called the World Bank. After the quick recovery of the most developed countries, the work of the IBRD shifted towards providing support to less developed countries (LDCs).

Objectives and tasks

The mission of the World Bank group is to fight poverty and improve living standards in developing countries. Over the decades the focus has shifted from economic development projects (such as projects concerned with agriculture, industrialization, infrastructure-building, etc.) to projects that support the improvement of other supply-side factors, such as education, health, etc. Now its activities are focused on the achievement of the whole array of Millennium Development Goals (MDGs). The different agencies of the WB group are specialized according to task. The IBRD is oriented on middle-income and creditworthy poorer countries, while the IDA focuses on the world's poorest countries and provides loans on very soft terms and grants. Another member of the group is the International Finance Cooperation, which provides funds for the improvement of private enterprise. The Multilateral Investment Guarantee Agency has been set up as a response to the global debt crisis to guarantee the investment in LDCs against risks such as political unrest, currency inconvertibility, etc.

Membership and power structure

Originally the number of members was limited, but over time new members have been accepted, so that the membership now includes almost all sovereign countries. Only countries that are members of the IMF can become a member of the WB. Voting in the World Bank is on a weighted basis (with capital as the criterion), so the World Bank (like the IMF) is in practice controlled by the major Western countries.

Internal structure

The way the World Bank is organized bears a strong resemblance to the set-up of the IMF:

- The Board of Governors (meeting once a year) sets the general policy.
- The Board of Executive Directors is responsible for the translation of this general policy into concrete terms. It consists of 24 directors of whom five are appointed by the largest shareholders and the other nineteen represent groups (constituencies) of other shareholders.
- The President of the Bank, elected by the executive directors, is responsible for the management of the operations of the Bank. The staff of the organization is very large; it numbers about 8,000 at headquarters in Washington, DC, and some 2,000 in the field.

7.5 The World Bank: governance[15]

7.5.1 General

The main objective of the World Bank is to support the development process in LDCs. Given its specific role, the World Bank does not make use of the regulatory method. It does to some extent use the coordination method, in the sense that it makes regular analyses of the dynamics of the factors that determine (the lack of) progress in individual developing countries. These reports, together with those of the IMF, serve as a basis for consultation with individual developing countries. So, the World Bank Group uses mainly the financial method (both in the form of loans and grants) to finance development projects such as infrastructure (e.g. a dam for irrigation) or industry (a local bank financing small and medium-sized industries).

7.5.2 Loans

The World Bank generates funds in several ways. One is by selling triple-A-rated bonds on the global financial markets. These bonds have a low risk premium[16] and thus also a low interest rate. Moreover, the Bank mobilizes resources in the form of donor governments' deposits in trust funds. These are created to foster specific development initiatives, such as the Global Environment Facility (GEF).

These funds are then used for lending to developing countries. As the World Bank needs only a small margin[17] on its operations, it can lend at rates that are much below the ones the developing countries would have had to pay if they had raised the money themselves.

The World Bank (IBRD) concessional loans are basically of two types. Investment operations finance economic and social development projects. Development policy operations (formerly known as adjustment loans) provide financing that supports a country's policy and institutional reforms.

The World Bank assesses each proposal from a borrower to ensure that it is economically, financially, socially and environmentally sound. During loan negotiations the Bank and the borrower agree on the development objectives, outputs, performance indicators and on an implementation plan, as well as on a loan disbursement schedule. The Bank monitors the realization of the policies and projects for which the loans were given.

This *conditionality* has been the subject of much debate.[18] Many authors have indicated that *ex ante* conditionality that is intended to induce reforms has not worked very well. One reason is that there are many reasons why the World Bank cannot enforce such conditionality (e.g. Kilby 2009). So, there is now a tendency to limit conditionality as a punitive device and to stimulate recipients to make reforms (see the next subsection; and see, for instance, Collier *et al.* 1997; Dijkstra 2002; Morrissey 2004).

7.5.3 Grants

The IDA branch of the WB uses two forms of financing. The first is interest free long term loans to the least developed countries. The amount of interest not paid is actually the grant element. The second is a real grant. The IDA funds have to be used for programmes that boost economic growth, reduce inequalities, strengthen institutions and improve people's living conditions. In some cases IDA funds can be used for debt relief. The grant element is more important the poorer the recipient country. Countries with the biggest problems (low GDP per capita, risk of debt distress, etc.) get 100 per cent grant; countries with less problems 50 per cent.

IDA is replenished by both developed and developing countries; an important contribution is also made by the other parts of the World Bank (IBRD and IFC), this is financed by their return on their regular banking operations.

7.5.4 Advisory services and capacity-building

Many countries in the world that are beneficiaries of considerable amounts of development aid suffer from poor governance. Consequently, growth in these countries has often been weak (Rodrik *et al.* 2004). Notwithstanding decades of development support, the problems in matters of poverty and governance have persisted. Some blame the dependency on aid for this lack of progress and speak about the "curse of aid".[19] On the other hand, there are also indications that conditional aid can avoid such effects. It may increase quality (decrease corruption) because it decreases the discretion of the recipient country's officials, removes pressure by increasing the salary levels of the public service, etc. (Tavares 2003).

The World Bank has analysed the gravity of the problems in several reports (Kaufmann *et al*. 1999a, b, 2009). It has quantified the indicators I introduced in section 4.6. The general picture that emerges for developing countries is not very positive. In general their scores are significantly lower than those for developed countries. Moreover, many problems tend to be cumulative: poor quality of regulation often goes hand in hand with high levels of corruption. This is clearly a factor that hinders investment and hence growth.

So, the World Bank has launched programmes to support developing countries in setting up institutions that are capable of effectively handling the many tasks involved in assessing problems, programming development and administering projects. The WB offers expertise in improving administrative procedures and training staff.[20]

7.6 Evaluation of the past and options for the future

7.6.1 Major achievements

We can distinguish between, on the one hand, the achievements of the IOs as a whole in matters of provision of official development aid, and, on the other, the performance of the World Bank in particular. Let us start with the former.

There have long been many misgivings about the lack of effectiveness of ODA. The international community agreed to take action to improve the situation, resulting in 2002 in the Monterrey Consensus and in 2005 in the Paris Declaration on Aid Effectiveness. The latter set out five principles: ownership, harmonization, alignment, managing for results and mutual accountability. Progress on these principles has been measured through twelve indicators by the OECD's Development Assistance Committee (DAC).

The *effect of the financial effort* devoted to development aid can be measured in several terms. One main indicator has been defined in terms of *input*: to spend at least 0.7 per cent of GNI for development aid. Most developed countries, including the European Union and its member states, fall short of this indicator. The *output* indicators could be more relevant; the most important are reduction in global income disparity and in absolute poverty. In the course of the 1990s many observers saw that on all these indicators progress of the recipient countries was either very slow or absent. So, concern about the (lack of) effectiveness of Official Development Assistance started to grow. A whole series of evaluation studies (both on a project level and on a more macro level) came to a wide variety of conclusions. Some were positive about the effect;[21] others said that aid does not work.[22] Yet others found that there is a positive effect of aid on growth; however, in too many cases this is countered by the adverse effects of associated rent-seeking activities (Economides *et al*. 2008), the unpredictability of aid (Kodama 2012) and the fragmentation of aid by donor and sector (Kimura *et al.* 2012). The recent improvement in growth of many developing countries (and hence in the improvement of global income distribution) is attributed not to aid but to other factors of dynamism (participation in production chains, reforms).

Multilateral aid can be more effective than bilateral aid (there is less political influence and better conditionality, and the aid is less tied; see section 7.3.4). So, one might expect multilaterals to perform better than bilaterals. This does not show up in the data: there was no significant difference in the outcome performance (growth) between the two forms of aid (Rajan and Subramanian 2008).

A final point on which performance can be measured is the increase in *consistency* between sectoral and development policies of donors. On this score the reality is less impressive than the rhetoric. For instance, many developed countries have for a very long time kept in place an agricultural policy that has been particularly negative in relation to their capacity to foster their own production and exports of food. Although in recent years things have changed for the better, quite a few problems still await solution.

Progress on the score of *policy coherence for development* is slow and limited. It took the DAC member states almost a decade to include statements on coherence in their policy documents. Recently the situation has changed for the better (OECD 2009a). Many member states are now taking concrete action, which has resulted in a reservoir of practical experience (UN 2011a). However, so far only limited evidence can be found of clear positive results in terms of policy change (see Box 7.5). One of the reasons may be the very large uncertainty as to who is accountable for each of the goals. Indeed, for each of the goals one has identified at least three multinational organizations that claim it as their prime task and two that consider it also as part of their responsibility (Reisen 2010).

The *performance of the World Bank* was above donor averages for all indicators that seek to measure donor performance.[24] The same was true for the efficiency of its actions: the World Bank group ranked high compared to both other multinationals and many bilaterals.

BOX 7.5 PROGRESS TOWARDS THE MILLENNIUM DEVELOPMENT GOALS (MDGs)[23]

The main targets for goal 1, *eradicate extreme poverty*, are as follows:

- Halve the proportion of people living on less than $1 a day. Sustained growth in developing countries, particularly in Asia, is keeping the world on track to meet this target.
- Achieve decent employment (again worked out in targets such as a rise in the employment rate and productivity). Economic recovery has failed to translate into employment opportunities; this target is unlikely to be met.

The main targets for goal 7, *ensure environmental sustainability*, are as follows:

- Reduction in the emissions of CO_2. This target is disappearing out of sight; despite the recent downturn in economic activity, greenhouse gas emissions continue their ascent.
- Reduction of the depletion of resources such as forests. The achievements here are mixed: forests are disappearing rapidly in South America and Africa, while Asia – led by China – registers net gains.

The targets for goal 8, *partnership for development*, are as follows:

- Develop further a rule-based, predictable, non-discriminatory trading and financial system. The score here is mixed; readers should refer to the specialist chapters of this book for an assessment.
- Address the special needs of the least developed countries.

The target, *deal comprehensively with the debt problems of developing countries*, is subdivided into a number of sub-targets that are particularly relevant:

- Step up the proportion of ODA to donor GNI to reach the targets set by the DAC. In 2010, aid to developing countries was at a record high; however, it fell short of promises made in 2005.
- Increase the proportion of untied aid. On this indicator, considerable progress has been made since the turn of the century. The vast majority of DAC members have untied their aid, with the result that by 2007 some 80 per cent of total DAC bilateral ODA was untied. Some of the remaining members have announced that they will untie it very soon. Peer pressure is being put on the remaining countries to comply as well (OECD 2010a: 23).
- Improve market access in developed countries, specifically measured by the increase in the proportion of LDC exports admitted duty-free and the decrease of tariffs on agricultural products. Protection has been averted, notwithstanding bad times, owing to strong international cooperation in the framework of international institutions.
- Increase debt sustainability (worked out as decrease in debt service as a proportion of exports) and increase debt relief. There has been a slight improvement on this score, but the crisis has brought the progress to a halt.

Sources: For the goals, see UN MDG website http://un.org/milleniumgoals/; see also the MDG progress chart (several years) of the UN statistics division and UN (2011b).

7.6.2 Inadequacies and challenges

The major shortcomings of the development "system" stem from the *extreme fragmentation of the donor community*. In section 7.4 I succinctly described the main players and indicated the large number of small and very specialized players. Over time, these numbers have even increased. Moreover, there has been considerable "mission creep": each of the players has tended to expand its remit in the light of new emerging needs, such as the concern for the environment. This has increased the overlap between agencies (see Box 7.6) and the need for a clear role assignment (Riddell 2007; Easterly and Pfutze 2008; Reisen 2010).

This fragmentation is a source of *considerable losses of efficiency and a lack of effectiveness*. The effectiveness problem has been assessed in the previous section, so let us now look in more detail at the efficiency question. We recall that efficiency is defined as the benefit–cost relation (or output–input relation; see Chapters 2–4).

BOX 7.6 A MULTITUDE OF ACTORS, LEADING TO OVERLAP AND LACK OF COORDINATION

The establishment of each new multilateral fund or agency has usually occurred because of international pressure to address a particular need perceived to be inadequately addressed. However, the remit of many, if not most, new agencies or funds has inevitably encroached on those of existing agencies, adding to the overlap and complexity of the multilateral aid system.

Ironically, coordination itself is another area of overlap. The UNDP and the World Bank have both taken an active role in trying to coordinate the activities within particular countries, but there often remains a lack of clarity over precisely which agency (if either) has the mandate to coordinate the activities of other aid agencies, and what such coordination entails, especially if this is perceived to challenge the authority of the host country itself.

It should also be noted that these sorts of problems extend well beyond the UN system. The regional development banks have sometimes developed niches in which they are specializing; but often they compete. The same is true for the bilateral and regional donors of grants. They are further aggravated by the host of private sector and non-governmental organizations.

These problems persist because the world of official aid is still dominated by the discrete actions of different donors and agencies, driven predominantly by their own assessments of how to use aid and to whom to give it. Institutions strive and struggle to maintain their own survival, sometimes expanding into new areas to ensure self-preservation, even when they have passed their sell-by date.

Source: Cited from Riddell (2007: 86–88).

The literature is very negative about aid efficiency; in all donor–beneficiary relations, many resources are wasted. The reasons for this bad situation are manifold.

On the *donor side* all organizations tend to fragment their efforts over many types of projects in a large number of countries and sectors of activity according to political priorities. They tend to spend significant resources on overheads: internal management and administration. They are not willing to coordinate their efforts effectively and to specialize in a particular area. Among the bilaterals, some EU countries tend to perform well (such as the United Kingdom and France), while others tend to perform badly (Germany and Spain). The score for EU aid is very low. The main causes for this have already been indicated in the previous sections. Among them we find complexity of administrative and political procedures, affecting both the Brussels administration and EU delegations in developing countries, which are rather deficient by comparison with those of the most important bilateral and multilateral donors. The situation for most multilaterals is not very brilliant either. Notably, many UN agencies perform very poorly. On the other hand, most financial institutions rank very high, both multinationals (such as the World Bank) and regional development banks (such as the Asian Development Bank (Easterly and Pfutze 2008)).

On the *recipient side* there are similarly important losses in efficiency. The multitude of donor bureaucracies dealing with development aid, each with their specific demands on project planning, management and audit, put a very heavy burden on the limited administrative capacity of the recipient countries and divert these resources from other uses.[25]

Specific shortcomings of the present situation relate to the institution that has been analysed in more detail in the previous sections: *the World Bank*. Even according to its own evaluation many things can be improved:

> The Group's decision-making process is widely seen as too exclusive, offering many member countries too little voice and too few opportunities for participation. Insufficient institutional accountability for results weakens the World Bank's effectiveness and legitimacy. And certain conventions and practices have contributed to the perception that the institution is accountable and responsive only to a handful of shareholders at best.
>
> *(World Bank 2009: ix)*

7.6.3 Proposals for improvements

The main proposals for improvement concern on the one hand the total institutional architecture of global development aid in order to improve its effectiveness and efficiency and on the other hand the structure of the organization on which we have focused: the World Bank.

From "non-system" to consistency

The excessive fragmentation and the ensuing considerable losses in efficiency have led to some policy action. The 2005 Paris Declaration called for increased complementarity among donors to reduce the transaction cost created by the lack of specialization, and established five principles for improving the effectiveness of aid delivery:

1 *Ownership.* Developing countries should set their own strategies for poverty reduction, improve their institutions and tackle corruption.
2 *Alignment.* Donor countries should align themselves behind these objectives and use local systems.
3 *Harmonization.* Donor countries should coordinate their efforts, simplify their procedures and share information to avoid duplication.
4 *Results.* Developing countries and donors should shift their focus to development results and ensure that results get measured.
5 *Mutual accountability.* Donors and partners must be held accountable for development results.[26]

On the basis of an in-depth study (OECD 2009b) of the size and character of all multilateral and bilateral aid flows, the OECD has developed criteria to determine the relevance of flows. It suggests that donor organizations should withdraw their irrelevant flows. Notwithstanding the fact that the number of donor organizations has continued to increase in the past years, it seems as if these recommendations have indeed been followed (OECD 2011d). Action has also been taken for a more performance-oriented allocation of resources within donors (see, for instance, IDA 2007, 2010).

There have been proposals to arrive at concentration through a better assignment of roles among donors. One of these concerns the UN agencies, which should start working as "one UN". Unfortunately, this initiative has not led to concrete measures. Another proposal is to attribute to a single agency the responsibility for a Millennium Development Goal and charge that agency with the task of coordinating the work of all the others (Reisen 2010). A third proposal has been to improve the situation by better donor coordination. This has given rise to a debate on which agency should lead the coordination in each recipient country. The World Bank, the IMF, the European Union and the UNDP have all claimed to be in the best position to assume such a role. In line with the Paris Declaration, this approach has been abandoned and now the recipient country is supposed to programme its own development and to negotiate with donors on the optimal points for them to join in.

The World Bank

The *remit* of the World Bank has been changed over time. Initially it provided low-interest loans to countries for them to develop their infrastructure; gradually it has diversified into all areas of government, such as health (the fight against AIDS), the environment (global warming), gender equality (education for girls in Muslim-dominated countries), etc. Further concentration on the basic tasks would be in order. This can also imply the limitation of its activities to those countries that are really in need of its services (excluding middle income countries and countries with considerable own capital resources, such as energy exporters).

To remedy the weaknesses of the *institutional structure* of the World Bank, several proposals have been made. Under the impetus of the G20 many countries have urged a change in the weight of the developed and developing countries. This concerns the redistributing of votes from the developed world (in particular the United States and the European Union) to the emerging and developing countries. It concerns also the internationalization of the staff so that it becomes more responsive to non-Western concerns (see World Bank 2009). A final suggestion has been to limit the remit of the WB to the most important global concerns and to increase the role of the regional development banks. Interesting to note is that the WB has institutionalized coordination with the major regional development banks (Kingah and Salimzhuarova 2012).

7.7 Summary and conclusions

- The world is confronted with considerable differences in wealth between countries. They are felt to be morally unjust and economically inefficient.
- A balanced wealth distribution is considered a global public good. There are several ways to contribute to achieving it (e.g. giving LDCs better access to markets of the developed countries). However, another important means is by alleviating the LDCs' need for capital and knowledge.
- There is a plethora of organizations dealing with development aid. Many of these are public; others are private. In the former group are organizations that give bilateral aid and ones that are organized on a multilateral basis. Among the former, the European Union and its member countries stand out as the largest donor. Among the latter the World Bank takes pride of place.
- The main instrument of the World Bank is a loan on advantageous terms (primarily, a low interest rate). The Bank can make its loans concessional – that is, dependent on a good development programme. Next to this the WB can give grants to the least developed countries.
- The overall performance of the aid "industry" is not very satisfactory. In general, its effectiveness and efficiency are low. This is largely due to the extreme fragmentation of the aid. However, the World Bank's loans have in many cases been used well, hence many observers judge the results of World Bank interventions to have been positive.
- Greater specialization and concentration of the aid efforts would improve the overall impact. An effort has been made to realize this. The recipient countries need to assume responsibility for the programming of their own development and assign roles to the relevant donors for each segment of the plans.

8

THE ENVIRONMENT

8.1 Introduction

The world is confronted with a number of very serious environmental problems. Some of them have been with us for a long time (e.g. soil pollution), others have only cropped up since the middle of the last century (e.g. climate change). Some of them are of a local character, others have a global dimension. Coping with the latter is a matter of great complexity.

The *objective* of this chapter is to show the rationale, main features and effectiveness of the regimes that have developed to cope with global environmental problems. We will focus on the problem of global warming.

The *structure* of this chapter follows the sequence that has been used for all the sectoral chapters. We start with a definition of the problem: the deterioration of the global environment. In the next section I describe how we can define a global public good of sustainable development and the principles on which a regime should be based to deliver such a public good. I also set out there the responsibilities of public and private actors on both the national and the international level. In the following section I describe the essential features of the major organizations involved and mention the main instruments they use to put their policies into effect. In a special section we will go into the governance aspects of the regime that has been set up to combat climate change, the Kyoto Protocol. I conclude this chapter with two elements: first, an evaluation showing that for the time being we have to work with a highly fragmented structure; and second, a perspective for a better response to the environmental governance problems the world is facing.

8.2 The main problems

8.2.1 Categories of environmental problems

Economic activity implies the use of resources for production and consumption. Each of the links in this chain has a number of environmental consequences. Some of the most significant ones are as follows:

- *Exploitation* (extraction or production). Here several problems arise. One of them concerns the use of renewable resources such as forest and fisheries. Unsustainable exploitation leads to depletion of the resource and to several other problems such as loss of biodiversity, loss of capacity for regeneration (e.g. in the case of tropical forest), etc.
- *Processing.* The production of many goods implies the use of energy resources both for the transformation of raw material into finished goods and for the transport of these goods to the market. Most energy is still provided by fossil fuels. Burning these fuels produces gases that tend to lead to global warming.
- *Consumption.* Some consumption also involves energy use, and the effect thereof adds to the effect of processing. However, most consumption eventually results in the disposal of the used good as waste. To this problem there needs to be added the disposal of waste that occurs at different stages of production. Together this waste leads to pollution of the air, water and the soil.

Many of the effects just described can be seen in economic terms as negative externalities. This means that the costs they generate are borne not by the producer or the consumer but by a third party, often society at large. Such externalities constitute a failure of the allocation mechanism. Take the case of coal-burning. The fumes resulting from coal-burning are disposed of in the atmosphere that people need for breathing. Because the company or person responsible for burning the coal does not have to pay a cost for keeping the air clean, there will be an overuse of the atmosphere as the waste bin of the energy users, while clean air for the whole population will become in short supply.

8.2.2 Examples of major global problems

A number of environmental problems have a fairly local character, such as waste disposal. These problems can be solved on a local or national level, as most of the time the externalities do not spread beyond national borders. Some other environmental problems, however, tend to cross national borders. Many of these problems can be dealt with on a regional (supranational) level by cooperation between neighbouring countries (e.g. river basin pollution), however, there are also problems that span the whole globe. These fall into two categories:

- depletion of global resources, such as the loss of biodiversity (due to the extinction of species) or the depletion of reserves of water and certain raw materials;

- pollution of the atmosphere, leading to global warming. Greenhouse gases spread all over the globe and combine in the atmosphere, so the whole world feels the negative consequences.

We will limit ourselves in this chapter to the second category.

The problems of environmental damage are going to become ever more acute as a result of demographic pressure (9 billion people in 2050) and the increasing demand on resources per person as wealth levels increase. Notwithstanding an increased awareness of the problems, the need for action is not felt in the same way in the major countries of the world. Part of this difference can be explained by differences in wealth levels. Indeed, a positive relation between economic development and the concern for sustainability can be observed (see, for instance, Somanathan 2010 and the literature cited therein). An important factor here is the world trade and investment regime (see Chapters 5 and 10). Investors may shift the location of polluting activities to countries with a lenient regime (see Box 8.1).

BOX 8.1 DOES OPENNESS TO GLOBAL MARKETS LEAD TO A DETERIORATION OF THE ENVIRONMENT?

The relation between trade and the environment is the subject of much controversy.

Many people think that an *open regime for trade leads to more pollution*. The reasoning is simple. Highly developed countries in general have a low tolerance level for pollution, so they will have strict regulation. Polluting firms that want to avoid abating cost will relocate to LDCs, which usually have low environmental protection. These will become a sort of "pollution haven". The rich countries will then import the products of these firms from the LDCs. At the end of the day this leads to an increase in global pollution. This reasoning might imply the need for a policy of restricting free trade and applying checks on the way goods have been produced. Some argue that in case goods have been produced under poor environmental conditions, import restrictions should be introduced (e.g. Ederington 2010).

Others think that trade helps to *improve the environment*. The reasoning here is more complex. It starts with the consideration that trade increases wealth levels. It presumes next that wealth levels have a positive effect on the strictness of environmental policy. Abatement will be stepped up and pollution levels will thus decrease. This is reinforced by the fact that industries that are characterized by high pollution levels are usually very capital-intensive. The conditions for such investments in LDCs are not always optimal. So, firms will not move to LDCs but prefer locations in capital-rich countries and accept a strict environmental policy. This reasoning leads to a quite different recommendation on the preferred policy package: stimulate open borders and transfer good practices in terms of environmental policy and make an appeal to responsible corporate behavior (Antweiler *et al.* 2001).

A considerable amount of effort has gone into empirical measurement of the environmental effect of trade. The results show in general that the various channels of influence are very intricate and diverse, so that no general conclusion is warranted (see, for example, various contributions to Marsiliani *et al.* 2003; Benarroch and Weder 2006; Costantini and Crespi 2008; Grether *et al.* 2012).

8.2.3 Climate change: global warming

A very substantial number of economic activities lead to the emission of so-called greenhouse gases. These are gases that trap heat in the atmosphere, thereby leading to an increase in the earth's average temperature, commonly called global warming.

Problems associated with global warming are manifold. The main ones are as follows:

* *A rise in sea levels* leading to a danger of inundation of coastal areas. As many urban areas have been developed along coasts, preventing inundation will incur very high infrastructure costs (Bosello *et al.* 2007).
* *Desertification.* Reduced precipitation in traditional agricultural areas leads to loss of capacity of food production.
* *Increased imbalance.* In the rich countries the effects will be limited and the capacity to deal with them is large. In the poor countries the effects will be large (alternative agricultural investment opportunities are small) and their resources limited.
* *An increased risk of contagious diseases* (malaria, etc.), possibly leading to extra costs for health care.
* *Loss of non-human ecological diversity.* The habitats that are now characterized by high diversity tend to be at risk, which in itself represents a loss. Moreover, the need for agricultural land to replace the land that is presently suitable but has become less so will further limit the ecological diversity on these lands.
* *A perverse effect on energy use.* The increased use of refrigeration and air conditioning will increase the use of energy, in turn accelerating the production of greenhouse gases.

The diversity of the problems and the wide spread of the sources of emissions make it very difficult to establish the cost of warming, the cost and benefits of abatement and the capacity for adaptation to new circumstances (for an early overview, see Swanston and Johnston 1999: 33–38; see also Helm and Hepburn 2009).[1] Estimates of the cost of abatement (i.e. of reduction of emissions) leading to stabilization of the levels over an extended period are of the order of magnitude of 1 per cent of GDP. The benefits of abatement are most difficult to measure. Estimates of the cost of adaptation range between some 1.5 per cent of GDP for developed countries to very high percentages for low-lying islands that are threatened with complete disappearance. The negative impacts on the economy become more serious with higher rises in temperature (Tol 2012). Any serious cost–benefit analysis is hampered by the problems posed by the long period to be taken into account and the uncertainties as to the development of the influencing factors, such as technology, change in public preferences, etc.

8.3 The main public goods[2]

8.3.1 Objectives

Climate change or global warming is clearly a global public "bad", hence the absence of such a "bad" must be considered as a global public good. The two criteria of public goods, namely "non-rivalry" and "non-excludability", clearly apply. For instance, as soon as air pollution has abated, nobody can be excluded from the breathing of the clean air. Moreover, it is non-rivalrous: if somebody in Japan breathes clean air, he or she does not preclude someone in South Africa from doing the same (see, for instance, Heal 1999; Perman *et al.* 1999; Pearce and Turner 1990).[3] The main public good in matters of environment is often called "sustainable development". It was defined by the Brundtland Report as development that "meets the needs of the present without compromising the ability of future generations to meet their own needs". The *objective*, then, is to realize such sustainable development. Often this imprecise outcome variable is translated into other terms such as the reduction of pollution, so that the general objective can be translated into concrete targets. Such targets have been negotiated for a number of issues, the most important being the reduction of greenhouse gases.

A number of structural factors make *collective action in environmental matters* difficult. Some of the most relevant ones are as follows:[4]

- The *pervasiveness of sources of pollution.* Environmental problems are created at each stage of the production–consumption chain. Decisions on production and consumption are taken in a decentralized way by millions of enterprises and by billions of consumers. Each of them is only a small contributor to a series of problems and a small beneficiary of the solutions to be found.
- *Entrenchment of the problem in ways of life.* A good example is motor transport. The widespread use of cars has led to the spatial separation of work, home, leisure and education. As people have adjusted to this spread, it has become very difficult to limit the use of cars.
- *Uncertainty as to the cause–effect and cost–benefit relations.* In environmental matters, uncertainty exists as to the real causes and the type of damage done, the cost of prevention or of cleaning up, the seriousness of the impact, etc. The chances

for change are better the stronger the public concern, the scientific consensus as to the cause–effect relation, the seriousness of the problem, the economic substantiation of the cost–benefit relation, the actions of lobbies and the influence of the media.

- *Time preference*. In many cases the cost of environmental improvement will have to be borne immediately, whereas the benefits will tend to take years to materialize. So, there is a strong tendency to postpone action.
- *Unequal distribution of costs and benefits*. For some measures, the costs fall more on one group and the benefits accrue to another. This would be justified if the "polluter pays" principle led to the costs being charged to the major producers and users of the goods and services that cause environmental damage. However, the implementation of this principle has been very difficult, both at the level of national states and at the level of groups within countries. The economic cost prevents even rich countries from accepting abatement.[5]
- The *institutional framework* has weaknesses; new forms need to be invented for coping with new problems.

8.3.2 Principles

The values and basic attitudes that support the promotion of the global public good of sustainability converged to a large extent during recent decades. This is also the case for the *principles* that determine the architecture of the regimes that need to be set up for the preservation of the global environment. Three such principles are of particular importance: the precautionary principle, the common but differentiated responsibilities principle, and the polluter pays principle.

The precautionary principle[6]

In matters concerning the environment, one is often confronted with uncertainty as to the seriousness of the problem, the cause–effect relation and the best instruments to deal with the problem. As we have seen in Chapter 2, such problems of uncertainty and incomplete information do have a bearing on the behaviour of actors. However, in environmental matters we are often confronted with irreversibility. An ecological system that has passed a certain threshold, will not be able to recover, the end result being a permanent loss. In order to cope with this problem the precautionary principle is adopted. In day-to-day terms it means "better safe than sorry". In more elaborate words:

- When an activity raises threats to the environment, precautionary measures should be taken even if cause–effect relationships are not (yet) fully established scientifically.
- The proponent of the activity, not the public, should bear the burden of proof.
- The process of applying the principle should be open, informed and democratic, and should include potentially affected parties. It must examine the full range of alternatives, including taking no action.

The polluter pays principle

There is a tendency in market economies for polluters not to incur the cost of pollution prevention or of abatement themselves but to let others deal with it. A good example is the pollution of surface waters by a chemical industry. It permits consumers of the products of that industry to buy cheap goods. However, its implication is that water companies have to invest heavily in treatment to produce safe water, with the result that the consumer of water pays for the cost. The polluter pays principle is intended to arrive at a correct allocation in the economy. It obliges the chemical industry in this example to avoid disposing of waste in the surface water. If to that end it has to make investments that increase the cost of its products, it means that these costs are internalized and borne by those who consume the relevant good. The consumer of water will have a lower price. So, the application of this principle obliges economic actors to internalize the environmental costs of production, consumption and distribution.

The common but differentiated responsibilities principle

The common but differentiated responsibilities principle has as its main elements the recognition by all states that they are collectively responsible for the solution of a global problem, yet that they will contribute to its solution in a differentiated way. This differentiation applies notably to developing countries, which are permitted to do less than the developed countries. The difference in efforts is justified not so much on the basis of the limited capacity of the LDCs to contribute but rather on their limited responsibility for the present problems. Indeed, most of the problems have been (and sometimes still are) caused by the developed nations. The application of this principle facilitates, first, the concluding of multilateral environment agreements and, next, the compliance with obligations (Matsui 2002).

8.3.3 International responsibilities

Coping with environmental problems that go beyond the national level is clearly a matter of international responsibility. It is not only a moral obligation but also good economics. For instance, the costs of timely global action against climate change are considerably less than those of ill-coordinated and postponed national actions (Stern 2008).

Many international environmental regimes are created by means of a framework convention. The choice of this form can be explained on the basis of elements of the theories of collective action (see Chapters 2–4). Multilateral environmental agreements (MEAs) cover in general objectives (e.g. in terms of reduction levels of pollution), distribution of tasks (over signatories) and implementation (instruments such as monitoring and enforcement mechanisms).

In order to bring as many countries as possible into the sphere of the agreement, a number of measures can be taken:[7]

- *Incentives.* Environmental agreements are made easier to reach if the burden-sharing is done in a way that is perceived as fair by all. In international matters this may lead to the use of the instrument of side payments to countries that have a particularly high cost of pollution abatement and little direct benefits or little capacity to do something about the problems (see, for example, Carraro and Siniscalco 1993, 1998; Petrakis and Xepapadeas 1996). Industrial countries have accepted that they should make side payments to LDCs covering the incremental cost of compliance. Moreover, project support by, for instance, the World Bank can be made conditional on joining the protocol (see Box 8.2).
- *Free rider deterrence.* Signatory countries may apply trade sanctions to non-parties that continue to trade substances that have been ruled out or goods that contain such substances. This may be a serious threat, as it may lead to relocation of economic activities to countries that have taken measures to comply.
- *Minimum commitment.* The setting of a minimum threshold for the number of signatories creates a strong incentive for hesitant countries to sign up, because the effort put into the reaching of an agreement and the public good provided by the agreement would be lost if the threshold in terms of minimum number of countries were not passed.

BOX 8.2 INTERNATIONAL AID TO LDCs TO STIMULATE COMPLIANCE WITH MULTILATERAL ENVIRONMENTAL AGREEMENTS

Institutional and financial support is often needed to enable certain weak countries to meet their obligations. To that end the 1992 UN Rio Conference on Environment and Development created the *Global Environment Facility*. This has been set up as a joint undertaking of UNEP, the UNDP and the World Bank. Its objective is to help developing countries finance the incremental cost of new environmental investments in the following areas: climate change, preservation of biodiversity, protection of the ozone layer and protection of international waters (see www.thegef.org).

There are several *instruments* available to realize the production of a public environmental good. They are not all equally effective in an international setting. Let us analyse the most relevant ones.[8]

Direct regulation has two disadvantages when applied in an international environment. First, the cost of designing rules is very high, as they have to take into account a considerable diversity of situations, economies and legal and institutional systems. Second, enforcement is difficult, as there are often no means of coercion. Sanctions could be considered, but these are difficult to agree on (asymmetry between rich and mighty versus poor and weak) and to make effective.

Market forms have the advantage to stimulate an optimal allocation of resources of investment for abatement (e.g. via tradable permits). The efficiency of national systems of *tradable permits* can be much enhanced if the market can be organized on a global scale. Such a global trading framework brings order into the diversity of the various national (or regional: EU) systems. It would permit to elaborate minimum standards as to aspects such as the definition of the quantities, the interchangeability of the various pollutants, the price-setting system, the guarantees against price manipulation, etc.

In a national context, *taxation* is a much-used instrument, as it has the advantage of hitting the polluter and producing income for the state. In international matters the instrument of taxation is less relevant, as most governments do not accept inroads into their sovereignty in matters of taxation and are very reluctant to hand over considerable resources to an international institution. A system of harmonized national taxes would be easier to negotiate and implement, but is unlikely to be effective in reaching the targets of lowering the global public bad.

Litigation is another possibility. In environmental matters, self-enforcement is very important. Some MEAs open the possibility that a country can be taken to the International Court of Justice for failing to comply (but only with the defendants' permission). So, few cases are brought before the ICJ. Even after a Court decision there is no mechanism for enforcing compliance. So, many have considered the possibility of private litigation. However, this is an instrument that is not easy to transpose to the international level. It can only be done on the precondition that governments sign an international convention that specifies the standards that all polluters have to respect. This is very unlikely to happen, because it would encounter all the difficulties I cited in the paragraph on direct regulation. And even if such an agreement were to be reached, large-scale polluters have the power to stall lengthy procedures, while the sanctions that the Court might eventually impose are difficult to make effective.

So, if we consider the various options as a whole, it seems as if a combination of direct regulation and market forms is the best instrument for the realization of international environmental agreements.

8.3.4 National responsibilities

National governments shape international environmental agreements in complicated negotiation processes. Once such an international agreement has been ratified, it has to be implemented by nation-states.[9] In many cases they have quite some leeway as to the choice of instruments, provided they deliver on the agreed targets. The most important instruments national governments deploy to reach objectives have already been mentioned in general terms. Here, I will discuss the specific aspects of their application in a national context.

Command and control: direct regulation

The command and control method consists in instructing the subjects of the regulation on the norms they have to meet. This is the most-used instrument in national matters, because it has two advantages:

1. *Transparency*. Rules specify clearly for everybody the limits to pollution and the punishment for offenders.
2. *Certainty*. Resources committed to enforce the rules make compliance credible.

However, in environmental matters the linear view of regulation (problem → goal → instrument → implementation) does not hold, as there are many points of interference between the various stages, In many cases the degree of discretion by the administration in applying general rules in view of effective goal attainment is very important (Huppes and Simonis 2009).

Market forms such as pollution rights: tradable quotas

The point of departure for tradable quotas is to limit (by regulation) the total quantity of pollution that will be permitted (so, this instrument is very good in terms of effectiveness). The next step is to design a system for distribution that is efficient in economic terms by dividing the total into a maximum number of permits to pollute.[10] The third step is to design a system of trade that determines who has access to the market and that sets the rules for trading. The big advantage of this method is that it provides certainty as to the quantitative targets in terms of pollution.

With the instruments of tradable pollution rights, polluters themselves choose the modalities of abatement, which has three advantages:

1. It permits the optimal (cost-effective) choice of investment projects. Those who face the highest cost of abatement will buy permits and those who face abatement costs that are lower than the price of a permit will sell them.
2. It avoids the problems of application of outdated and hence inefficient technologies because of time pressure. Sectors that need to adapt their technology get sufficient time to do so.
3. It makes minimal demands of the institutional set-up, and avoids bureaucracy.

There are, however, some complications with this system. These are in the following domains:

* Putting property rights on free goods is politically very difficult and the initial assignment of property has proved a very delicate matter to decide on.
* Establishing a market regime is difficult; it involves the design of a minimum institutional set-up, avoiding high transaction costs in trading, making sure that

there will be no dominant player, limiting the risk of fraud and, finally, ensuring that inter-temporal trading is possible.

These problems can be overcome, as evidenced by the tradable pollution rights systems that have been put in place in some countries (see Bertram 1992; Smith 1992; Tietenberg 2006).

Taxation and excise duties

The basic idea of taxation in this sphere is to affect the price of polluting goods by taxing the polluter. The first advantage is that it stimulates clean production and consumption. The second is that it mobilizes resources for governments that can be used to compensate the damaged. Price changes due to differential taxation are theoretically more efficient than quantity controls (see Pizer 2002).[11] The effectiveness of the method depends on the capacity of the authorities to set the level of taxation at the point that is necessary to arrive at the desired reduced level of pollution. The use of the tax instrument by national governments has the advantage that it can be applied without much international coordination. Moreover, governments have some leeway to share the burden in a manner that is perceived as equitable (Boyd and Ibarraran 2002).

Litigation

National governments have the means to make their citizens and companies comply (taking offenders to court and using force). The problem of implementation and compliance can be further lowered by permitting private litigation – that is, by giving any person, firm or NGO the right to sue offenders against environmental law before any national court of their choice.

8.4 Organizations involved in the provision of the public good

8.4.1 Major players

The effective protection of the environment calls for an international regime. The elaboration of such international environmental regimes necessitates the co-operation of a number of major actors (national states, business and NGOs). All three have seen their role change over the past few decades. These changes have also influenced the global governance of environmental issues (see Biermann *et al.* 2009a).[12] It now involves more norm-setting actions by non-state actors, more self-regulation (codes) of business and "adoption of standards" elaborated by scientific communities.

Nation-states

Nation-states have become increasingly aware of the need to take environmental concerns into account. The increased capacity to deal with the relevant problems at home has contributed to the acceptance of practical solutions for problems that transcend the national borders. The most advanced states were the first to take collective action to improve the quality of the environment. This group tends to be joined by countries that give only lukewarm support, because for them the balance between perceived benefits and costs of action was only marginally positive. LDCs have in general taken the position that environmental problems have been caused mostly by the developed countries, so that the latter should also take the responsibility for finding solutions. LDCs have tended to ask for compensation for the costs they would incur if they joined other countries in collective action.

Business

Business logic has increasingly integrated environmental concern in firms' strategies. Many firms have embraced environmental concerns because of the responsibility they have in societal matters (WBCSD 2010). Others have been compelled to conform to this larger responsibility because they have been the subject of specific targeting by NGOs (non-compliance would have meant a considerable negative commercial impact due to a loss of reputation). Finally, many firms have understood that the greening of products and production processes is just good economics. A technology lead (e.g. in car engines) gives a competitive edge. New production technology may lead to substantial cost savings.

Non-governmental organizations

NGOs include scientific associations such as the International Council of Scientific Unions and a wide range of organizations that advocate improved protection of the environment in general, or specific items in particular (e.g. marine biological diversity). The best known among them are Greenpeace and the WWF. All these NGOs have improved their finance, their organization, their technical know-how and their capacity to get the media interested in their actions and points of view. Consequently, they are increasingly capable of influencing public opinion and, hence, decision-makers. The increased means of low-cost communication via the Internet has greatly enhanced their effectiveness. This increased professionalism and expertise means that they are sometimes invited to participate in the official delegations of countries to negotiations (Boehmelt 2012). The higher their access the stronger the commitments governments accept (Boehmelt and Betzold 2013).

8.4.2 Main international organizations

There are a large number of international organizations that take responsibility for global environmental problems. The most relevant ones are the following:

- *The United Nations.* At the time the United Nations was founded, there was very little concern about environmental problems, so it is not surprising that the UN Charter does not mention the issue explicitly. However, during the 1970s a number of new scientific results and major disasters sparked off UN action. By the end of the 1980s the Earth Summit at Rio de Janeiro engendered a whole series of initiatives and fixed a number of the principles that govern environmental policy. However, the United Nations did not establish an organization that covers all aspects of environmental protection and sustainability. At the moment, more than 170 international environmental treaties have been signed. Paramount among the United Nations' activities is the United Nations Environment Programme (UNEP), established in 1972. Most countries in the world are participants in it.[13] Other relevant institutions are the UN Commission on Sustainable Development and the Global Environmental Facility (see also the World Bank, later in this list).
- *The OECD.* The environmental policy committee of the OECD was formed in 1970. The OECD exchanges information about best practices in national environmental policy-making and regulation. The quality of the policy process is enhanced by a system of peer reviews. The OECD also stimulates the negotiation and signing of international environmental commitments (see, for example, OECD 1999a, b, 2000; Ruffing 2010). These include codes of conduct and directives for multinational firms. Past experience has shown that such codes are effective, as stakeholders in many a multinational firm check the compliance of their company with the code.
- *The G8 and G20.* Environmental matters have taken an increasing part in the attention of the G8 and G20 over the past decades. Sometimes this institution has been used to try to break stalemates in negotiations. However, their role in the total effort to reach international environmental agreements has been limited. It is probably more important as a medium for customizing national policies to international objectives (Kim and Chung 2012).
- *The WTO.* There is a close connection between trade and the environment. The WTO starts from the premise that trade measures apply to goods and services, not to the way they have been produced. So, its rule of non-discrimination does not allow countries to take action against products from countries that do not respect the importers' sustainable production standards. NGOs have consistently tried to change this situation and to "green" the trade regime. As yet these efforts have not resulted in consistency in the WTO's stand and the main organizations responsible for environmental issues.
- *The World Bank.* The Bank has been rather slow to integrate environmental concerns in the selection of the projects it supports. In the early 1990s it started to integrate the environment in its analysis and its instruments. It finances the GEF that provides funds on favourable terms to projects that have a beneficial effect on the global environment (now notably climate change and biological diversity; see Box 8.2, earlier). The environment has now taken an important place in the Bank's development considerations.

- *Specialist schemes (regimes)*. More than 200 multinational environmental treaties have been concluded for specific issues. They differ greatly as to mandate, principles, norms, rules and instruments.
- *Regional schemes*. Many environmental problems that extend beyond national borders have a regional dimension not a global dimension, so a large number of regional integration schemes have been created to deal with a variety of environmental matters (see Box 8.3).

If one surveys the institutional structure as a whole, one is struck by the fragmentation both vertically (national, regional and international) and horizontally (over different organizations on each level). Moreover, this fragmentation is even enhanced by the fact that for many specific regimes there is internal differentiation: some countries adhere only partially to certain agreements, creating a multiplicity of sub-regimes. The disadvantage of this situation is that many of the bureaucracies involved have developed their own ways of thinking and acting without a clear idea of a coherent and efficient action (see in this respect Biermann and Siebenhüner 2009).[15]

BOX 8.3 SELECTED REGIONAL SCHEMES FOR ENVIRONMENTAL PROTECTION

Regional economic integration schemes that cover environmental matters as well often start with the interrelation between trade and the environment; a case in point is NAFTA. The EU has gone beyond that stage and has developed an environmental policy in its own right. We will describe the basic features of both schemes.

The *North American Free Trade Association* (NAFTA) integrates the markets of the United States, Canada and Mexico. Right from the start of the negotiations on this scheme, environmental concerns were taken into account. The preamble to the NAFTA agreement calls on the contracting parties to pursue their programme of trade liberalization so as to promote sustainable development. This is given substance in a number of ways. First, NAFTA acknowledges that members are permitted to maintain environmental policies even in cases when these impact on trade. If a dispute with both trade and environmental aspects arises, the agreement provides for procedures where environmental experts have their role next to trade experts. In such trade disputes, members are not allowed to refer to WTO procedures. Moreover, the NAFTA negotiations have been paralleled by environmental cooperation negotiations. These have resulted in an environmental side agreement to NAFTA. This side agreement set up a development bank to support investments in environmental infrastructure on the US–Mexican border. It also set up a

Commission for Environmental Cooperation that serves as a forum for cooperation on environmental issues and monitoring of compliance.

The *European Union* started its activities in the 1950s at a time when environmental concerns were not yet on the international agenda. Since 1972 the Union has had formal competences in its environmental policies.[14] The various enlargements from six to twenty-eight members have resulted in a very wide geographical coverage of the policy. The EU policy aims at a high level of protection. The treaty specifies that the policy shall be based "on the precautionary principle and on the principle that preventive action should be taken, that environmental damage should as a priority be rectified at source and that the polluter should pay". In practice the policy is given direction and substance via action programmes. The Union has developed a range of instruments to put its policy into effect. A whole series of "directives" (EU law) have in the meantime been adopted on a whole series of environmental subjects. The Union pursues a proactive role on the global scene and cooperates with the competent organizations to promote measures at the international level that can improve the environment; it has assumed a particularly active role in the field of climate change. The EU may enter into agreements with third parties; it tends to refer to environmental issues in bilateral (trade) agreements (see Chapter 5).

8.4.3 The Framework Convention on Climate Change (FCCC)

Emergence

The basic text (the Framework Convention) was agreed on during the 1992 Earth Summit in Rio de Janeiro. In a follow-up conference held in 1997 in Kyoto, the so-called Kyoto Protocol (KP) was adopted. It was agreed that it would enter into force after having been ratified by fifty-five countries, accounting for at least 55 per cent of all 1990 emissions. Ratification became uncertain, as the United States decided not to ratify.[16] However, the European Union was determined to proceed and has succeeded in mobilizing sufficient support for the final entry into force of the Protocol. In a conference in Bonn in 2001, 170 countries finally came to an agreement about a detailed filling in of the KP's targets and instruments. The protocol entered into force in 2005. In the meantime, several other conferences have been held that have specified further details of the agreement for an increasing number of countries (191 by the end of 2011). The quantitative targets for each group and for each country are set for 2012 (later extended to 2015); the agreement (including the setting of new targets) for the post-2015 period is now under negotiation.

Objectives and tasks

Solving the problem of global warming requires reduction of the major cause: the emission of greenhouse gases. The Kyoto Protocol *commits* the signatories to realize concrete targets by a specific deadline. The targets have been translated into the form of emission rights.

The allocation of pollution rights has been an example of political horse-trading. Each country or region (e.g. the European Union) has finally negotiated a level of pollution that it considered feasible in technical terms, acceptable in political terms and fair in comparison to the effort of its negotiating parties. So, the targets for reduction vary from country to country. The major developed countries (responsible for most of the present levels of pollution) are required to reduce emissions by about 7 per cent with respect to 1990 levels. The KP has adopted the principle of "common but differentiated responsibility". It implies that *no targets have been set for LDCs*. This was understandable from the point of view of their minor contribution to the problem. It could also be understood from the point of view of transaction costs (it would probably have held up the negotiations indefinitely). However, this exclusion now poses a number of problems. First, there is the problem of effectiveness, as many of the larger LDCs have become substantial polluters. Second, the exclusion of LDCs prevents the levelling out of the marginal cost of abatement over all polluters in the world.

These arguments have carried the day. In view of the very quickly rising emissions by the emerging countries (in particular, India and China have moved into the top rank of polluters), the 2011 conference, held in Durban, agreed that after 2015 all countries would participate in the reduction efforts.

The national targets for emission reduction have been translated into specific targets on the level of various actors by every country in the way that best suits its internal situation. Countries act on:

- the main polluting plants, by setting emission limits and by structural measures (fuel switching). This implies investment in projects that reduce the emissions of such plants;
- the multitude of smaller emissions, by product regulation, price incentives, civic behaviour and tax incentives;
- the capacity of the country to absorb emissions by so-called carbon sinks. As carbon is fixed by wood or by other vegetation, the more vegetation, the less the need to use the above two instruments.

Members and division of power

The KP has been signed and ratified by almost all countries in the world. The European Union too has signed. Notable exceptions are the United States (for a variety of reasons) and Canada (for maintaining competitiveness with respect to the United States). The distribution of power (all countries negotiate as equals) makes progress very slow. A leading role has been played by the European Union.

8.5 FCCC governance

8.5.1 General

For the Kyoto Protocol a number of possible instruments have been considered. Many of them have, for several reasons, been discarded. This is the case for regulation: the reaching of an agreement on a long list of detailed technical subjects and on an operational system of checking compliance was considered politically unfeasible. Similar reasoning applies to taxation, as countries in general are unwilling to give up their sovereignty in matters of taxation. So, the option that has been chosen is to adopt mostly market-related instruments. It is then left to the individual country to see what other instruments it wants to put in place to reach the targets.

The cost of pollution abatement can differ greatly from one country to another. Countries that already have high standards and use modern technology will face high marginal costs for further abatement. Countries that still use older technology may realize considerable environmental improvements at relatively low cost. It is thus good economics to stimulate common efforts so that worldwide abatement is done in an efficient way.

The way to do this is to accept that reductions need not be realized in a particular country itself; they may instead be realized in other countries. This realization appears in the KP in two forms. Joint Implementation applies to countries that are both signatories of the KP.[17] An example of such a project would be investment by Shell in clean technology in Poland. The Clean Development Mechanism (CDM) applies in cases when the host country is not a signatory of the KP. An example would be investment by Shell in a clean technology project in Ghana.

8.5.2 The international emissions trading system

Fiscal and market type instruments are the most effective for combating emissions of greenhouse gases (e.g. Parry *et al.* 2012). The basic method of the KP is of the second type; it comprises the setting of maximum pollution levels and the trading of emission rights (see section 8.3). The KP obliges developed countries to make at least half of the reduction of emissions in the country itself. The rationale for this is twofold: first, to avoid a situation in which LDCs sell their most obvious possibilities at a low price now, with the risk of being confronted with the more costly projects later;[18] and second, to stimulate the highly developed countries to search for innovative ways to decrease the cost of abatement and to develop new clean technologies.

In recent decades a number of countries have been experimenting with the setting up of national systems of emission rights trading. Consequently, a number of differences exist between these systems, bringing the risk of incompatibility. The institutional way out of this problem would be to link these systems – or rather, to create a new international system. The realization of this idea is fraught with difficulties, in particular because several of the major actors (e.g. the United States and China) do not want to participate. As the EU system is the most sophisticated and has shown that a multilevel governance set-up can work (see Box 8.4), many (both inside and outside the European Union) think that it could be used as the backbone of a global system (see, for example, Kruger *et al.* 2007; Ellerman 2008; Jaffe *et al.* 2010).

BOX 8.4 BASIC FEATURES OF THE EU SYSTEM FOR COMBATING CLIMATE CHANGE

The European Union has been the leader of the vanguard countries promoting internal policies to combat climate change. After a failed attempt to set up a structure according to the first-best solution (i.e. using the taxation instrument), it has successfully set up an EU-wide system (integrating the twenty-seven national systems) for the second-best solution: a cap and trade system (Convery 2009). The main characteristics of this system are the following (EC 2006):

- *Attribution of rights.* Each country can use its own rules as to the allocation of rights to companies. National plans have been set up and submitted to the European Union for approval. Since 2008 it has been possible for rights to be auctioned.
- *Trade.* Companies can use their rights for their own purposes. If they exceed their right, they have to pay a fine of up to €100 per ton. To avoid this, companies can buy the rights of those that have not exhausted their rights. The price is settled by the market.
- *Coverage.* In the first instance the system has been set up for the industries that are responsible for the largest part of the emissions (40 per cent). It takes in some 4,500 companies in the Union in the sectors of oil refineries, basic chemicals, fossil fuel-fired power stations, steel, cement, pulp/paper and ceramics.

The effectiveness of the EU system is a matter of considerable debate. An initial problem has been that the member states have been fairly generous in attributing emission rights, so that the system has not been as tight as is necessary to make substantial reductions. Moreover, the causal relation between reduction and policy is not very clear: emission reductions are influenced by many other factors too. They depend, for instance, on the number of old installations scrapped (owing to transition and economic recession) and on new installations put in place. These problems can be circumvented by comparing the emissions from existing plants over time; one then clearly sees a reduction (EC 2011).

However, it is clear that for meeting targets an extra effort is needed. To that effect, the post-2012 system will be changed in the following respects:

- *Rights.* The caps will no longer be set at the national level but at the EU level. The Union intends to reduce them by 20 per cent with respect to 2005. EU-wide rules will apply to transitional free allocations.
- *Trade.* Trade periods will be longer and more of the available rights will be auctioned, which will introduce more flexibility and hence efficiency.
- *Coverage.* Other polluters (such as air transport) and pollutants other than CO_2 will be included.

8.5.3 Compliance and enforcement

How likely is it that the efforts that were agreed under the KP will lead to the actions needed and finally to the intended effect? The following factors are important in this respect:

- *Monitoring.* Transparency of compliance by partners is effectuated by the obligation that all partners designate a national authority to administer the inventory on greenhouse gases and the trade in emission rights. They have to submit regular reports to the secretariat of the KP regarding their emissions. These reports are reviewed by a compliance committee. The effect of this factor is based on reputation. NGOs can hold governments accountable for any non-compliance, which may increase the political support for the measures needed.
- *Sanctions.* The use of this instrument is very controversial as sanctions are very difficult to make effective internationally.[19] A threat by partners to maintain a high emission level if a country does not meet its abatement commitments is hardly credible, as countries are unlikely to pursue self-damaging policies. Financial measures, for instance fines for non-compliance, did not survive in the negotiation rounds that preceded the conclusion of the KP.
- *Dispute settlement system.* The KP does not provide for such an instrument. Yet it might have been helpful to use the experience of the WTO as an example of best practices in this respect (see Box 5.7).
- *Incentives.* Some incentives are actually used in the KP. They come notably in the sense of other international organizations (e.g. the World Bank) linking aid with environmental issues (see Box 8.2).

The general *conclusion* of this analysis is that the KP is still in the infancy stage of an MEA. In order for it to develop to the maturity stage, several conditions need to be fulfilled (see Chapters 2–4): the problems need to become more visible and acute, the diversity of interests need to decline, the instruments need to become more effective and the means of persuasion that can be employed on non-participants (including LDCs) need to become much stronger.

8.6 Evaluation of the past and options for the future

8.6.1 Achievements

In recent decades, global environmental concerns have attracted considerable public interest. This has prompted national governments to cooperate on a range of issues. Such international policy-making has resulted in a rapid expansion of the number of global environmental regimes. The main legal form used was the multilateral environmental agreement (MEA). MEAs concern notably the preservation of biodiversity and the promotion of lower emissions and cleaner production. Most MEAs have created conferences of parties that do most of the decision-making. The elaboration of major new regimes has gone hand in hand with the use of innovative instruments such as tradable pollution rights. An important element in this whole set of international conventions is the Kyoto Protocol on Climate Change, which has started to tackle this important problem. On this issue the target variable is pretty clear: the reduction of greenhouse gases. Unfortunately, the progress on this score is very diversified, fragile and overall unsatisfactory.

The concern for sustainability is still mostly felt by people in developed countries. This applies also for the burden of environmental policy according to the principle of "common objectives but differentiated obligations." Moreover, developed countries support (financially) developing countries that are willing to accept international obligations.[20] A clear example of this is given in the Kyoto Protocol.

8.6.2 Inadequacies and challenges

There is considerable and widespread concern about the inadequacy of the present regimes and organizations to deliver the global public good of environmental sustainability. This inadequacy is closely linked to the *organizational weakness* of the environmental regimes. Over the past decades a broad range of regimes has developed on a case-by-case basis, all concerning very specific issues. This development can be explained by a range of factors, such as institutional inertia (Vijge 2013). UNEP has not provided a unifying framework for an encompassing environmental regime; neither is there a standard format of obligations and instruments. This incoherence and lack of standardization means that the transaction costs for participants in the process and the information costs for stakeholders are higher than necessary. They mean, moreover, that there are very few mechanisms to internalize externalities that underlie global environmental failure.

The ensuring of *compliance* with environmental agreements is essentially based on non-judicial instruments (e.g. transparency and reputation). It applies not only to governments but also to firms. UNEP, for instance, promotes the Global Reporting Initiative, developed in partnership with leading multi-stakeholder organizations to encourage voluntary environmental reporting by companies around the world. Non-compliance often results in further diplomatic activity and negotiation. It often involves the search for means that can facilitate compliance by the defector, rather than punishment (see, for example, Faure and Lefevere 1999). Dispute settlement mechanisms are very rare and, even when in place, have very rarely been used. The International Court of Justice has so far never dealt with a purely environmental conflict.

Given the weak compliance instruments, there is reason for concern about the (lack of) *effectiveness* of many of the MEAs (e.g. Andresen 2007a). In order to improve compliance, some incentives have been put in place. The GEF can provide financial support to countries that have difficulty in living up to their commitments. However, there is widespread concern (notably among developing countries) about this facility's lack of resources, the priorities it sets (not always felt to be in the interests of the developing world) and finally about its cumbersome procedures (unsuited, given the limited administrative capacity of LDCs).

Unfortunately, the measurement of effectiveness is very difficult for many agreements. Only in cases where concrete targets for abatement have been agreed is a quantitative assessment possible. This has been the case for the Kyoto Protocol on greenhouse gas abatement. The results are disappointing: targets are not met. This is partly due to the fact that major polluters have not ratified and that the instruments have not been sufficiently constraining. International conferences where these problems have been addressed have been unsuccessful in promoting change, due to the widely diverging interests of major players.

The effectiveness of many MEAs is negatively impacted by the *irregularity of their financial resources*. This makes the room for manoeuvre of the organizations involved subject to significant uncertainties.

A final point to be mentioned is that the interface between the environment and other policy areas has not adequately been clarified. This applies in particular to the relation between environmental standards and trade.[21]

8.6.3 Proposals for improvement

The world is thus in need of better environmental governance. However, a change for the better will be difficult, given the very large differences in interests that exist between the major players: the United States, the European Union and the major emerging and developing countries (e.g. Andresen 2007b). This applies both to the general issue of global environmental governance and to the specific issue of the regime for climate change. I will deal with them successively.

Many proposals have been made to remedy the *organizational weakness* of world environmental governance. They mostly address the following two aspects:

1. Reducing the organizational diversity and improving consistency between regimes. This starts with more and better coordination among the various MEAs, notably between those that cover similar areas (biodiversity, toxic waste, etc.). It ends with a call for a fully fledged World Environment Organization (see Box 8.5).

BOX 8.5 Proposal for a World Environment Organization

To remedy effectively a number of the problems many favour the replacement of all global environmental organizations by a newly created *World Environment Organization* (WEO) along the lines of the WTO or ILO (see, for example, Whalley and Zissimos 2002; Tussie and Whalley 2002; Biermann and Bauer 2005; Esty 2009).[22] The basic elements of the proposals can be described as follows.

Objective

The WEO would facilitate, encourage, administer and take actions aiming to advance cross-country negotiations on the environment whose effect would be to raise environmental quality. The WEO would manage all MEAs, working on the harmonization of their objectives and structures. The most important aspect of this integration is, however, that comprehensive (cross-issue) deals would be possible that would make sure that every partner would obtain some benefit (compare the tariffs rounds of the GATT and, later, the WTO). The seeking of comprehensive deals limits the problem of free-riding.

Compliance

In most cases, the partners in environmental agreements have to verify themselves whether a commitment is put into practice. On the level of the WEO one could, however, foresee a more effective instrument where independent judgment prevails. This could take the form of an Environmental Policy Review (similar to the Trade Policy Review in the WTO). Such a surveillance mechanism would not necessarily have to be intergovernmental; accredited NGOs could also be given the right to lodge complaints.

Centralized dispute settlement mechanism

There is a need for the creation of an international body to analyse cases of conflict and give a judgement. The forms in which disputes are likely to arise in a WEO are different from those in the WTO. In the latter they tend to apply to the interpretation of general rules; in the WEO it would be more about the individual fulfilment of collective deals. However, the mechanisms to deal with the issues need not be much different. They could even imply a set of measures that the international community could apply in order to sanction violators. In this respect there is strong pressure from environmentalist NGOs to use trade sanctions against countries that do not comply with MEAs. They point towards the fairly direct relation between policy measures concerning production, consumption and the environment. This view is opposed by trade specialists, who fear "corruption" of the regime. It is also opposed by certain security specialists who claim that trade sanctions have generally proved to be ineffective in trying to force countries to comply with other values, such as racial equality and human rights. So, sanctions should be rather of the type of withdrawal of incentives (financial support to programmes for environmental improvement). As yet, support for this proposal has been very limited; the reasons for such lack of enthusiasm were given in Chapters 2–4.

2.   Stabilizing and enlarging the financial basis. This applies in the short term notably to the GEF. The financial basis needs to be considerably enlarged and it needs to be made more predictable (that is, commitments must be made for several years).

The United Nations has not waited for the realization of such organizational solutions and took the initiative to reinvigorate the actions for global sustainability and for global environmental governance by calling a Conference on Sustainable Development in June 2012 in Rio de Janeiro as a successor of the earlier landmark conference (see section 8.4.2). The results of the conference were very meagre: only a small extension of the role of UNEP in the surveillance of environmental agreements for all UN members has been accepted. Proposals for enhancing the status of UNEP to a UN agency were not accepted (UN 2012). So the multilateral route seems to be very difficult in the future. Progress will depend on the willingness of individual states to make voluntary commitments to a better environment.

Among the many proposals for improvement few mention the *regional option*. For one this is due to the fact that the regional level is not adequate to deal with truly global issues (such as climate change, the depletion of resources or the extinction of species). For another it is due to the lack of empowerment of most of the present regional integration schemes in environmental issues.

Many proposals have also been made for an improvement of the *regime on climate change*. Given the considerable investment made in the Kyoto Protocol and its relative merits, many tend to build on the present set-up and propose to eliminate several of its weaknesses, notably through the participation of all major polluters (industrialized, emerging and developing countries), and a stronger set of instruments. Others tend to consider that this is infeasible and would rather go in the direction of the gradual linking of the present national and regional systems and alternative ways of combating emissions (see reviews by Kuik *et al.* 2008; Aldy and Stavins 2008).[23]

8.7 Summary and conclusions

- The world is confronted with a number of environmental problems that have a truly global character. Many consider global warming to be one of the major problems.
- To cope with such problems, global regimes have been elaborated, with the objective of providing the global public good of sustainability. Environmental regimes are based on three principles: (1) precaution, (2) the polluter pays, and (3) common but differentiated responsibilities.
- There is a plethora of international environmental agreements, most of which have very weak organizational structures. The strongest among them is the United Nations Environmental Programme, which has the custody of important regimes, such as the one combating global warming (the Kyoto Protocol).
- Governance aspects differ widely from one regime to another. In many cases, regulation is used. In other cases, market-based instruments have been chosen. One of the most salient features in this respect is the system of internationally tradable emission permits that is elaborated in the framework of the Kyoto Protocol with the objective of stopping global warming.
- The *effectiveness* of environmental regimes is mixed. On the positive side we see an increasing compliance with international commitments. On the negative side we see that improvements fall short of targets set in the past and that progress on new commitments to face future challenges is very slow. These challenges are threefold: to strengthen the organizational structure, to integrate the various regimes into a single framework (a WEO, comparable to the WTO for trade) and to improve the instruments' effectiveness.

9

LABOUR AND SOCIAL PROTECTION

9.1 Introduction

The possible negative consequences of globalization on employment and labour conditions are major concerns of large sections of the population and hence of their governments.[1]

The *objective* of this chapter is thus to explain the rationale, the modalities and the effectiveness of the international regime on the social protection of workers.

The *structure* of this chapter is as follows. First I will describe the problems that have arisen in work conditions and social protection as a result of increased globalization. In the next sections I will show that it is in everyone's interest for there to be global standards concerning work conditions, both for reasons of human rights and for maintaining fair competition. I pursue the demonstration by describing the organizations that provide that collective good and the instruments they use to safeguard it. A separate section deals in particular with the governance aspects as given form in the most important organization: the International Labour Organization (ILO). The chapter ends with an evaluation of the present regime, an assessment of the future challenges, and a set of proposals for improvement.

9.2 The main problems[2]

9.2.1 Exploitative forms of employment

The world is confronted with many labour-related problems. Some of them are morally unacceptable – in particular, exploitative forms such as forced labour and child labour. The latter problem is related to underdevelopment; families in very poor countries seek employment for their children to obtain additional income. In Asia the problem affects hundreds of millions of individuals. In other areas, such as

Latin America and sub-Saharan Africa, the problem is less serious in numerical terms but nevertheless very significant. It is difficult to measure exactly the evolution of the problem (e.g. Hagemann *et al.* 2006).

9.2.2 Vulnerable labour market institutions

Globalization, in the form of greater openness to trade and to capital movements has an effect on the way national labour markets function. Labour market institutions differ considerably from one country to another. They have been developed over a long period with a view to improving social standards and correcting outcomes of market processes in the light of societal preferences. Many fear that global openness is causing at best the erosion and at worst the total breakdown of these institutions. So, they want to see high standards applied worldwide. However, many newly developing countries see the application of high standards as a loss of competitiveness and hence as a brake on their growth potential.

Labour market regulation concerns a whole group of subjects. The most important are employment protection, unemployment benefits (level and duration), payroll taxes and minimum wages. However, industrial relations aspects such as collective bargaining, employee councils, etc. can also be mentioned. So too can working conditions, such as the protection of health at the workplace (against toxic and dangerous substances), working hours and a ban on child labour.

The situation as to labour regulation is very diversified. Table 9.1 gives some figures by income classes as defined by the World Bank. The indexes run from 1 to 100; the higher the index, the more elaborate and strict the regulation. The last column gives the arithmetical average of the five previous columns. The fourth row gives the average for all developing countries. If we compare rows four and five we see the traditional picture: in developing countries the protection levels are

TABLE 9.1 Strictness of labour market institutions by income category of country (index)

	Labour conditions	Employment law	Collective relations	Wage-setting	Hiring and firing	Average of columns 1–5
Lowest	46	39	37	48	61	46
Lower middle	46	50	46	50	62	51
Upper middle	43	51	48	51	65	52
Average LDC	45	47	46	50	63	50
Traditional developed	43	52	46	58	64	53
Recently developed	36	42	40	44	58	44

Source: Adapted from Freeman (2010).

low; in developed countries they are high. The differences are, however, less pronounced than many would have expected. Note that these figures mask important differences within groups. For instance, there is a big rift within the developed category between the Anglo-Saxon countries (the United States and United Kingdom) with low indicators and the continental EU countries with high ones. Particularly interesting are the low indicators that are exhibited by the recently developed countries.

Strict regulation is often found as inhibiting competitiveness, employment and growth. This negative effect is thought to affect developing countries in particular. However, the effect of strict labour regulation on growth is inconclusive (see for example Djankov and Ramalho 2009; Feldman 2009; Freeman 2010).[3]

9.2.3 Welfare state

Many observers fear that the pressure globalization puts on labour reduces the capacity of countries to sustain typical provisions of the welfare state such as insurance against illness, old age, unemployment, etc. The argument for less developed countries is somewhat involved (see, for example, Rudra 2002; Scharpf 2002). It hinges on the deterioration of the position of the lower-skilled that exacerbates the collective action problem – in other words, globalization erodes the capacity of labour to put pressure on governments in their favour. The situation is different for developed countries, where the organizing capacity of the relevant groups is apparently stronger and institutions are more resilient. Yet here too, trade unions hold globalization responsible for the jeopardizing of welfare state provisions.

9.3 The main public goods

9.3.1 Objectives

The problems listed in the previous section can be considered a public bad. This is notably the case for a potential race to the bottom in terms of the quality of labour conditions. The public good can be defined in terms of the consistent improvement of the quality of employment and work conditions – in particular, a ban on the most painful forms of labour exploitation.[4] It is recognized that the public good of high-quality labour conditions around the globe (including industrial relations) can best be realized by international regulation – in practice, by setting labour standards. There are essentially three reasons for standards:

1. *Moral.* Certain labour standards are part of the essential universal human rights. This set of standards needs to be respected and should not be part of any discussion.
2. *Economic.* Standards oblige firms to internalize the external effects of their functioning, including firing and hiring. Labour standards avoid the loss of social

and human capital that accompanies sudden and profound economic restructuring. Moreover, standards are an asset to any country, as they represent a stabilization of the social fabric. This results in higher productivity due to increased motivation, higher investment in specific skills and a decrease in conflicts. Setting labour standards enhances total welfare provided that it is done in a gradual way, that it permits flexibility in forms and pace, and that it is done in line with the productivity growth of individual countries.

3. *Social.* Labour markets are highly influenced by power relations on both the demand side and the supply side. In some cases, social groups are at a disadvantage because of such factors. Standards prevent the inequality between social groups from widening.

So, the *objective* is to define standards and to make countries comply with them. This objective can be measured in terms of output by the number of countries that do indeed comply. In terms of outcome the objective is somewhat less clear. In terms of the three reasons mentioned above, it is not really possible to measure the improvement in moral terms; and even in social terms it is not easy, although disparity in income might be a good indicator. In terms of the economic argument, one might adopt an increase in productivity and growth as the final indicator.

9.3.2 Principles

In matters of work and social protection there is some consensus as to fundamental principles that should guide the setting of standards. This consensus took shape in 1998 with the "Declaration on Fundamental Principles and Rights at Work". It states four universal principles deduced from *basic human rights*:

1. freedom of association and the effective recognition of the right to collective bargaining – that is, the right of workers to form organizations of their own choice and to negotiate freely their working conditions with their employers;
2. elimination of all forms of forced labour (slavery) and compulsory labour;
3. effective abolition of exploitative forms of child labour, such as bonded labour and forms of child labour that put the health and safety of children at serious risk;
4. elimination of discrimination in employment and occupation – that is, the right to equal respect and treatment for all workers.

Although seldom mentioned in the context of international labour-related issues, two more principles seem to be applied in practice. The principle of *solidarity* is at the basis of all national systems of social security. The principle of *common but differentiated responsibility* (similar to the one in sustainability) requires some more explanation. The word common is used because high-quality labour conditions in one country do, via many channels (among them international trade), influence the situation in other countries. The word "differentiated" is used because the specific situation in countries at different stages of development means that they have to contribute according to their resources to the general improvement of conditions.

9.3.3 National responsibilities

Markets tend to function well only under certain institutional conditions. This is particularly true in labour markets. As a consequence, most countries have passed detailed regulation on labour markets. Labour standards are an important instrument in this respect. Labour standards are norms and rules that govern specific aspects of the labour market – they may concern prices (minimum wages), quantities (maximum working time), all sorts of conditions (such as health and safety) and the behaviour of actors (industrial relations). On the national level, labour standards represent important choices as to the way in which a society wants its labour market to function, taking into account the country's social values and level of development.

The choices that many countries (developed and developing alike) have made in the past are now coming under heavy criticism. Critics claim that the density and level of regulation on work and social protection distort the efficient allocation. They point to the waste of resources through rent-seeking, to a lack of competition and hence innovation, and to constraints on investment and hence on economic growth. They claim that in many cases the benefits of regulation have been annihilated by the cost. So, national regulation needs to be reviewed and has to justify itself in terms of effectiveness and efficiency criteria. However, the right balance to be found between the advantages of regulation and deregulation is a very difficult matter and depends very much on political choices and the cultural and institutional preconditions.

The next section introduces the reasons for international standards. Some of them are considered universal – that is, that they have to be applied by all countries, irrespective of their degree of development and the character of their institutions. Others are optional, and the suggestion is that they are applied as soon as a country is ready for it. Indeed, LDCs tend to comply better with core labour standards the higher their income levels, the more open their trade and the higher their human capital (Busse 2004). For that reason, the national compliance with global standards is considered to be a dynamic gradual process of improvement. This is in line with the principle of common but different responsibilities: developed countries observe all and developing countries an increasing number of these standards in line with their development level.

9.3.4 International responsibilities[5]

The need for labour market regulation on a national scale is justified by the considerable improvements in social public good provision. Supporters of international labour standards tend to draw a parallel with the national level. Opponents of such a transfer to the global level have a quite different set of arguments.

The arguments of those *in favour of setting international standards* come principally from workers who benefit from high labour standards in their own country, and employers who are bound by them. They raise their voices against the perceived unequal conditions under which the stiffened competition in open markets is taking place. They accuse countries that do not observe high labour standards of unfair competition and social dumping. The argument runs as follows. Countries that have low labour standards can produce at low cost. Countries that want to enter the market for certain goods are then obliged to match this low cost level, which will be possible only by accepting the same low standards. Hence, the openness of markets leads to a race to the bottom in terms of standards. This loss of labour protection standards is a public bad. International standards have to protect notably the categories of labour that are most vulnerable to international shocks.[6]

The *arguments of those against* are mainly economic. Two strands of thought can be distinguished:

1. *International standards are not needed.* No straightforward relation between labour standards and (lack of) trade performance and/or growth exists. The most important determinants for growth are technology and labour qualification. Labour standards have only a small weight in the total balance. For instance, there is no clear relation between workers' rights of association or collective bargaining and trade (for overviews, see for example OECD 1996; Brown 2000).[7] So, countries will choose their optimum labour standards according to their competitiveness.
2. *International standards are damaging.* Markets need to function well in order to improve the chances for growth. If standards are set too high, this will actually diminish total welfare. This can be very detrimental to countries that are in the course of catching up. They need to be as efficient as possible. International standards cannot take the diversity of national situations into account. National governments are the closest to the problem, so their choices in matters of specifying labour standards tend to reflect best the optimal positions in aggregate welfare. In other words, competition of regulatory systems does not lead to a race to the bottom but to optimality in regulation.

However, the transposition of the arguments pro and con labour standards from the national to the global level (as done in the previous paragraphs) is fraught with difficulties. On the national level there is in general full freedom of movement of goods, services and the production factors capital and labour. Often there is also a way of compensating the regions that suffer from the imposition of such standards by means of regional development policies. On the international level both aspects are deficient. Rich, high-standard countries do restrict both trade and migration and are not always generous in compensating poor countries that accept to set higher standards in terms of development aid.

9.4 Organizations involved in the provision of public goods

9.4.1 Major players

The major players in matters of labour and social protection are on one hand from the private sector and on the other hand from the public sector. In the former we mention representative organizations of employers and of labour. In the latter we mention governments and public authorities such as labour exchanges. Most of their activity is on the national level. However, in view of the external effects of international commercial activity on labour they have also come together on the global level. The role of national governments has been detailed in the previous sections, so we will focus here on the role of the social partners.

Employers have gradually become more positive about standards. Initial support has come from employers in developed countries and from multinational firms (MNFs). Many European MNFs have adopted a socially responsible asset management strategy (Te Velde 2008). An increasing number of MNFs have found that compliance with formal international labour standards did not seem enough to give substance to their claim of corporate social responsibility (Murray 2004), so they have tried to operate corporate codes of conduct. These are partly morally motivated. However, there is also some basic economics in the motivation. Firms do realize that they face a cost disadvantage by observing them. On the other hand, they count on gaining better market access in developed countries, where critical consumers judge products not only on their value for the user but also on the conditions under which they have been produced.

Trade unions too have diversified positions as to standards. Those in developed countries have always been staunch supporters; increasingly, those in developing countries want to see them applied.[8]

9.4.2 Main international organizations

The most important international labour standards have been set by organizations such as the ILO and OECD, whereas other UN organizations have had some involvement as well.

The International Labour Organization

The conventions of the ILO constitute the most comprehensive set of international labour standards. They are binding on all member countries that have ratified them. The fundamental principles as elaborated in the 1998 declaration are binding on all members, irrespective of their ratification.

The Organisation for Economic Co-operation and Development

Traditionally the OECD has given much attention to the key aspects of economic growth, including the production factor labour. Among its publications we mention its landmark *Jobs Study* (OECD 1994), its annual *OECD Employment Outlook* and its Country Reviews. Moreover, the OECD carries out specialist studies on labour-related issues.[9]

The United Nations

The United Nations has addressed core labour standards in several acts as well. These provisions are similar to but less detailed than the ones contained in the corresponding ILO conventions. They are important in the sense that they have to be observed by all UN members, so have almost universal application, whereas many ILO conventions are applicable only in the subset of countries that have ratified them. Moreover, the United Nations has recently adopted guiding principles on business and human rights that are based on the Universal Declaration of Human Rights and fundamental labour rights.[10]

Other multilaterals

There have been numerous attempts to introduce labour standards into trade agreements. A first case to be mentioned happened in the immediate post-Second World War period with the aborted International Trade Organization. Other cases targeted the GATT and afterwards the WTO. They all fell victim to the fierce opposition of the less developed countries, which see them as disguised forms of protection.[11]

Regions

In several continents regional organizations have developed, that have in some cases taken labour related issues on board. The EU has developed farthest in this respect, but NAFTA has also introduced labour concerns into its rules. Other regions have only very timidly gone along this path, sometimes referring to ILO standards.

9.4.3 The International Labour Organization[12]

The ILO was created in 1919 at the end of the First World War. The initial motivations were mainly humanitarian (concerning conditions of labour), political (a desire to avoid revolutions) and economic (fair competition conditions). However, a leading idea was also that lasting peace cannot be obtained without social justice. The organization adopted a set of international labour conventions dealing with a diversity of aspects, such as hours of work, night work for women and young persons, and maternity protection. During the interwar period its activities were rather limited, as many governments that were struggling with the effects of the First World War and the economic crisis of the 1930s complained about the constraining nature of many of the standards adopted. After the Second World War the ILO became a specialist organization of the United Nations.

The ILO has recently reformulated its mission (ILO 2008). It pursues four core *objectives* that are inseparable, interrelated and mutually supportive. It promotes:

1. employment, by creating a sustainable institutional and economic environment in which individuals can update their necessary capacities and skills, and enterprises can generate income opportunities for all;
2. social security and labour protection measures which are sustainable and adapted to national circumstances, including measures that provide a basic income for all in need for such protection; healthy and safe working conditions; and policies with regard to wages and labour conditions that permit a just sharing of the fruits of progress;
3. social dialogue and tripartism as the most appropriate method for consensus-building on relevant national and international policies and law-making on employment relationships, and for the development of good industrial relations and effective labour inspection systems;
4. respect for the fundamental principles and rights at work – in particular, freedom of association and the effective recognition of the right to collective bargaining.

Membership of the ILO is open to all members of the United Nations. At the moment there are 183 members. The unique feature of the organization is the tripartite composition of the national delegations (government, employers and workers).

The *internal structure* of the ILO consists of the following bodies:

1. The International Labour Conference (ILC) meets once a year; each member state is usually represented by its cabinet minister responsible for labour affairs and persons representing both employers' and workers' organizations. The ILC is a forum for discussion, and formally adopts the texts of standards and conventions. All members have equal rights to speak and vote. Sometimes workers' representatives vote against the government and employers, and vice versa.
2. The Governing Body (GB; executive council) takes decisions on the ILO's policy. It meets three times a year. It is composed of twenty-eight government members, fourteen employers' and fourteen workers' members. Ten countries have a permanent seat (Brazil, China, France, Germany, India, Italy, Japan, Russia, the United Kingdom and the United States). The others are elected by the ILC.
3. The International Labour Office is the permanent secretariat of the International Labour Organization. It is headed by the director-general. Its main departments

are respectively concerned with standards, employment, social protection and social dialogue.

9.5 ILO governance

9.5.1 General

The ILO uses a small range of governance methods. The most important one is regulation, mostly done through the setting of standards. Most of the remaining action of the ILO is through soft methods – in particular, coordination. This comprises monitoring of compliance with ILO regulation and moral persuasion to stick to standards. The budgetary method is used to some extent as the ILO can provide technical assistance to countries to help them improve their situation. The ILO does not have a mandate to apply stronger governance methods, such as the establishment of blacklists on performance (compliance with standards). It can engage in litigation, but this results only in public shaming; the ILO does not have a mandate to use sanctions.

The formal governance processes (detailed in what follows)[13] are not the only way in which the ILO's social standards impact on the global society. There is also considerable informal influence. Indeed, the very existence of standards influences the behaviour of many actors, such as domestic courts, investment advisers, risk analysts, NGOs of many sorts, and consumer associations. And even if the inclusion of ILO norms in trade matters is not accepted by the WTO, reference to them in the proliferating regional and bilateral trade agreements is becoming a common phenomenon.

9.5.2 Regulation: core labour standards

The main instrument used by the ILO is a form of regulation that finds its materialization in *conventions* and *recommendations*. Conventions are international treaties that are open to ratification by member states (see Chapter 4). A country that ratifies a convention thereby commits itself to a binding legal obligation. Under ILO rules, countries are free to "de-ratify" – that is, to withdraw from obligations in case they find them too constraining. ILO recommendations are intended to guide national action but are not legally binding (de Wet 2010).

In many ILO conventions there are several types of labour standards. Some of them have been called *core labour standards*, mainly because of their reference to universal human rights.[14] They have to be respected by all members, irrespective of whether they have ratified them or not. Among them are:

- conventions 87 and 98, providing freedom of association (i.e. organizing trade unions) and collective bargaining (negotiating wages and working conditions with employers);

- conventions 29 and 105, prohibiting all forms of forced labour (particularly slavery) and compulsory labour;
- conventions 100 and 111, providing non-discrimination in employment – that is, equal treatment for all workers;
- conventions 138 and 182, abolishing exploitative forms of child labour.

The ILO has also designated some conventions as *priority* and encourages member states to ratify them. These apply notably to labour market and social protection institutions, and are referred to as *Governance Conventions*. They concern:

- labour inspection (81 and 129);
- employment policy (122);
- tripartite consultation (144).

There are several conventions that imply standards, including conventions dealing with:

- access to social security;[15]
- employment: minimum level of employment security, standard contracts, etc.;
- social policy: minimum level of living standards; access to education, training;
- conditions of work, such as minimum wages, maximum hours of work, etc.;
- social security: sickness, maternity and unemployment benefits, pensions;
- employment conditions for vulnerable groups such as for women, children, old and young persons;
- migrant workers.

Gradual improvement on all these scores should lead to the enhancement of *decent work* – that is, employment that permits a decent living under conditions of liberty, dignity, equity and security. The ILO has stated explicitly that these standards are not to be used as protectionist devices in trade policies.

9.5.3 Coordination: monitoring and surveillance; promotion and persuasion

The monitoring of compliance by member states with the standards is done through annual reporting by the member states, including the views and opinions of workers' and employers' organizations of those states. Moreover, the International Labour Office makes a Global Report that often highlights specific themes.

Cases of non-compliance are entrusted to the committee of experts on the application of conventions and recommendations. The committee members can make a further investigation by asking the allegedly violating member state to clarify its situation. The facts thus established in reports are the basis for a discussion between the ILO (delegates on the Governing Body) and the member states. This aims at the identification of problems and the suggestion of solutions. It also helps to identify areas where technical cooperation can be helpful for realization.

The procedure depicted and the actors involved make it clear that the application of the coordination method has a highly political character.

9.5.4 Dispute settlement

The ILO has instituted several means for stimulating compliance that is based on various forms of litigation. It has opened the possibility to complain to both the private and public actors.

1. Employers' or workers' organizations can file a *representation* with the Governing Body of the ILO (in practice the secretariat). The GB establishes a committee that investigates the case by asking for information from the complaining organization and from the governments against which the complaint is addressed. The committee makes a report that it submits to the GB. The strongest sanction the GB can take is to publish the report, so it relies on naming and shaming.
2. Member state governments that are not satisfied with the effective observance by another member country that has ratified the convention can file a *complaint*. It is mostly invoked in cases of persistent violations by a member of ILO standards. The complaint has to be lodged with the GB. The latter appoints a commission of inquiry to examine the case and to make a report. This report may contain recommendations aimed at removing the cause of the complaint. The report is communicated to the supposedly offending government. The commission of inquiry reports to the GB; its report is published. If the government of the defaulting state follows up the recommendations of the commission, the procedure is closed. If the government does not accept the "ruling", it may submit its case to the International Court of Justice (ICJ), whose decision is final. In an extreme case where a government chooses not to comply with an ICJ decision sanctions can be envisaged.

The two methods depicted are not used very much, largely because of the complex power relations between the three constituent partners, and those between developed and developing countries. The possibility of sanctions is largely a dead letter; it has only been invoked in very exceptional cases (for the first time in the early 2000s against Myanmar). The ILO relies mostly on the other governance methods (persuasion) depicted in the previous sections.

9.5.5 Technical support

Technical assistance ranges broadly and covers such diverse aspects as advising on specific reforms of national legislation and enhancing administrative capacity through training of government officials and representatives of the social partners (organizations of workers and employers). Most technical assistance targets primarily vocational training, labour law, industrial relations, occupational safety, social security, etc.

9.6 Evaluation of the past and options for the future

9.6.1 Major achievements

Many observers fear that the weakness of the governance instruments used by the ILO must lead to weak results. The reality is somewhat different, however, as may be deduced from three types of analysis.

The first makes use of *simple output indicators*. On this score the record of the ILO is positive. For instance, the number of countries that have ratified the various ILO conventions (in particular the core ones) has significantly increased. Moreover, the number of conventions has increased: since 1919 the ILO has established about 200 conventions and the same number of recommendations.

The second uses more detailed *quantitative* or *qualitative output indicators*. The construction of such indicators is fraught with difficulties. However, a few attempts have resulted in assessments of the situation in each country with respect to the observance of each of the core standards and of many of the other labour standards (e.g. Kucera 2008). They show considerable differences between countries in performance and that national scores for individual indicators tend to be highly correlated. Unfortunately, the indicators are not yet sufficiently developed to produce a reliable basis for seeing the extent to which the general situation as to compliance has improved or failed to improve. However, they do give a basis for the ILO to assess the situation in, and monitor the progress of, individual countries and to base its programmes for improvement on such detailed indicators.[16]

The third output method makes use of a comparison of individual countries with respect to global and regional benchmarks. Disregarding the recidivist behaviour of some pariah states, the comparison produces clear results: the ILO monitoring system and the instrument of shaming have reduced the risk of governments' renouncing core international labour standards. The same positive result is found for the incentive structures (bilateral agreements and World Bank conditional loans; Weisband 2000; Onida 2008).

With respect to *outcome* indicators, one might point to the positive relation between standards and growth. The causality of this relation is in two directions, as growth certainly also has a positive influence on standards.[17] Moreover, there is some evidence that labour market regulation also improves equality in the distribution of income (Calderon and Chong 2009).

So, it seems as if the overall picture is positive, even if some observers doubt this.[18]

9.6.2 Challenges

There does not seem to be any need for a new institution or for new legal measures. Most of the needs with respect to labour standards can be taken care of through an extension of the present ILO system. The main challenges would be:

- better coverage of the present conventions (more countries ratifying);
- further extension of subjects;
- a search for equality of standards in countries with similar levels of development;
- better compliance with the present conventions.

9.6.3 Proposals for improvement

There are two main ways in which the ILO system could be improved, but they have certain disadvantages:

1. As there is a relation between level of economic development and observance of standards, the first suggestion would be to step up growth through enhanced development aid. The effectiveness of classical development aid is, however, questioned by many (see Chapter 7).
2. As the ILO relies mostly on monitoring and persuasion, it seems necessary to strengthen the surveillance instruments of the ILO. One suggestion is to improve transparency by a change in the procedures of reporting and coordination. This would replace the present highly politicized procedure by a more technical and administrative procedure (Hartlapp 2007). Better dissemination of the results would also be needed. Bear in mind that suggestions for more detailed definitions of labour standards and enhanced international inspection powers are considered unacceptable inroads into national sovereignty by many countries. A problem here is the limited budget the ILO has available for such activities and the unwillingness of many countries to accept an increase in the budget.

There are also suggestions that support for ILO standards could be improved if progress in other multilateral institutions and in bilateral agreements were made conditional on the observance of ILO standards. These apply to all subjects dealt with in the previous chapters.

- Using the WTO trade sanctions. This is a very controversial issue. There are many reasons not to follow this route. First, the WTO instances are not equipped for this role and many countries do not want to mix trade issues with labour issues. Second, the effectiveness of the trade sanctions instrument is open to doubt. Finally, the welfare effects of sanctions in both the targeted country and the imposing country are so intricate as to make use of this instrument very problematic. (For a short literature review, see Onida 2008: section 4.1.)

- Making macro and monetary support loans (from the IMF) conditional. Many difficulties arise here. First, the instrument is applicable only for countries that applied for such loans. Second, it can be counter-productive in the sense that denying access to such loans might stop the country concerned from emerging from a crisis and recovering growth, so it would risk locking countries into a poverty trap.[19]
- Making grants and loans for development (from the World Bank, the United Nations Development Programme or the United Nations Environment Programme) conditional. This has not been done in the form of sanctions for non-observance but rather in a positive way: as incentives for countries that increase compliance. The World Bank group has started with this in the form of International Finance Corporation performance standards.
- Making regional or national programmes. In this respect, trade measures (the Generalized System of Preferences of the United States or the European Union, or the regional trade agreements of the same countries)[20] and/or the development assistance provided by these countries can be cited. The effectiveness of this instrument may be very good, as bilateral trade advantages and aid are often given in the framework of a more intimate donor–recipient relation, which could cope with the intricacies of a set-up with such conditionalities.[21]

Finally, more confidence might be placed in the *private sector*. Firms are becoming increasingly aware of the negative reaction of consumers towards products that have been produced under conditions that lack respect for core labour standards. They will want to be known as socially responsible corporate citizens and to make sure that their subsidiaries comply with standards. There will, however, always be discussion about the level of social protection that would qualify for such social labelling.[22] .

In view of the set of problems that comes with each of the avenues depicted, one can only conclude that improvement of the present regime will be done in a piecemeal way and will take much time. Economic necessity does indeed point towards flexibility. Progress will be gradual and will depend on the occurrence of favourable constellations of interests leading to partial compromises between workers and employers and between (groups of) countries.

9.7 Summary and conclusions

- In a globalizing world there is strong competition, and that means that there will be a very strong drive to reduce costs. As labour costs make up a considerable part of the total cost structure of many products and services, there is pressure on them. In developed countries with high labour costs, this may lead to unemployment and to pressure on wages in the exposed sectors. In developing countries it will lead to low levels of labour protection against health risks, etc.
- The protection of labour against the risks of exploitation is a global public good. It cannot be realized by private action, or by independent national actions, given

the external effects. The main objective is to achieve decent work all over the globe.

- The main body entrusted with the task of social protection is the International Labour Organization. It has a specific characteristic that differentiates it from all other international organizations: it is tripartite. Alongside representatives of governments there are also representatives of trade unions and employers' organizations.
- The main instrument of the ILO is the setting of international labour standards. These have an important function: to safeguard social values and human rights principles. ILO members do not have to adopt the whole set; they can adhere to part of it.
- The effectiveness is rather satisfactory if one looks at the output; over time the number of such standards has increased and so has the number of countries complying with them. However, it is less so if one looks at the outcome; although there is some evidence of a parallel improvement in both labour standards and welfare growth.
- There remain many insufficiencies. A further strengthening of the ILO-centred global regime would be desirable for a wide array of detailed subjects.

PART III
Coping with insufficiencies

10
COMPLEMENTS

10.1 Introduction

The previous chapters have described in detail how the major constituent parts of the global socio-economic institutional system have gradually evolved. We have focused on the evolution of the global regimes that directly affect the economy: those concerned with trade, finance, development, the environment and social matters.

Many observers have pointed to the deficiencies of this system and have suggested the filling in of some missing elements. I have grouped such suggestions under two main headings.

The first concerns the *global markets of production factors* – in practice, capital and labour. In the first main section of this chapter we concentrate on capital and, more specifically, on direct investment, as this is an essential part of the workings of modern production systems and value chains. We will then go somewhat further into the migration of labour, a subject that is very rigidly regulated by national governments, with the objective to limit the influx of persons.

The second element that needs to be covered better is the *functioning of markets*. There is a pressing need for some form of global regime-building in matters of competition; we will deal with this issue in the third main section. I discuss in the fourth section forms of international commerce that have been revolutionized by the Internet. For the moment the Internet is still highly unregulated; I will evaluate some ideas to better safeguard public goods in this domain.

As usual, the chapter is rounded off by a short section that gives the major conclusions and an outlook into the future.

10.2 Production factors: investment[1]

10.2.1 The main problems

Foreign direct investment (FDI) has grown very quickly during recent decades. Table 10.1 gives an idea of this development and of the importance of FDI for the global economy. It can be seen that FDI has grown much faster than GDP and that it has engendered similar growth of the total international exchange of products of foreign plants. For the developing countries, FDI is of particular relevance as it accounted during the past decade for the lion's share of total capital flows to these countries.

The very rapid increase in FDI is the consequence of the progressive liberalization of FDI flows. However, this has not been facilitated by a multilateral regime (see the next sections) but is the result of the efforts of many countries that have unilaterally or bilaterally done away with restrictions on incoming FDI. The rationale of these policies can be found in the better allocation of resources that this provides, benefiting both receiving and sending countries. This growth continued up to 2007 and has since decreased under the influence of the global crisis and under the influence of a change in the policy towards more protectionism by many governments. The reason for the latter trend is that more and more governments are concerned about the disrupting effects of the speculative element in FDI and want to develop FDI in line with their industrial and external policies.

The liberalization policies of individual countries and of regional groupings (such as the European Union and NAFTA) have created a situation in which much of the global FDI flows are now formally free. This is definitely the case for the flows among developed countries and to some extent also for many emerging and developing countries. However, FDI is still confronted by two main types of problems:

1. *Barriers.* Many obstacles to FDI come in the form of so-called performance requirements, obliging the multinational firm (MNF) for instance to abide by minimum levels of local procurement or to accept the transfer of certain technologies. Even where FDI is liberalized by a national policy, a problem of credibility remains. Indeed, as long as this policy is not locked into a multilateral commitment, it can be unilaterally suspended.

TABLE 10.1   FDI and foreign production ('000 billion of $)

	1980	1990	2000	2010
FDI flows	0.1	0.2	0.7	1.3
Total assets of foreign affiliates	2.0	5.0	25.0	57.0
Exports of foreign affiliates	0.7	1.5	2.6	6.0
Gross domestic product	10.8	22.0	32.0	63.0

Source: UNCTAD (2002, 2011).

2. *Distortions*. The main problem is the behind-border government influence on investment. Governments tend to compete for FDI with incentive schemes (subsidies and other advantages such as tax relief). However, once the investment has been made, the investor is hostage to changes in the rules of the host country; major problems may occur, such as competition with subsidized local firms and even expropriation. Governments have responded to these challenges in very different ways, resulting in a huge multiplicity of regimes, increasing costs and producing uncertainty for international investors. Moreover, there are distortions arising from geopolitical considerations of large investors that function under the direct influence of the public sector in their home country.[2]

10.2.2 The main public goods

The relevance of a comprehensive multilateral regime for international investments has been identified on several occasions in the past (see, for instance, Goldberg and Kindleberger 1970; Brewer and Young 1995). In the first instance, attention has been on forms of international insurance against actions by host governments that could jeopardize the value of the FDI (e.g. by expropriation). Subsequently the emphasis has been on liberalization to do away with barriers and on the setting of common standards to limit distortions.

A *multilateral investment regime* would be an important public good, as it would enhance predictability and legal security, and thereby bring down transaction costs for private investors, adding to an optimal distribution of capital.

Some doubt the need for an international regime. They consider that countries that want to attract investment have no interest in discrimination. They consider, moreover, that the transaction cost argument should not be exaggerated, as MNFs anyway have to come to grips with the intricacies of the legal and regulatory system of the country they invest in.

Others are much in favour of a multilateral regime. They consider that it is the best instrument to do away with the credibility gap facing countries with a poor record. Multilateral arrangements lock in national reforms and in so doing enhance the confidence that investors have in the continuity of the national regime. They can also help to achieve other goals such as reduction of corruption, money-laundering and tax evasion. Of course, these advantages in regime-building come at a cost: a reduction in the capacity of national and local governments to choose the combinations of policy measures they prefer.

A multilateral FDI regime will typically be designed on the basis of the following principles:[3]

*   freedom of entry: giving foreign firms the right to invest in the host country;
*   national treatment: foreign firms will be treated in the same way as local firms;
*   most favoured nation treatment: the host country will not discriminate between investors from different nations.

These principles need to be worked out in practical arrangements. Much like the WTO provisions on trade, these mostly concern three aspects.

The first aspect is *transparency* – that is, all national regimes should be published so as to permit all interested parties to check their conformity with international rules.

The second concerns *national treatment*. The putting into practice of this principle raises a set of very difficult issues for both developed and developing countries. The former are very concerned about geopolitical side effects of FDI coming from state-owned enterprises. The latter tend to be greatly concerned about the negative effects of across-the-board liberalization of FDI on their capacity to maintain development-oriented macroeconomic and industrial policies. Host and home governments alike are very much concerned about the possible ability of MNFs to elude national regulation concerning taxation due to transfer pricing systems that favour tax havens. They thus want to set specific rules for MNFs to avoid such behaviour.

The third concerns a *dispute settlement device*. This could be done on lines similar to the WTO's Dispute Settlement Procedure (see Box 5.7): a type of consultation and dispute settlement between states. For investment one might envisage the possibility of a firm versus state procedure.

10.2.3 Organizations

The most important rules with respect to foreign direct investment come from the following international organizations.

The Organisation for Economic Co-operation and Development

The OECD's involvement begins with the 1961 Codes on the Liberalization of Current Investment Transactions and on the Liberalization of the Capital Movements. In 1976 these were followed by the National Treatment Instrument. The OECD guidelines for multinational enterprises are a set of recommendations (which means they have no binding character and represent no legal obligation) by the governments of the OECD countries to MNFs operating in their country.[4] They ask firms not only to behave in accordance with rules and laws of the host countries, but also to respect certain standards concerning such diverse issues as the environment, competition, industrial relations, etc. The OECD has tried to go beyond this by setting up the Multilateral Agreement on Investment (MAI). However, the initiative failed (see Box 10.1). It then turned to the development of a policy framework for good practices on FDI (OECD 2006), specifying aspects such as trade, tax, competition, labour rights and good governance.

BOX 10.1 ABORTED FDI REGIMES: THE OECD
MULTILATERAL AGREEMENT ON INVESTMENT

In the early 1990s many OECD countries became increasingly concerned about the safety of their FDI. In 1995, official negotiations started for a *Multilateral Agreement on Investment* (MAI) that would set high standards for the protection and rights of foreign investors. The group of negotiating partners was limited to OECD members (accounting for some 90 per cent of outgoing FDI at the time). Other partners would be invited to join the agreement later. By 1997, negotiations resulted in a draft text.

This draft for the MAI had the following *characteristics*:

- It would be *free-standing*. The MAI would not be part of an existing international organization. It would be an agreement among signatories, like GATT (see Chapter 5).
- It would be *comprehensive,* covering all types of investment and all sectors of activity, and applying obligations to all levels of government (federal, national and local).
- Its *principles* would be that signatories would have to observe both "national treatment" and "most favoured nation treatment".
- It would offer *protection*, providing the highest standards of treatment of investors against expropriation. Free transfer would be given to all payments related to the operation.
- It would be *balanced*. MNFs would have to recognize societal concerns, such as environmental protection, labour standards and rules of responsible corporate citizenship.
- It would include *performance requirements*. It would be prohibited to set conditions concerning transfer of technology, location of headquarters, employment of locals, domestic content, etc.
- It would include a *dispute settlement mechanism*. Disputes between states were to be settled by an arbitral panel. Disputes between states and MNFs were to be settled by arbitration.
- There would be *safeguards, exceptions, etc.* There would be the possibility provisionally to install certain regimes such as restrictions on capital movements in the event of serious balance of payments difficulties.

On the basis of the progress made in negotiations, it looked as though the MAI would successfully enter the ratification stage. However, matters took a quite different course.

The *support* from the business community vanished in the wake of increased opposition. A possible reason for this was that many large MNFs did not really

need the MAI as they are able to exert strong pressure on individual governments to obtain tailor-made advantages in return for investing in a particular
location.

The *opposition* to the draft text came essentially from developing countries.
Accepting the MAI in the form presented would strip them of the possibility of
using certain instruments they think of as essential for reaching policy goals.
They were supported by a rainbow coalition of pressure groups that considered
that the MAI would in practice remove all checks on environmental, labour and
societal consequences of FDI.[5]

In the face of this strong opposition neither the business community nor
governments saw a sufficient need for committing themselves to a binding
multilateral agreement and the text was abandoned.

Source: Witherell (1995).

The World Trade Organization

The WTO has concluded the Agreement on Trade Related Investment Measures
(TRIMs). The agreement limits the range of goods-related performance
requirements (such as requirements for using local goods). It mostly addresses trade-
distorting policies rather than investment issues. It has left many ambiguities, and
therefore the implementation is far from perfect. The WTO has made an attempt
to come to a multilateral investment regime as part of the Doha Development
Agenda. However, for a number of reasons this attempt has failed (see Box 10.2).
Nevertheless, the WTO seems to be most adequate organization for the development of such a regime, given the very strong interlinkages in modern production
systems between trade and investment, and the experience of the WTO with the
investment aspects of, for instance, services (see Chapter 5).

BOX 10.2 ABORTED FDI REGIMES: THE WTO DOHA DEVELOPMENT AGENDA

In the framework of the Doha Development Agenda (DDA) a number of
negotiations went on in parallel. In the 2000–2004 period a Working Group on
Trade and Investment did tackle the issues related to foreign direct investment.
These covered aspects such as definitions, scope, principles, etc.

The *support* for the new WTO-based set-up for FDI came in particular from
the European Union, with some support from other developed countries. They
used the standard arguments in favour of a multilateral deal on FDI.

> The *opposition* to the proposals came essentially from changing coalitions of developing countries. They were convinced that the form in which the agreement was proposed would not deliver significant development benefits, while unduly constraining their policy options.
>
> An agreement might have been found, as interests on many points seemed to converge. There is evidence for this convergence in the number of regional and bilateral agreements in which both developed countries and developing countries are partners. Also, the specific conditions of the WTO project seemed in some cases even better for developing countries than certain of the bilateral deals.
>
> Nevertheless, the initiative did fail, which may be attributed to two factors. One is procedural. According to WTO rules, negotiating takes place on packages of different issues but nothing is agreed until the package is agreed. Developing countries had made a strong case for improvements on the issue of agriculture. Seeing no progress there, they stalled the discussions on other issues, in particular FDI. The second factor is of a political nature: the civil society pressure groups that had successfully worked to stop the MAI considered that the WTO project was essentially subject to the same flaws.
>
> *Source*: Sauve (2006).

The International Bank for Reconstruction and Development

In order to provide insurance against political risks for investments, the World Bank in 1988 set up the Multilateral Investment Guarantee Agency, which has since been joined by over 100 countries. The notion of political risk covers a number of categories: currency restrictions, repudiation of contracts, expropriation and armed conflict.

UNCTAD

UNCTAD has gradually assumed responsibility for FDI. Its activities are mainly in the field of monitoring developments in the flows and stocks of FDI and in the national regimes of FDI. Particular attention is also given to the monitoring of international investment agreements; these mostly are of a bilateral character. Moreover, UNCTAD has started to move to the setting up of a policy framework for sustainable FDI (UNCTAD 2012).

Regional arrangements

Many regional arrangements (in particular the European Union and NAFTA) include rules concerning FDI.

10.2.4 What could a new regime look like?

The form in which international regimes develop is very much dependent on collective action problems (see Chapter 3). Most problems occur with respect to the development of comprehensive regimes. Fewer problems occur if one decreases the coverage in terms of subjects (sectoral limitation) or in terms of club members (regional limitation). We will work out three alternatives below.[6]

Multilateral

Since the misadventures of the MAI and the WTO Doha round, no more attempts have been made to come to a comprehensive multilateral system on FDI. As the development of such a system would still be of interest to many it is necessary to analyze the conditions under which such a multilateral option might be advantageous to the main actors. It would mean that the details of the regime have to be checked on their contribution to development. This concerns coverage as to type (with or without portfolio investment and short time flows), sectors (manufacturing, financial services) and aspects (such as incentives, accounting, corporate governance, tax and repatriation of funds).

Sectoral

The WTO has already integrated some of the issues related to FDI for a limited number of sectors. It could develop more of these partial agreements. Given that the bulk of the problems as to FDI now relate to service industries, it seems as if the General Agreement on Trade in Services (GATS) is the first candidate to be extended in this way. In the goods sector, however, there are also many opportunities for further specific issue agreements, including on market access. A way to select further subjects would be to study the content of regional and bilateral agreements and then generalize the elements that seem to be common to most of them.

Regional

Regional arrangements have been made by the European Union, NAFTA and ASEAN. They are likely to develop further in future. The European Union is furthest advanced on this front. Since its creation, it has acquired responsibility for direct investment within its borders. The recent treaty adaptation has also given it the responsibility for external aspects of FDI. The Union is now in the process of specifying the different components of its external policy in this respect: objectives (protection of FDI), standard procedures (dispute settlement), partner choice, etc. FDI issues are likely to be integrated in EU trade and investment agreements with third countries, which also tend to include related points such as standards on labour, corporate governance and the environment, and development issues. Given the large share of the European Union in total global FDI flows, the outcome will have a big impact on regime development on the global level.

Bilateral and regional international investment agreements have proliferated over the past decade; they have increased in number from some 4,000 to some 6,000 (UNCTAD 2011: 100). Of the total stock of FDI, two-thirds to three-quarters is covered by an international investment agreement (IIA), split about half and half between regional arrangements (such as those of the European Union) and bilateral ones. In terms of actors involved, the developed countries have the highest numbers. But an increasing number of such treaties are concluded on the one hand between emerging countries (in particular China) and developing countries, and on the other hand among developing countries. In terms of content, about half of the treaties contain stipulations about double taxation, the other half only about liberalization. The new treaties often contain specific arrangements for dispute settlement and the number of arbitrations has grown very quickly.

This proliferation of bilateral agreements has significant disadvantages, as many treaties overlap, which creates confusion as to interpretation. On the other hand; the lack of uniformity also has an advantage, as the IIAs have been custom-made to fit the context and the specific interests of the partners.

10.3 Production factors: migration

10.3.1 The main problems

In recent decades, international migration of persons has increasingly been felt as problematic for a whole series of reasons. The most important are felt by the *host countries*:

- *Sheer size.* Massive inflows have been registered for the major host countries such as the United States and the European Union, but also for other developed countries. Emigration movements are driven by problems of security (war), famine (climatic or environmental disasters), politics (repression of human rights) and economic factors.
- *Unpredictable character.* The huge variability in influx makes it extremely difficult for a host country to react adequately.
- *Large number of origin countries.* The increased diversity of immigrants increases the difficulties of integration for each host country. Migration movements stretch over the whole globe and are not confined to the same region. This is due to the increase in the possibilities of communication (mobile phones, television) and the decrease in transport costs.
- The *illegal situation* of many immigrants. Their mere presence poses a challenge to the basic principles of the rule of law in host countries. Moreover, they are thought to use public services while not contributing to their financing.
- A *sense of insecurity* for the existing population of host countries, induced by evidence that some sending countries tend to stimulate the emigration of criminal or terrorist elements.

On the other hand there are also problems on the side of the *sending* countries. Emigration may relieve unemployment and poverty, but it also involves a drain on human resources – often, scarce talent that is badly needed for development. These problems may be mitigated in part by the secondary effect of migration, which is remittances. Indeed, for many developing countries this item has become one of the most important sources of income and considerably eases their balance of payments situation.

To many, the problems caused by the present migration flows are only a foreshadowing of what is to come. They point to the considerable potential for international migration that is building up. The three factors that determine migration (push, pull and friction) are all likely to lead to larger migration flows. The main push/pull factor is the very large difference in wealth levels between the developed countries and the poorer ones. Notwithstanding improvements in many developing countries (see Chapter 7), the differences remain very marked. On the push side we find the problems mentioned in the first bullet point of the previous paragraph. On the side of friction factors we observe that the costs of communication and transport have significantly decreased (see the third bullet point in the previous paragraph), while the friction costs are lowered further by the development of international traffickers who convey people to the destination countries by all sorts of means. On the pull side there is in the developed countries a constant demand for immigrant labour coming from the black economy and from the group of activities that are threatened by international competition. Policies to stem migration by doing something (providing development aid, putting in place sanctions concerning non-registered employment, etc.) regarding the causal factors tend to be rather ineffective in the short term.

10.3.2 The main public goods

The question of how to deal with international migration receives quite different answers depending on the theoretical basis from which it is approached (compare social embeddedness in Chapter 2). To individualists, the freedom to migrate is seen as an inalienable right. To those who put the interests of the community first, the migration decision resembles a decision to become a member of a club: the individual applies and the club can impose conditions on individuals before accepting them.[7]

Many economists see a clear advantage in openness; the textbooks say that international migration will improve the allocation of labour and thereby increase overall welfare. This would in theory lead to the adoption of the *principle of free movement of labour*. However, this macro view does not take into account three major countervailing aspects. One is the distribution of benefits and costs. For those whose source of income is threatened by immigration, there is a cost and they will oppose immigration. Another is that (unlike for goods) there is no such thing as comparative advantage; in migration terms it is absolute advantage to all those involved that counts. Finally, there are important externalities to migration; these bring additional costs and benefits, and challenge the assumptions of the macro neo-

classical theory (e.g. a brain drain for developing countries and the further concentration of wealth in a limited number of areas).[8]

The quantification of these positive and negative elements has proved to be a
difficult exercise,[9] but the available evidence[10] suggests that the net benefits are
dependent on the specific characteristics of the host country (its labour market,
social security benefit schemes, etc.) and of the length of stay of the migrant. As
the results from empirical economic studies into the net effects of immigration are
not conclusive, there is ample room for political arguments to shape the policy.
These involve state sovereignty, public security and national cultural identity, and
mix with economic policy aspects such as competitiveness and the safeguarding of
investments of human capital. In most cases this leads to the adoption of restrictive
and selective policies by host countries.

So, the present "non-regime" is largely constituted by unilateral rules about
immigration. Indeed, each national state wants to keep the right to determine who
will belong to its community and who will not. So, as yet countries have preferred
to do without a multilateral regime for migration.

This non-system is coming under increasing pressure, as it is apparently incap-
able of coping with the increasing problems. The main failure is in the incapacity
to control migration flows effectively. "Once national governments closed the *front*
door of legal immigration more or less strictly, most of the entrance . . . occurred
through the *side door* (asylum seekers, refugees, family reunification) or through the
back door (illegals)" (Straubhaar 2006). This is increasingly a problem in the sense
that the nation-state as a club of citizens can no longer provide the sort of goods
to the members of the club that these members expect from it. Illegal users challenge this exclusivity criterion, which leads to a rise in congestion cost for existing
members without a corresponding decrease in the membership fee.

10.3.3 Organizations

The present situation with respect to regime-building for international migration
is very fragmented. As is true in many other fields discussed in this book (e.g. the
environment, or development aid), there is no single international organization
dealing with migration. On the contrary, there is a whole network of different
intergovernmental organizations that deal with specific aspects of migration, such
as refugees, human trafficking, etc. Often they tend to compete with each other;
only rarely can one see examples of cooperation to fill certain gaps in the global
regime. There is no common terminology for defining problems, no agreement
on the type of public goods that should be provided, let alone on the governance
methods that should be deployed to provide them.

The following organizations (each of them dealing with a specific aspect of
migration) are involved:

- Migrants have *rights* under core human rights treaties and the UN convention
  on migrants.[11] Unfortunately, the UN convention is poorly ratified and

compliance remains a matter of concern. The United Nations and its specialized agencies have realized various other conventions. The objective of these conventions is to safeguard the rights of migrant workers and to establish standards for the way these persons and their families are to be treated.[12]

- *Labour migration.* Both the International Labour Organization and the International Organization for Migration are weak institutions in matters of migration. Neither of them has much regulatory power in this field. In principle, migrant workers need to be treated on an equal footing with autochthonous workers.
- *Refugees.* The United Nations High Commissioner for Refugees is a fairly strong organization that has emerged because of the need of governments (particularly those of the least developed countries) to deal with sudden upsurges in migration or with the persistent presence of masses of migrants. The principle is that asylum has to be given in cases when there is a "well-founded fear of persecution".
- *Services.* The World Trade Organization (WTO) has included in its General Agreement on Trade in Services (GATS) some stipulations that relate to those who need to cross borders to deliver a service.

It is clear that this set-up is not capable of dealing with the types of problems listed in the previous sections.

10.3.4 What should a new regime look like?[13]

So, some sort of multilateral solution needs to be worked out. To see what sort of solution would be possible, one needs to look for common interests among the participants. In the past, transaction costs could be minimized in a national setting, which is actually an institutional solution based on territorial exclusivity and legal rules for citizenship.

Theory (see Chapter 2) predicts that it will be easier to come to grips with the problems of openness in a *regional setting* than within a multinational setting. This does not seem to lead to concrete actions, though. The European Union still struggles with the setting up of a common external regime, although it has passed some agreements with neighbouring countries to protect it from excessively heavy pressure, notably of illegal immigrants. For the United States the same concern has led to some coordination between it and Central American states. However, as we have seen already, these arrangements tend to be at best only partial solutions, as the migration problem is now really a worldwide phenomenon. So, multilateral solutions need to be worked out.

The basic long-term *principle* of the new regime should in theory be that people can freely choose where to live and work. This principle prevails within most countries, and also in a supranational or regional setting such as the European Union. Taking away barriers, notably in combination with trade, might provide significant benefits (Anderson and Winters 2009). However, it is unlikely that this principle of free movement will be applied on the global level in the near future to all migrants.[14] So, the demands on the regime will be rather to improve the conditions for orderly movements of people and crisis management.[15] There are three requirements.

First, the regime would need to *provide effective measures for preventing the occurrence of sudden mass movements*. In this respect the following elements need to be looked at:

- National policies that promote growth and development in potential source countries. These include efficient markets, good governance and democratic government.
- National measures with respect to human rights, minorities, etc.
- International measures with respect to market access, development aid, stability of the financial system, etc. – in other words, making sure that the other international regimes work out well for economic growth in potential emigrant countries.

Second, there is the need to *facilitate orderly movements of a regular character*. In this category fall such elements as:

- International principles regarding labour rights, taxation, social security; pension for migrants and their dependants abroad. There is a clear case for the extension of the ILO conventions in this area.
- Rules for entry, exit and re-entrance to which source and host countries agree.
- Rules regarding illegal migrants.[16]

Third, there are the rules seeking to *balance the benefits and cost for both (potential) sending and host countries*. These include matters such as:

- A migration tax, to compensate sending countries for their loss in investment in human capital or to compensate the host country for the investment in club goods to which the newcomers have not contributed. This tax[17] has a number of side effects that make it difficult to implement in practice while at the same time substantiating as far as possible the basic principle of freedom of movement.[18]
- Standard agreements between countries on waiving the migration tax if there is sufficient bilateral compensation in terms of other aspects of the migration regime (e.g. development aid).[19]

So far, the analysis has been primarily inspired by economic considerations. However, there are more aspects to regime-building for such a sensitive subject as migration than economics. These refer to criteria such as comprehensiveness, transparency, accountability, etc.[20]

10.4 Market order: competition

10.4.1 The main problems

The WTO trade rounds have removed a great number of problems that inhibit international trade. That puts the accent on other aspects that can impinge on fair trade. I listed a few of them at the end of Chapter 5; they constituted the so-called "trade and" agenda. One of the major topics in this respect is the issue of competition (see Hope and Maeleng 1998; Waverman 1997).

With increasingly global markets, it is clear that many mergers and acquisitions and global business practices that restrict competition will affect the situation in individual countries. On the other hand, the regulation of anti-competitive behaviour by both private and public parties is still a national affair. This coexistence of global markets with national jurisdictions poses two sets of problems with respect to competition.

Behind borders

The removal of many obstacles to trade has opened national markets to foreign competition. This is supposed to have positive welfare effects. These effects can, however, be reaped only if the markets are really contestable – that is to say, if the exporters can effectively access such markets under normal competitive conditions. However, anti-competitive behaviour by local producers may impinge upon such access. This can take several forms; an example is collusive agreements among importers. Particularly negative is the practice of bid-rigging in public procurement processes. Competition law should place sanctions on this type of behaviour. If national competition authorities apply different rules to foreign companies as compared with domestic ones, the principle of non-discrimination is violated, which could have strong effects on trade. It would even have a negative effect on development; there is ample evidence that a good competition regime decreases corruption and directly fosters total factor productivity (e.g. Voigt 2009).

Beyond borders

National competition authorities in general exercise their jurisdiction on cases that have an effect within their borders, irrespective of the location of the firm (at home or abroad). In so doing they may take decisions that have implications far beyond their borders. Many smaller countries will not have the capacity to investigate such cases with extra-territorial effects, so they may go unchecked. On the other hand, large countries may take decisions that have strong extra-territorial effects and hence may lead to conflicts with partner countries. For instance, if for domestic reasons EU authorities block a merger of two MNFs with global activity, this may lead to a loss in efficiency in other countries where there was no threat to competition. Many such cases have indeed occurred (e.g. Klodt 2001). Avoiding the ensuing conflicts requires a global view on the objectives and principles of competition policy. The same is true for reasons that have to do with the effectiveness of the implementation of competition policy. MNFs may have their headquarters and hold their assets in a country outside the one where the offence takes place. Competent authorities are thus handicapped to investigate the case as they have no access to the relevant documents; and under the assumption that they have been able to judge the case they have no means to make firms comply.

10.4.2 The main public goods

The definitions of competition policy vary considerably in scope between different countries. A fairly restricted definition limits competition policy to anti-trust policy (in other words, to the control of cartels) and to the prevention of abuse of dominant positions. A wider definition would also encompass questions of dumping and state aid. This wider definition of competition policy is not very adequate here, as the latter aspects are already dealt with under the present WTO trade regulations and dispute settlement mechanisms.[21]

Anti-competitive business practices can have a serious negative effect on the economy. Mainstream economics provides clear recipes for competition policy (see, for instance, Neumann 2001) and defines the public good of a fair competition regime. However, the problem is that many countries have very different views about the need for a textbook-inspired competition policy.

There is much debate over the *principles* on which a multinational competition regime should be based. Among the group of developed countries there is considerable convergence, in particular between the European Union and the United States. However, it should not be forgotten that even in the European Union some countries have only recently started to adhere to the principles of the EU Treaty, which boil down to three rules: no cartels, no abuse of a dominant position and no state aid.[22] Developing and transition countries have only recently started to enact competition laws and create competition authorities. There is much diversity in approaches (Metha and Evenett 2006).

The *arguments for intervention* on a global scale and the conclusion of a WTO-based multilateral agreement on competition (MAC) came mainly from the European Union. The Union argued that the adoption by all WTO members of common principles on competition and on procedures for dealing with disputes would reduce the legal uncertainties and the number of conflicts between jurisdictions. This in turn would lead to a decrease in transaction and compliance cost (e.g. Meiklejohn 1999). It was said that a MAC would make it possible to:

*   avoid discrimination; this would improve allocational efficiency;
*   recover the effectiveness in competition policy disciplining MNFs; this would enhance growth.

The Union was aware of the fact that many developing countries did not have much experience with competition policy, so proposed technical assistance.

The *arguments against* came from different strands. Opposition from developing countries was particularly fierce (e.g. Singh 2004; Bhattacharjea 2006). They argued that the proposition was based on Western ideas and practices and that a development-oriented competition policy had to be studied first. To these arguments were added those of other groups, which can be summarized as follows:

- The proposal was not needed because the present trade-related measures cope with most of the problems.
- It was unfeasible because of difficulties in international cooperation due to the absence of universally accepted principles and notions about contribution to growth.
- It was unfair, as Western MNFs would gain extra power to wipe local companies off the national markets of LDCs.
- It was unjust, as it impinges on national sovereignty.

So, to sum up, many are convinced that anti-competitive practices need to be addressed in an international setting. There is, however, much disagreement as to what any multilateral agreement should include and in what organization it should be sited.

10.4.3 Organizations

There is at this stage no international body that is responsible for competition matters. The international organizations that have dealt in one way or another with the issue are the following:

- *The OECD.* Since 1967 it has analysed options and and in the following years has adopted several recommendations on multinational enterprises that contain some codes on anti-competitive practices (see, for example, OECD 1987, 1995).[23]
- *The United Nations (UNCTAD).* In 1980 a set of Multilaterally Agreed Equitable Principles and Rules for the Control of Restrictive Business Practices was adopted. However, these are recommendations and are not binding on member states. Since then, UNCTAD has notably served as a forum for debating the best practices in pro-development competition policy and as a provider of services for administrative capacity-building.[24]
- *The WTO.* The attractiveness of the WTO for taking on board competition matters is based on a series of features. First, extending the remit of an existing organization seems easier than creating a new one. Second, the WTO is the only international organization that has both the competences (strong powers) and the experience in using them (including dispute settlement) that are a *conditio sine qua non* for an effective competition regime.[25] Third, there are strong linkages between competition and trade, the prime task of the WTO.[26] On the initiative of the European Union, the WTO ministerial conference of

1996 agreed to set up a (study) working group on competition policy. However, it is precisely these strict and universal features that are unacceptable to developing countries. Consequently, during the 2001 Doha conference the EU proposals to include competition in the agenda of the new trade round were not accepted; the issue was taken off the negotiating agenda in 2004.[27]

In view of the present stalemate on the multilateral front, a number of other solutions are now applied:

- *Bilateral solutions.* The most important in this respect is the United States–European Union relation. Indeed, here the potential conflicts are as yet the most important and the need to come to some sort of solution is the most pressing. The 1991 EU–USA (transatlantic) Agreement has come under severe strain on several occasions when either the EU or the US authorities judged cases in a way that was considered to harm the interest of the partner country's firms. Both entities now cooperate better in matters of fact-finding, principle-setting, etc.
- *Regional solutions.* The European Union and NAFTA have set competition rules for their areas. The former regime is very strong and effective; the Commission has many powers to investigate anti-competitive behaviour and to impose fines for infringements. NAFTA has as yet a much weaker regime. In other areas, such as ASEAN, the subject is under study. Both the European Union and the United States have tried to cope with the problem of the absence of a MAC by including rules about competition in bilateral agreements on trade and investment.

10.4.4 What should a new regime look like?

Multilateral

Notwithstanding the advantages that a WTO-based multilateral competition regime might have, political economy considerations make it unlikely that one will be realized in the future. Indeed, many factors inhibit for the time being the setting up of a MAC. Yet the problems are real and have to be addressed.

Sectoral limitation

Collective action problems are much less important in cases when the number of issues to be debated is limited. This has been demonstrated very clearly in the field of the environment, where many regimes have been worked out for coping with specific problems (see Chapter 8). Such a more limited set-up might take the form of a free-standing regime or organization.[28] One could start work with the very basic instruments (see Chapters 2 and 4), namely information and coordination. The main actors would then be national competition authorities, which see an advantage in cooperation. Subjects to be covered could be:

- exchange of general information;
- mutual technical assistance;
- consultation on the application of law in specific cases;
- support in investigating and judging cases;
- mechanisms for settling disputes.

Such a regime might develop gradually and could very well create a start from which it is easier to move to a next stage. Specific issues that are in the interest of developing countries, such as hard-core international cartels, could then be negotiated first. Theoretical work (Beverelli and Mahlstein 2007) does indeed indicate that with the increasing complexity of their international linkages in both consumption and production, developing countries become increasingly interested in agreements on the external aspects of the conduct of their competition policy.

Regional/bilateral

The second option that may develop further is the *bilateral* one. This would evolve along the lines indicated in the last bullet point of section 10.4.3. It would have some similarity to the stipulation on investment (see section 10.2.4). Notably, the EU is very active in pursuing this strategy and up till now has been rather successful both in introducing the subject in bilateral and regional agreements, and in exporting its ideas on best national practices.[29]

10.5 The Internet

10.5.1 The main problems

The very quick spread of the Internet has brought with it a multifaceted set of problems (e.g. Graham 2001). I have selected the following four for further scrutiny.

Dominance over content

The characteristics of the Internet mean that there is an increasing risk of commercial or special interest groups taking over control of certain parts of it. This may lead to a de facto limitation of information. Limits to information may come from two other sources. The first is the Internet service provider. Most consumers are unlikely to subscribe to more than one. Some of these gateways are run as a largely integrated sub-web with a wide range of services. Under such conditions, consumers are unlikely to access another supply of services. The second is the browser. This determines what is found and what not. If the cost of switching is high, consumers can become locked into one system.

Provision of illegal goods and services

In moral terms the provision of illegal goods and services is particularly important in cases when there is a breach of universal values and rules; a case in point is a film related to paedophilia. However, in economic terms the illegal copying is much more important. Many people think that information, books, games, music, etc. should all be available for free, and the Internet gives them the technical means to obtain them for free. However, the law protects intellectual property on cultural goods in order to let novelists, songwriters, musicians, actors and filmmakers earn a financial return on their investment.

Cybercrime in commercial activities

Many people and firms now rely on the Internet to do business or to operate transactions. The Net is the marketplace, but transactions that are made there have to be followed by some physical delivery and by a compensating financial transaction. Each element of this chain may be the subject of fraud and crime: the quality of the good is not what has been promised; credit card numbers are used for other purposes; money transferred is diverted, etc.

Breach of privacy of individuals

Exchange of information for medical purposes brings with it the danger of these data falling into the hands of third parties. Other problems arise with the use of data on patterns concerning personal preferences (shopping, information searches, etc.).

10.5.2 The main public goods

The previous subsection has made clear that many aspects of the functioning of the Internet have a public "bad" character.[30] So, avoiding them provides just as many public goods. They can be listed in line with the five public bads from the previous section as follows:

- *Diversity of sources of information.* The Internet provides an unprecedented means of instant information-gathering at very low cost. It opens possibilities such as tele-education. The right of access of citizens to such diverse sources of information is certainly a public good. A first instrument to be used to realize this public good is regulation. Governments may oblige providers to realize a minimum of interconnectivity, so that consumers are not trapped in a subsystem. Moreover, they may step in with public production in the event that the private market shows important failures. A comparable case is that of public broadcasting.
- *Good functioning of the market.* Fundamental to the market economy is fair competition. The new forms under which competition presents itself on the

Internet needs further analysis and, on the basis of the results of that analysis, new forms of regulation need to be elaborated. The instruments that governments have on this score form part of regular competition policy; they are not specific to the Internet. The specific features of the Internet make their application far from easy, however (Graham 2001; Cave and Mason 2001).

- *Absence of illegal services.* Countries wanting to protect their citizens from attacks on certain values will want to block the transmission of offensive material such as publicity for drugs, or information about terrorist methods. They will want to prevent children from being confronted with hard pornography. The main instrument by which they can do so is of a technical nature; it consists in the filtering of information that can be accessed by the users of the Internet. Some governments, such as China's, have tried to do such filtering themselves. Others, like the French, have tried to implement policy with this instrument by obliging the providers to comply with national law and make sure they do the filtering. Although a number of such cases are clear universal public goods, many others are subject to considerable controversy. Indeed, values differ, and what seems a basic right in one civilization may constitute an offence to public morale in another (an example is drinking alcohol). The universal character of the Internet poses a clear challenge to policymakers in this respect.
- *Smoothly functioning e-commerce.* The Internet opens up a whole set of possibilities for new types of business. It brings down transaction costs for many users (an efficiency criterion). Moreover, it presents opportunities for improved distribution: firms that are located in distant places will now be connected to potential partners in a similar way to those in central locations. This holds also for developing countries, which should be better able to catch up with developed countries, as the Internet makes very low demands on the cost of infrastructure. The instrument by which to realize this is of a legal character: the recognition of such elements as the electronic signature. Most of the instrument is again of a technological nature: firms wanting to make sure that the partners they deal with are sound have to accept identification rules and verification rules that often pass by specific devices on their computers. Governments may oblige Internet firms to apply standardized devices.
- *Safeguarding of privacy of individuals and firms.* The public good character of privacy is clear from the very strict laws that some countries have passed on the subject. However, there is controversy about this point, as some countries consider that the "excessive" protection of the individual constitutes an undue limit to normal commercial practices on the one hand and on the capacity of the state to safeguard security on the other hand. Here, technical devices (including software) are essential. Governments should make sure that such software is applied by Internet service providers.[31]

If there are so many public good aspects involved, the question then is "Should one intervene or not?" In the first instance, intervention would imply public regulation. *Arguments for intervention* are that regulation:

- prevents public bads, such as paedophilia and loss of privacy; prevention cannot be effectively done by other means;
- stimulates the type of technical progress (filtering of information) and legal progress (effective regulation) that is necessary for taking things forward.

Arguments against intervention are that regulation is:

- Bad economics; it bridles market forces, while unleashing them would produce growth of new services and hence overall growth. Moreover, it risks fossilizing structures that may have only a temporary value,[32] given the great uncertainty as to the direction of development of the system.
- Unconstitutional; people have the right to free speech and free gathering of information; public surveillance of information access can give rise to bigger problems than letting it carry on freely.
- Ineffective; even if it were desirable to regulate it, regulation would not work as people can always bypass such measures.
- Unneeded; self-regulation has (for the time being) worked out rather well.
- Unfeasible: bringing all states together would be too lengthy a process and the chances of its leading to any good solution would be limited.

10.5.3 Organizations

The Internet has a very idiosyncratic form of governance (Mueller 2010). It actually functions without a central governing body.[33] It has developed from the bottom up; its rules are the result of consensus-building among its users.[34] This has been made possible as the initial users and designers of the net were notably engineers and computer scientists who had their strong professional codes and shared understandings. The technical infrastructure of the Net is the remit mainly of two organizations, the IETF and ICANN.

The IETF

The process of policy formulation is largely carried out by the Internet Engineering Task Force (IETF). This body functions as an online community of interested parties (an open forum) and is in charge of the development of technical standards such as communication protocols. The IETF represents in a sense the basic spirit of the Internet; it has no formal legal status, it has no fixed membership and its objective to facilitate open discussion of the Internet's architecture. The IETF is financed by meeting charges.

ICANN

Coping with the problems of names is the Internet Corporation of Assigned Names and Numbers (ICANN). It is a hybrid form of an online community (like the IETF) and a traditional government structure. It comprises individuals drawn from global business, academic and civil society organizations, and representatives from accredited organizations such as the World Intellectual Property Organization.

So far, this original bottom-up decision-making structure has proven remarkably resilient and robust, notwithstanding some inherent flaws. The question is whether this self-regulation can survive. The pressures for regulation have grown, given the increased importance of the Web. Two types of solutions have been tried out

First, *national governments* try to regulate access to parts of the Net. However, national regulation cannot ultimately be the solution; on the contrary, the diversity of the sort of national regulations may constitute a new problem.

Second, *international action* has come from some existing major organizations (G8, UNO). However, as their initiatives have not been followed by much progress a limited number of players with large interests have tried to establish a new organization (ACTA). I detail these as follows:

- The G8 has on several occasions expressed its concern with Internet security. It has not initiated any negotiation, however; in conformity with its structure it has invited interested parties to invest in the safeguarding of international principles.
- The Internet Governance Forum (IGF) is an organization created under the auspices of the United Nations. It comprises four stakeholder groups: governments, the private sector, civil society and intergovernmental organizations. The legitimacy of the public-sector would justify a certain tendency towards regulation. However, not much has materialized over the past (Gutterman 2011).
- The Anti-Counterfeiting Trade Agreement (ACTA) is designed as a self-standing multilateral treaty outside existing organizations such as the WTO. It has the objective of better protecting intellectual property through rules on enforcement. It targets counterfeit goods, generic medicines and copyright infringements. It notably wants to stop the very large rise in the piracy of movies, music, etc. over the Internet. As such, it is supported by a coalition of large-business interests and the most developed countries. It is opposed by a coalition of Web-based groups in favour of freedom of information and of developing countries that are fearful of having to pay excessively high prices for imported medicines and NGOs afraid of breaches of privacy. As a consequence the ACTA has run into serious difficulties, the more so because important groups in major signatory countries (in particular in the EU) have voiced very serious concerns about privacy protection and have stalled ratification.

10.5.4 What could a new regime look like?

The tools that governments have for making sure that the provision of the basic public goods identified in the previous sections is safeguarded fall into a number of categories. The first is in the confirmation of the *basic principle* of the freedom of information. The second comes in some form of regulation, supported by technical means of access to the Net and/or surveillance of actions on the Net. Most fundamental in this respect is the basic physical infrastructure on which much private and public activity depends. So, the security of the Net is of the utmost importance. For the time being, however, it is unclear how robust the structures are against major cyber-attacks.

So, the *conclusion* must be that it is increasingly necessary to harmonize national regulations and to rethink the governance of the Net, including international regulatory institutions and codes of conduct. As yet, however, these have not been crystallized out. The IGF does not seem to be the nucleus of a regulatory body.

10.6 Summary and conclusions

- The global "system" of regimes as described in the previous chapters is not complete: there are important "missing links" that call for action. These missing links are strongly concentrated in the areas that have to do with markets and allocation. In this sense they are all closely related to trade issues.
- *Direct investment* is a first case where action is needed. After the aborted attempt of the Multilateral Agreement on Investment, a new regime should be elaborated. It should take more regard of the interests of non-Western countries, should best be grafted on the existing framework of the WTO, and should be composed of the best of bilateral and regional arrangements.
- The situation for *migration* is in stark contrast to the one for goods: the present international regime is very embryonic and, in practice, national controls dominate the situation. Migration movements do not need a WTO-type regime; what is needed here is a regime that is capable of preventing (and, if necessary, dealing with) sudden mass movements (crisis prevention and management).
- Diverging national *competition* rules risk distorting increasingly international economic exchange. Given the close link with trade and the need for some sort of dispute settlement procedure, the WTO framework would be a good locus for global regime development on this issue. However, for the time being reasons of political economy preclude such solutions, so the most likely future development is a free-standing regime that will improve transparency and mutual learning by the exchange of information and by cooperation.
- The *Internet* is still in the development stage. The world has not yet come to grips with the dilemma it presents to society. On the one hand it permits instant global switching of information, with entirely positive effects on innovation and growth. On the other hand, many public goods are not provided.
- The *general conclusion* is that for the topics discussed major advances in regime-building are very unlikely in the foreseeable future.

11

EVALUATION

11.1 Introduction

The preceding chapters have described how the growing interdependence between the various economies in the world has created the need for global public goods (GPGs) and this in turn has led to the development of international institutions. These chapters have also shown that this global international institutional system is far from ideal. Because of the difficulties of collective action, certain aspects are not covered, obsolete structures have difficulty in being adapted and there is a lack of consistency between the actions of many self-contained organizations. In the words of Nobel Prize winner Joseph Stiglitz (2002: 22):

> We have a system that can be called *global governance without global government*, one in which a few institutions . . . and a few players . . . dominate the scene, but in which many of those affected by their decisions are left almost voiceless.
>
> It's time to . . . think once again about how decisions get made at the international level – and in whose interests – and to place less emphasis on ideology and to look more at what works . . . Globalization can be reshaped . . . [to] create a new global economy in which growth is not only more sustainable and less volatile but the fruits of this growth are more equitably shared.

Since the publication of these words, some things have changed for the better – in particular, the growing importance of the G20. Other things have changed for the worse: for example, the stalemates in WTO and the climate negotiations. So, the basic criticism still holds. This citation contains two elements: an evaluation of past developments and a suggestion for future change. The first element is the subject of this chapter; the latter element is the subject of the next chapter.

In making an evaluation of the past, I will follow the same systematic set-up as used in the previous chapters. I give a comparative overview of the basic features of the regimes that were analysed in depth in the previous chapters. In the subsequent sections I will set out the most important findings for each of these features. In this way I will deal subsequently with the basic rationale for regime formation, the major public goods provided, the principles on which the regimes are based and the modalities for implementation (governance). I conclude with a short overview of the major achievements and shortcomings of the present institutional set-up.

As usual, I round off the presentation with a short summary of the main elements discussed in this chapter.

11.2 Evaluation

11.2.1 An overview of the main features of the regimes

Table 11.1 gives an overview of the main features (in the rows) of each of the major regimes (columns) that I analysed in Chapters 5–9. The subjects of the rows reflect the choices that I made in Chapters 2–4 for the set-up of the regime chapters in sections. The top rows refer to such basic notions as the definition of the common interest that countries have in getting together – in other words, the motive for their collective action. This is made more concrete in terms of specific public goods that need to be provided to the international community. The middle rows indicate the organizations that deal with the provision of public goods, followed by the basic principles that govern each regime. Next I specify some governance aspects, in particular the most important instruments that are used to get to results. The bottom part of the table describes the results obtained so far in the provision of the major public goods and the open issues that still remain.

11.2.2 Rationale

Globalization has spread rapidly, largely under the impetus of multinational firms. It has eroded the capacity of national governments to deal independently with problems and thereby increased the need for international cooperation in the framework of international institutions.

The efforts of these institutions need to be oriented towards a set of *basic objectives*. Among them, economic growth takes pride of place, in particular in those countries that have a considerable poverty problem. But other societal concerns also call for action. Among them are traditional ones, such as respect for human values and for sustainability. Also important in this respect is equitable development. These basic objectives have not changed profoundly over time, notwithstanding very rapid and profound changes in the structure of the economy, such as the change from manufacturing to information, the increased sophistication of products and services, the growing internationalization of business (trade and direct investment), the increase in the mobility of capital and the Internet.

TABLE 11.1 Basic features of the global order

	Trade/alloc. efficiency	Finance/stabilization	Development aid/equity	Environment/sustainability	Labour/social
Basic rationale	Enhancing economic growth	Enhancing economic growth	More balanced distribution of wealth	Safeguarding sustainable development	Labour rights are universal human rights
Public good provision	Enhancing free trade in goods and services	Stable financial relations Avoiding crisis and contagion	Provide capital Keep coherence in diverse policies	Stabilization of climate Prevention of ozone layer depletion Maintaining biodiversity	Improve labour conditions For social rights, prevent race to the bottom
Main organization	WTO	IMF	World Bank	UNEP	ILO
Basic principle	Most favoured nation Non-discrimination	Precaution Solidarity Conditionality	Solidarity Conditionality	Precaution Polluter pays Common but differentiated responsibilities	Freedom of association Elimination of exploitation Non-discrimination
Instrument	Dispute settlement Sanctions Retaliation	Standards Financial assistance	Loans Coordination of donors (grants)	Standards Pollution rights Tradable permits Bans on products	Standards Tripartite negotiation (labour unions, employers, government) Complaint
Results	Considerable progress (lower barriers in more areas)	Reasonable in prevention Limited in management	Mixed	Slow progress	Slow progress
Open issues	Maintaining other values Conflict of principles	Inherent instability Choice of instruments	Fragmentation Lack of effectiveness and efficiency	Further deterioration of situation No uniform framework	Tension between "social dumping" and gradual improvement

11.2.3 Delivery of global public goods: the factor "interest"

The changing structure of the global economy reinforces the need for existing global public goods and creates a need for new ones. Given the constraints on collective action, regimes come about only if there are very good reasons for them (see Chapter 2). We found that factors such as "awareness" and "knowledge" are important, but the factor that carries most weight is actually "interest". The sequence in which regimes have been set up and developed is very specific for each regime and depends on the changes in the constellations of interest. Note that such changes in interest can actually be entailed by the successful development of a regime in another area of public goods. A case in point is trade: it has increased the vulnerability of countries to macroeconomic shocks and to international differences in social protection.

The role of the factor "interest" on the global level is very clear in the *trade* field. The early creation of GATT for liberalizing trade in industrial goods and the subsequent development of GATT and later the WTO in matters of trade in services and allied subjects (such as intellectual property) was indeed based on clear economic advantages based on international specialization. It has even been able to integrate the work of a pre-existing specialist organization for telecommunications.[1] Lack of a clear common interest explains the absence of progress on related scores, such as competition and investment.

The case for *finance* and stability became very clear in the interwar period, when monetary unrest deepened the negative effects of the crisis. Since then the main problem, and with it the main public good, has shifted from stability on foreign exchange markets towards the stability of the international financial system. This seems to be a logical step in the sequence of regime-building. Indeed, the "interest" argument applies here in full, as actions for the improvement of exchanges in matters of trade (and investment) can only bear their full fruits if stable financial and monetary conditions prevail. The enormous importance of this factor has again become evident during the crisis that began in 2007, which has led to a strengthening of the regime.

The *development* problem came to the foreground immediately after the Second World War. The factor of interest for donors may not be immediately clear. However, two elements should nevertheless be brought forward. First, the (under)development problem also (albeit to a limited extent) constrains growth possibilities in the developed world. Second, security aspects have often been dominant in the allocation of aid. Otherwise, development aid has largely been motivated by equity aspects.

It is a well-known fact that the concern for *environmental* problems is taken seriously only after basic needs have been settled. The emergence of global environmental action and its subsequent development in the 1970s, then, fits into the overall picture of a gradual shift in "interest".

The case of the social aspects, notably of *labour standards*, has its own particularities. The development of the social aspects would have been stimulated by the almost universal interest in the subject. However, the perception by developing countries that standards are a barrier to growth has been a formidable obstacle to global regime-building and explains why progress has been slow.

11.2.4 Organizations

As we survey past developments, we see that many of the international organizations (IOs) that are responsible for governing the world economy were founded in the aftermath of the Second World War. This applies notably to GATT and the WTO, responsible for trade, and to the World Bank and IMF, twin institutions responsible for stabilization and balanced development. Some of the UN organizations are even older, such as the ILO, which deals with social and labour issues. Under the influence of new needs, these organizations have been adapted and new organizations have been created.

In cases when there was a strong pre-existing organization, it can be seen that organizational solutions to emerging problems have been made within the present frameworks. Examples are the switch from GATT to the WTO and the gradual expansion of the remit of the WTO into new areas such as services. Another example is the mission change of the IMF.[2]

However, for many – often political – reasons, it is often decided to create a new institution. An example is the creation of the Financial Stability Board in the field of stability. Political pressures can even lead to the creation of a multitude of organizations in a specific field; such organizational fragmentation is particularly problematic in the fields of development aid and environmental protection.

The formalization of institutions into international organizations with their detailed rules has been done for a very good reason: to create strong and stable answers to global problems. Such a rule-based system gives predictability and reliability and is conducive to investment in international relations. However, the advantages come at a cost: they have led to a lack of flexibility. In practice, stable formal institutions have much difficulty in adapting to new realities – hence the advantage of certain less formal institutions, such as the G7, G8 and G20, that have accommodated new players and are capable of operating in a network of formal and informal institutions (e.g. Sapir 2009).

The overall set-up of organizations suffers from four major *problems*. First, owing to mission creep for existing organizations and the creation of new ones, the responsibilities of the various organizations tend to overlap each other (e.g. the WTO and UNCTAD; the IMF and the World Bank), giving rise to high costs and uncertainty.[3] Second, there are gaps in responsibilities, leaving room for failures of the system (e.g. in regard to investments or competition). Third, the organizations (in the words of Stiglitz cited in the introduction to this chapter) provide a lot of governance but little government. Fourth, the power distribution is unbalanced: emerging countries and developing countries tend to be underrepresented in most of these institutions.

With respect to the solving of the first two of these problems, one might have expected a stronger role for the United Nations. The global sectoral organizations are all part of the UN system. However, the United Nations has not yet been able to coordinate the various regimes better, let alone integrate their actions in a consistent way. Moreover, the deficiencies of the United Nations in matters of effectiveness and efficiency make many countries doubt whether a gain in effectiveness could be obtained by moving from the present situation towards a UN-dominated one.

When it comes to solving the third and fourth problems, things have changed for the better during the past decade, notably because of the emergence of the G20. The G20 has taken a certain role in matters of *government*. It has taken the lead in the discussions about the best way to deal the crisis that began in 2008, redistributing the roles of the various international organizations. It is more legitimate than other institutions as it represents some 85 per cent of global GDP and includes all the world's major economies (including developing countries).

11.2.5 The role of values and ideology

The main regimes I have analysed have all been conceived as functions of the basic norms and traditions (ideologies) of the Western countries. They represent different blends of liberalism and public intervention. For some time this situation precluded universalism for these major regimes. However, two major developments have fundamentally changed this situation. First, the demise of the centrally planned economies and their transition to a market economy has meant that the values of the WTO have become acceptable to these countries. A similar remark can be made with respect to the group of developing countries. After decolonization a large number of the newly independent states that emerged tried to get to grips with the challenges confronting them by means of state interventionism. Most have seen the negative side of this choice and have moved to market-driven economic systems. So, transition countries (including Russia and China), developing countries (such as South Africa and Indonesia) and even some of the least developed countries have decided to become members of the global economic organizations described in previous chapters.

The dominant role of ideology can be illustrated for all three basic economic functions as follows.

Optimizing allocation

The fundamental economic function of optimizing allocation has been entrusted on the global level to the WTO. It is based on a liberal ideology (free access to markets for goods and services), which in turn is in line with the results of economic theory. For the movement of production factors the situation is less clear-cut. The abortive attempt to arrive at a direct investment regime (MAI) departed from a liberal ideology, and the regime was intended to create the conditions for optimizing the free flow. For other capital movements, liberalization has become wide spread, even without a formal regime. For labour movements, no regime has yet even passed the stage of proposal; but the liberal ideology does not find very fertile soil here.

Creating conditions for stability

The major institution in charge of creating conditions is the IMF. It creates the conditions for growth with respect to macroeconomic stability. The ideological basis for its activity has been shaped to a large extent by the dominant market economies, notably the United States. The recent changes in the IMF have made the institution more responsive to other sensitivities. Other public goods, such as a regime for competition, have not yet passed the stage of proposals, partly because of differences in the views of elites on the relative advantages and disadvantages of the regulation of economic forces.

Respecting social preferences

There is no clear overriding ideology at the foundation of the regimes dealing with social and environmental objectives. The world is very diverse in these matters. On the one hand the United States has a tendency to impose individualism and liberalism, and a minimalist involvement of the state. On the other hand, the European and Asian countries want their quite different values to be respected. The search for clarity and unity is still going on.

11.2.6 The role of principles

The elaboration of the basic principles has been done in very idiosyncratic ways for the different regimes; the various columns of Table 11.1 show that there is no "meta" principle that could serve a unifying role. The emergence of a leading principle is often dependent on a variety of contributions by different parties at the negotiation table. For reasons of transaction cost minimization it is efficient in an initial stage not to talk too much about details of organization and governance but to see how far it is possible to agree on principles. In emerging regimes we can observe this aspect very clearly; cases in point are the three principles governing the environmental regimes and those of the social protection regime of the ILO. The "non-regime" of the Internet (Chapter 10) is interesting in this respect; it is based on the principle of free access to information. This is clearly inspired by a liberal ideology. However, as this conflicts with societal preferences and corporate interests (intellectual property), adaptations have been proposed, although they have not been realized.

In a number of cases the emergence of dominant principles has been facilitated by unanimity in scientific circles about the basic working of the system. With respect to the contribution of the economics profession we see a diversified pattern. Economic theory supports strongly the case for the freedom of markets for goods and services. The economic case for free foreign direct investment (FDI) is strong as well. However, the advantages of the freedom of other capital flows are still not sufficiently convincing to favour the setting of general principles there. In environmental matters the "polluter pays" principle is based on the conviction that it limits possible economic distortions. For global labour movements the net advantages of a free regime for both sending and receiving countries are not very clear-cut (Winters *et al.* 2004), so no principle has been worked out yet. As regards stabilization at the global level, it has become abundantly clear that markets left to themselves cause very large problems. However, the regimes created have not been clearly vested in principles, although here too the principles of precaution and solidarity seem to apply in a similar way as in some other regimes.

11.2.7 Instruments (governance)

International regimes try to realize their objectives by imposing obligations on their members and adherents. So, these latter are major actors in the implementation stage of the former. Member states may use the instruments that seem most adequate nationally to realize objectives agreed internationally (for example, for the limitation of pollution, some may use taxation, others tradable permits).

To check compliance with those obligations (and hence the effectiveness of their actions), all IOs use surveillance and monitoring instruments. To make such monitoring effective, countries must observe the rule of transparency. Only under that condition is a system of monitoring and surveillance possible at relatively low cost. An example of such pressure for transparency can be found in the case of the WTO, which has urged the abolition of opaque measures such as non-tariff barriers. The monitoring does not need to be done by the international organization in question. Some regimes rely on monitoring by interested parties (e.g. in the case of trade); others depend partly on NGOs (in the case of the environment).

Once a good monitoring system is in place, *reputation* should then do most of the job of making countries comply with the international regimes they have committed themselves to. Compliance with standards, for instance, signals to the international community that you are part of a respectable set, which leads to lower costs of capital or to higher inward investment. This is the more so because partners know that the quality of the deals they will get in future will depend on their good reputation. NGOs target both companies and countries on the aspect of reputation to enhance compliance.

Many countries that are willing to live up to international commitments find it difficult to do so because of weaknesses in their institutions and administrations. To cope with this problem, two instruments have been used. First, the organizations dealing with development aid, such as the World Bank, have put in place support schemes (e.g. for helping countries to live up to environmental standards). Moreover, all major international organizations have put in place *technical assistance programmes* targeting improvement of the administrative capacity of countries to deal with specific details of implementation (for example, the WTO for trade regulation, the ILO for labour standards).

As the instruments discussed in the previous paragraphs are common to all organizations, they have been omitted from Table 11.1. The case is different for some other instruments for compliance referred to in Chapter 4 (in particular, those set out in Table 4.1). I will shortly comment on the use of each of them.

Regulation is the basis of most regimes. We saw in previous chapters that a wide variety of forms (treaties, protocols, codes) are used. Regulation is given form in the basic trade law of the WTO, the rules for stability in the banking sector, the standards set for environmental protection and the standards set for labour conditions of the ILO. The degree to which these regulations can actually be enforced is very different from one IO to another. The most developed system is operated by the WTO; it involves litigation. Its Dispute Settlement Procedure is very elaborate and can actually lead to sanctions; the WTO allows retaliation by the victim if an offending country fails to comply with the result of a dispute settlement procedure. This is not an optimal instrument. A better option would be to remove the cause of the problem.[4] However, the introduction of such better instruments has not been accepted by the member countries. A less developed system has been put in place by the ILO. Its complaints procedure can only be launched if the Governing Body appoints by consensus a committee of inquiry, and no sanctions can be brought to bear against a country that does not stop its infringements. It is much less used in practice than the WTO one.

Financial measures are less common in the present landscape of international regimes. Recall that no country has accepted the use of financial disincentives by IOs – certainly not in terms of taxes, but not even in the form of financial sanctions. So, the main use is in terms of incentives. Finances come in basically two forms – loans and grants – and both are extensively used. Loans are made notably by the IMF and the World Bank; grants by a host of development organizations, including a special branch of the World Bank group. Most of these loans are conditional on meeting targets in terms of budget deficits, etc. The IMF has the strongest position in matters of conditionality; if the recipient country does not agree to the terms, the IMF can withdraw support for national plans, and, as alternative financing will be hard to find in an extreme crisis situation, a country will in general comply.

Coordination measures can be found in a variety of forms. Actually, the monitoring discussed previously often flows over into a simple form of coordination (as described in section 4.3.3). For instance, the regular surveillance of the compliance with labour standards gives rise to coordination of positions and persuasion of the country under scrutiny. In a similar way, the surveillance of the macroeconomic situation in a country by the IMF leads to discussions between IMF staff and national civil servants and politicians on consistent policy-making. On a higher level one sees coordination between the most important countries in the G20, OECD and the Governing Body of the IMF. Such coordination has been of particular importance for the actions taken to overcome the crisis that started in 2007. The highest forms of coordination – the setting of common priorities, and agreements on the implementation of regulation – are seldom used. In practice we do not see any regular institutionalized coordination mechanisms of this sort in the major IOs.

11.2.8 Results

The global institutional system was devised in broad outlines more than half a century ago. Since then it has gradually developed. On many scores the system has been able to show progress; this is most visible in matters of trade and the environment. In other respects, progress has been rather limited (labour), or even absent (competition). Recently, progress on many GPGs seems to have come to a halt; examples are the stalemate in the WTO and the difficulties in renewing the climate regime. The (lack of) progress has been dependent on a set of factors (see section 2.7.5), of which the following are the most significant:

- *Effectiveness.* The delivery of a public good has had beneficial effects and hence the organization dealing with it has shown further progress. This has happened in the case of trade. On the other hand, many of the organizations we have discussed – in particular, many UN subsidiaries – are not very effective.
- *Power.* In the post-war period the dominance of the United States was instrumental in creating a number of regimes. However, US power is now often considered as a negative factor for further development, as it is seen as being used to favour the United States' own interests (e.g. concerning trade and climate) or its own ideology (finance), disregarding the interests of the emerging economies.[5]
- *Equity or fairness.* This point has bedevilled many discussions about regime change. It has even led to the creation of a new organization next to GATT, namely UNCTAD. Currently, many countries think they are not getting a fair deal in the present international organizations and for that reason do not want to continue to develop them further (trade is an example). In other cases the equity point has been dealt with by exempting a vulnerable group from bearing part of the burden (e.g. LDCs and climate change).

Progress should not be measured only in terms of new regimes being set up or existing ones being extended; there should also be progress in getting rid of the regimes that have been set up under specific historical circumstances and shown to be inadequate and ineffective. Many organizations in the field of development aid are cases in point. However, experience shows that these regimes are particularly resistant to change; the interest of those that want change is rarely sufficiently important to lead to collective action that exerts sufficient power to overcome the defences of the combined vested interests of sector representatives, international bureaucrats and beneficiaries.

The ultimate aim of many global institutions is welfare growth. Here a revolutionary shift can be observed in recent years. Emerging and developing countries are showing remarkable growth, while the developed world is tending to stagnate. In recent decades, poverty in developing countries has been halved. Moreover, the disparity in income between rich and poor countries has decreased considerably. The same is true when inequality is measured in other dimensions. such as quality of life and human development (McGillivray and Markova 2010).

Whether this decrease in disparity has been induced by the system or has occurred despite the system is still a matter of dispute.

11.2.9 Open issues

There are many open issues specific for each regime (see the bottom row in Table 11.1). I have commented on them in the various chapters. They are all related to the fact that there is no system, but a patchwork of organizations and regimes each of which has been created to cope with a specific (set of) global problem(s). The patchy character of the architecture causes problems of extra cost (or forgone benefits) and distortions in wealth distribution on three scores:

1. *Transaction costs.* Regulatory forms are very different for the different regimes (compare, for instance, multilateral environmental agreements, WTO resolutions and ILO conventions). This diversity imposes a high cost on economic actors, as they have to come to grips with a multitude of aspects of international governance.
2. *Negotiation games and collective action.* As there is no integrated organizational framework, there is little incentive to reach package deals that comprise more than one regime, of the type "if you agree to making progress in the ILO, I will agree to accept progress in the WTO". So, it is less likely that the most effective deals will come about.
3. *Special interests.* Specialist regimes tend to become influenced or even controlled by specific interest groups that are inclined to overlook broader societal interests.[6] A case in point is the IMF, which used to be very much dominated by treasury ministries, which in turn tend to be sympathetic to the interests of actors in the financial markets. The financial crisis that began in 2007 has seen a switching of risk from the private sector to the public sector, resulting in considerably increased charges for the citizens of many countries. (More participation by NGOs has not been a solution to this.)

This "non-system" has come under heavy criticism, mainly for lack of effectiveness.

The first problem is that the global "non-system" does *not address all the important problems*. Many gaps exist, for example with regard to competition rules and labour markets. These have been dealt with in the previous chapter.

The second general issue concerns the *lack of progress* in the major multilateral organizations. One main cause for this is the multitude of actors (presently almost 200), which makes collective action difficult, notably in view of the diversity of their interests and their views about effectiveness and fairness. These problems are exacerbated by the enhanced complexity of interaction (including non-state actors) and the emergence of regional actors such as the European Union. Other causal trends are related to the economic structure: one can mention the increased interdependence of the private and public sectors (as in the financial and debt crisis) and the lack of understanding of the intricate economic interrelations (and hence of the impacts of shocks). We see these factors at work in all areas investigated. In the field of trade negotiations the stalemate occurs because emerging and developing countries disagree on the way to design trade rules (to bring about growth). In the field of stability, further progress depends on the redistribution of power. In the field of the environment, many large schemes (such as those seeking to mitigate climate change) have little chance of succeeding, as all countries are very afraid of the costs involved.

Consequently, we are seeing *a move away from the large monolithic organizations with their extensive bureaucracies to more flexible arrangements with fewer participants and more diverse solutions.* Examples can be seen in all policy fields: the proliferation of regional trade agreements (RTAs) in trade, the emergence of several parallel regimes for climate change, and the integration of labour rights in regional and bilateral agreements.

Finally, the lack of effectiveness can also be attributed to the fact that member countries *do not want to give stronger instruments* to the respective international organizations. I have cited many cases, but the one that best illustrates this is the case for a better dispute settlement procedure in the framework of the WTO. The present system relies on retaliation, which is not a very efficient instrument. It would be better economics if retaliation were to be replaced by fines. One should keep in mind, however, that there is no central authority on the global level to permit the use of such an instrument. As countries are sovereign states, effective arrangements are limited to those instruments for compliance or enforcement that are acceptable to member countries.

11.3 Old forms and new needs

11.3.1 Divergent demands on an already inadequate system

The present global governance system is a relic from the past; its foundations and construction still reflect largely the world as it stood in the post-Second World War era. It has only very reluctantly reacted to the need for changes. This is largely due to the incapacity of the present system to take into account the diversified interest of the emerging market countries and the developing countries while dealing with important societal concerns such as poverty reduction, sustainability and labour protection.

In recent decades, the world has seen important shifts in the factors that shape the global economy and global governance system. Some of these have already been described in the introductory chapter (see section 1.2). Here let us recall a few very salient factors.

First, closer worldwide integration has made all countries *more vulnerable to shocks* that originate in quite distant parts of the world. Important in this respect is the fact that citizens have the impression that their governments no longer have the capacity to provide shelter from the fallout of international development; while international solutions are not found because of problems with taking collective action.

Second, the concerns about the possible *negative consequences of openness* have moved beyond relatively straightforward matters such as trade liberalization into the much more intricate issues (such as competition, the environment, access to energy, decent work) where the interests of the major players are much more diverse, with the result that cooperative solutions tend to be hard to find. The developing and emerging countries, realizing that they have not received a fair deal in the past, have become more critical of any initiative that may harm their interests.[7] Finally, the global financial and economic crisis has shown us all the dangers of an unchecked liberalization on the global scale.

Third, in recent decades there has been a considerable shift in the *geopolitical power balance*. Notwithstanding some recent changes in governance of the IMF and the World Bank, and the reorientation of the OECD to G20 concerns, there are many misgivings about the lack of voice of emerging economies and of developing countries in global institutions. The once dominant West is no longer the engine of world economic growth; its growth is very low. By contrast, growth in the emerging economies and even in many developing economies has shown remarkable dynamism and as a consequence these economies are assuming an increasingly important role in shaping world affairs. In other words, the time when the US–EU axis could impose its views is over. This changed power balance is reflected in many ways. The most visible ones are the positions that major countries like China, India and Brazil take in WTO, IMF and environmental matters. With the demise of communism the labels "First", "Second" and "Third World" had already lost their relevance; now the distinction between North and South has done so as well. So, it seems that these old categories need to be abandoned. The West used to think that it had the answers to the many national and international problems, as it had gone through a growth and integration process before the rest. However, owing to the failure of many of its policy recipes and of its socio-economic institutions, it can no longer justify the patronizing of the rest of the world with detailed prescriptions coming from "global" institutions that are based on Western ideology and are dominated by the Western countries.

Fourth, a considerable shift in the *relation between government and market* has occurred. This relates both to public enterprises and sovereign wealth funds. In a number of the BRICS[8] countries the government has a direct influence on the strategies of large public enterprises. This means that geopolitical considerations may overturn economic rationales. A case in point is China: the Chinese government has already for some time been selecting specific (public) industries for external growth and has targeted specific markets in which such growth should be realized. Another case concerns the so called sovereign wealth funds. These funds have their origin in the balance of payments surpluses arising either from manufacturing exports or from energy and raw material exports. By the end of 2012 the total capital of such funds was estimated to amount to some $5 trillion. About a third of these funds are Chinese; others are notably in the Gulf countries.

11.3.2 The need for consistency

The previous chapters have made it abundantly clear that the various regimes have developed largely independently from each other. As a consequence, there is *a lack of consistency between the various regimes*. The considerable numbers of organizations have different members, objectives, rules and governance instruments. Their dispersed actions are geared to effectiveness in a segment of the global "system", not on bringing about improvements in the total system.

Consistency between the various (sub-)regimes has become a policy objective. For some time, efforts have been made to improve consistency by enhancing *coordination* between the main multilateral organizations. This applies in particular to trade, development and finance (and to some extent to environment and labour). Cooperating organizations comprise in particular the WTO, IMF, World Bank, UNDP, UNCTAD and ILO (see, for example, UNDP 2008).[9] Links have been created in the form of mutual observer status at the level of the board members, and cooperation at the level of staff members of these organizations. The IMF and World Bank have even had formal talks about the division of tasks and rules for coordination. The United Nations has tried to play a leading role here, but the many efforts to achieve better coordination under the auspices of the United Nations have so far failed.

A few recent developments can be cited that show that some progress has been possible in terms of consistency on specific interfaces:

- The World Bank has included in its conditionality list respect for the fundamental labour standards of the ILO. However, this is limited to loans to governments for infrastructural projects, not for World Bank lending in general.
- There have been some results, mainly on the trade–development interface (WTO) and the development–environment interface (World Bank).
- The G20 has moved along this path by stressing the mutual influence of stability, sustainability and employment.
- The WTO has cooperated with the ILO to study the relation between increased trade openness and employment. It has tried to clarify the intricate relationships between openness and employment, and has stressed the many ways in which in country-specific situations with respect to economic and institutional structures determine the employment effects (see Jansen *et al.* 2011; Bacchetta and Jansen 2011). So, there is no simple long-run formula "more openness leads to more growth leads to more and better employment".

Although all these efforts to achieve better coordination have helped to some extent, they have produced neither conformity in governance nor consistency in results.[10]

The consequence of that absence of determined action for increased consistency on the global level has been the further growth of *regional integration schemes* such as ASEAN. Here the collective action problem is less severe than on the global level. However, regional schemes are generally limited as to their subject coverage, so they have not been able to solve the consistency problem. Another consequence of the lack of multilateral agreements has been the *proliferation of bilateral agreements*; these often make trade opening conditional on compliance with environmental and social standards. This does away with part of the imbalance between different regimes, but it creates a new risk of inconsistency because of the diversity of stipulations in each agreement and of the legal impact of the stipulations.

11.4 Summary and conclusions

- The global "order" consists of a set of idiosyncratic regimes showing very wide diversity on all relevant features such as rationale, principles and governance.
- Many of these regimes have been able to provide important global public goods and adapt themselves to cope with some new needs. However, the present situation is not adequate.
- This is the case for the organizations taken collectively as they do not provide a consistent and comprehensive world government. On the one hand, some global public goods are not provided. On the other hand, for other GPGs there is overlapping of organizations. In short, the set of organizations is a patchwork, not a system.
- It is also the case for organizations taken individually with respect to their specific field of competence. On many points they do not adequately respond to present needs. In many of them, progress has been stalled because of the increasing diversity of interest of the major players.
- So, we are seeing a move away from large, monolithic organizations with their extensive bureaucracies to more flexible arrangements with fewer participants and more diverse solutions.

12

OUTLOOK

12.1 Introduction

The previous chapters have shown that in many respects the global socio-economic system of governance is inadequate. As it is likely that more problems will arise in the future and that presently unsolved problems will get worse, it is time to try to see what can and should be done to improve the situation.

It is the objective of this chapter to present some *proposals for change* that would make the set of international organizations capable of responding better to future needs. Because of this move to prospective analysis, the approach changes. Whereas previous chapters were all based on theoretical and empirical studies, we now enter into a domain of speculation. However, using lessons from the past will help us to stay as realistic as possible while projecting lines into the future.

The chapter has two main sections. The first deals with the future of multi-lateralism, the second with its main alternative: regionalism.[1] Both sections will use the same line of argument. We start with the scenario of a bold new architecture encompassing the main public goods. I next describe the many factors that inhibit its realization. I then describe the most likely alternative: a sort of muddling through scenario that consists essentially of incremental improvements of segments of the present institutional set-up.[2] Finally, we discuss the ways in which the problems of consistency engendered by this new architecture can be solved. The chapter is rounded off by a short list of main conclusions.

12.2 Multilateralism

12.2.1 Grand ideas about an integrated world government system

From the previous chapters it is clear that major improvements are needed in the way the world organizations deal with global socio-economic problems. This has induced quite a few thinkers (see, for instance, Nayyar 2002b; Slaughter 2004; Yunker 2011) to make bold and imaginative proposals for change. Most of these ideas for a fundamental reform of world government take as their point of departure the concept of a united framework for the provision of all global public goods. They apply the "trias politica" rules to the world system, defining a Government, a Parliament and a Court of Justice. They detail these three functions in organizational and governance terms.

The setting up of such a system does not need to start from scratch. The presently available (albeit sometimes embryonic) individual regimes could be fitted into the new system. With respect to the function of government, the specialized agencies of the United Nations and various separate organizations could be seen as the world ministries of trade (the WTO), finance (the IMF), environment (UNEP),[3] etc. The General Assembly of the United Nations could be thought of as a sort of Parliament. The International Court of Justice could be seen as the Court.

The *advantages* of such a system would be considerable. First, such a world government could take a consistent view on all the major problems. Next, it would induce substantial savings in organizational costs by removing overlap. Moreover, it would save on transaction and compliance costs by adopting a common set of legal instruments and rules of governance.[4] Further gains could be achieved by adopting a common world currency, as this would remove much uncertainty for international business and would also remove some of the causes of instability in the financial system.

There would also be *disadvantages*. First, an important incentive for effectiveness would be lost, as competition between the present international organizations pushes them to be responsive to new, emerging needs and to avoid fossilization. Next, there would be adaptation costs: governance systems of the various IOs with their differing histories would have to be harmonized to bring them to a common standard, which would lead to uncertainty for all concerned (e.g. about the legal impact).

12.2.2 Factors preventing realization

The intellectual attractiveness of such a grand new institutional design is not sufficient to see it realized. Achieving it would require willingness and capacity on the part of national governments to work together on a common project.[5] Now, both these factors are clearly missing (see, for example, Kapur 2002). There are a number of reasons why that is the case:

- *Insufficient sense of crisis*. Regime-building is a complicated matter. The previous chapters have made clear that only very specific circumstances (such as those pertaining after the Second World War) force major systemic changes. Even the present very deep crisis does not seem to be sufficient for fundamental change. We are not in 1944, when the grand design of the present system was constructed and put into practice. And although further crises are looming, it is not likely that they will be deep enough to force fundamental change.

- *Conflicts over ideology and principles*. Much of the opposition to further progress in multilateral institutions stemmed from misgivings about the liberalization of markets without due attention being given to societal and development concerns. It is unlikely that this conflict will be resolved in the near future. A new overarching paradigm needs to be developed that offers sufficient leeway for adaptation to individual cases; this can take decades, as the analysis in Chapter 2 has shown.

- *Unequal distribution of power*. There exist very large differences in the voting power of the major countries in the various international organizations. The United States and (to a lesser extent) the European Union dominate organizations such as the IMF and World Bank by the one dollar, one vote practice. The emerging markets and the LDCs dominate the United Nations by virtue of the one country, one vote system. A solution would be a uniform system of weighted voting on the basis of population figures for all international organizations. However, it is difficult to see what factors would occur in future that would induce the various parties to abandon their strongholds.

- *Ineffective bureaucracy*. Many international organizations are both ineffective (that is, they are not good at delivering the products and services they promise) and inefficient (that is, they use excessive resources in getting results). Objective ways of measuring the performance of international organizations are lacking,[6] but public choice theory shows that bureaucrats of international organizations have particularly strong incentives to pursue objectives different from the stated objectives of their organization. Moreover, international organizations run the risk of being hijacked by specific interests. Those concerned about such problems tend to consider that a situation without international organizations is better than a situation with poorly performing monopolist international organizations. Their argument is that because the public good is not delivered by the IOs, there is no benefit from their existence, so the actual cost of their bureaucracies can be considered as waste. Recent initiatives to improve that situation have shown how difficult it is to realize more responsive and effective bureaucracies. The conditions for such change are unlikely to improve in the future, which means that the same reluctance to confer new competences on international organizations will prevail.

One can only conclude that in the near future the realization of a new grand design is out of reach, owing to the weakness of the factors that push for global regime development, the absence of consensus on the desirability and the feasibility of new organizational forms, the difficulty of coming to collective action and the lack of leadership.

12.2.3 Incremental improvement of present global regimes

In the past, change has been possible in cases where the problems of collective action have been overcome, owing to the urgency of the specific problems and an incidental convergence of interests (as, for instance, the adaptation of the IMF to the crisis that began in 2007). Such cases will certainly occur in the future as well. They will lead to a gradual adaptation and marginal improvement of present institutions. The path that such a piecemeal development will take in future cannot be foreseen. It will depend very much on the specific configurations of the factors that push towards regime formation and change.

I will not speculate about such detailed sector-specific developments. The number of proposals that could be discussed in this respect is just too large and the conditions that will determine their chances of being realized too uncertain.[7] However, to illustrate the approach I will briefly sketch an issue that concerns a range of international organizations: power.

A *better distribution of power* has to start with a reduction in the voting rights (shares) of the major Western powers in the main international organizations. As far as the EU countries are concerned, this issue is closely related to the introduction of a single seat for the European Union instead of seats for all its member countries (see Box 12.1).

BOX 12.1 THE ROLE OF THE EUROPEAN UNION IN GLOBAL INSTITUTIONS

The EU treaties stipulate that the European Union acquires external competences in matters for which it is competent internally. For some areas this competence is exclusive (e.g. trade); for many others (e.g. the environment, labour) it is joint with member states. The treaties that laid the foundations of the major institutions such as IMF, World Bank, OECD and ILO recognize only states as members, which is logical, as supra-state entities such as the European Union did not yet exist when they were created. There is only one exception to this rule: GATT and then the WTO have accepted the European Union as a full member. In others the Union has observer status. Later developments such as the Kyoto Protocol (see Chapter 8), the Bank of International Settlements, the Financial Stability Board and the G20 could take the reality of the Union into account (albeit sometimes with complicated institutional compromises, as in the G20). But for the older IOs there is a strong tension between old form and new reality.

Solutions to this conflict are difficult to find, for two reasons. One is internal to the European Union; the other is external.

Internal reasons

Complications arise as a result of the diversity of legal situations. For instance, some EU countries are not members of the eurozone, so their external monetary policy is not handed over to the European Union. Moreover, there is a tendency among many member states to stay involved in external actions even in instances where the Union has competence (e.g. in the WTO).

External reasons

Many members of the major IOs resist changes to the articles that would enable supranational organizations to be accepted as members alongside sovereign states. Power politics is another inhibiting factor: the European Union has made its change in position conditional on a similar retreat in voting power by the United States and on improvements in the governance model of the IO in question.

The organization where the tension is greatest is certainly the IMF. It is clear that in the long term the European Union will move towards having a single seat. The change would need to go hand in hand with a very important rebalancing of voting power in the IMF.

12.2.4 Improvement of the consistency of existing regimes

A major problem with the present institutional set-up is its lack of consistency. The solution to this problem looks very different in the two scenarios that were depicted in the previous subsections.

In the framework of the new *grand design* (discussed in section 12.2.1) the consistency problem is supposed to be solved by the creation of an overarching institution that resembles a world government and can set strategic priorities and act as a great arbitrator in conflicts among policy domains. It is unlikely that member states will be willing to confer such huge powers on a "distant" international institution in the foreseeable future. So, here too we will have to go back to a more modest scenario. The most likely development here seems a stronger guidance role for the G20, and the strengthening of its status by introducing governing roles corresponding to boards in the diverse international organizations (e.g. letting the composition of the governing board of the IMF coincide with that of the G20). In the past the G20 has shown itself to be capable of improving the coordination between activities of IOs, and of allocating tasks to each of them.[8] In the future it might take this role more seriously, for instance in cutting out overlap. But even to realize such modest changes in the role of the G20 would involve many difficulties. Discord among the G20 members in strategic and defence matters (e.g. between China and Japan) and in macroeconomic matters (between the United States and Brazil) may impede the effective decision-making of the G20, and hence its leadership role.

The solution in the *incremental scenario* to the consistency problem is by improving horizontal coordination – that is, by encouraging the major socio-economic organizations to take better account of side objectives. In the past, this road has been followed with some success. It involves the adoption of measures that can bring a solution to a related problem without jeopardizing the provision of the major public good in the remit of the international organization in question. A case in point is the acceptance by the WTO of the Generalized Systems of Preferences for facilitating access of LDCs to the markets of the developed countries (see Chapter 5). Another case is the preferential financing by the World Bank of environmental projects (see Chapter 7). In many other cases such initiatives have not been successful. From the many examples of unresolved coordination problems, I have picked out two interfaces to illustrate the likely path that better coordination may take in the future.

A case that is still to be settled by WTO is the use of trade protection measures (including retaliation) against countries that do not comply with *labour standards* agreed internationally. Now, there are some reasons to expect that the conflict between the developed world (which seeks to link trade measures and labour conditions) and the developing countries (which are opposed to it) can be attenuated. Indeed, the universal character of many of these norms is likely to be increasingly recognized. So, it might be possible to achieve a linkage via a reinterpretation of Article XX of GATT, which permits member countries to ban products that have been produced by prison inmates.

Equally unresolved is the *environment–trade* conflict. Recent cases may illustrate this. The decision by the European Union to apply its emissions regime to the aviation sector has been opposed by China, which has even threatened to stop buying EU aircraft. Another example is the discussion about restrictions in the trade in fresh water, given the looming global water scarcity. Yet other examples have to do with the emission limitation measures in certain countries, which will lead to a transfer of polluting activities to countries that have less strict measures.[9] Similar conflicts are likely to arise in the future. All these examples show that environmental and trade issues can no longer be dealt with independently. The solution is not easy. For environmental norms a reinterpretation of Article XX (in the same way as for labour) seems unlikely; it presupposes a conclusion of the discussion about the fundamental character of a very large diversity of product norms. So, most hopes are vested in the gradual erosion of countries' opposition as they become increasingly aware of the economic cost of environmental damage as their income levels increase. This may lead to a change in the balance in favour of trade measures for environmental protection.

12.3 Regionalism

12.3.1 Grand ideas about regions as the hinge between nations and multilateral organizations

Action by small groups forming clubs is much easier than action by large groups, which explains the emergence of regional groups of countries. The many regions created in the past are cooperation devices for the governments of their member countries. But regions can also be conceived of as the building blocks of a global system.[10] This would take the form of a three-layer hierarchy (global, regional, national). At present the middle part is incomplete as to coverage and embryonic as to power. In a new design the regional layer could take a much enhanced role in two respects. First, it could be charged with the provision of a series of public goods for the member nations. Second, it could represent the national level in the organizations active on the global level. Realizing this option would imply a great many fundamental changes at each level. Many questions arise in this respect.

On the *regional level* the major question is whether full coverage of all countries in the world by regional integration schemes can be realized. Some of the great national powers are likely to shy away from this. If they do, can such large countries stand alone in this new set-up? (For example, can China and Russia be considered a region?) A further question concerns the competences of the new regional organizations. Would they cover all major socio-economic fields discussed in this book or limit themselves to a selection of them? Would they be mandated by the members to negotiate on their behalf, in the framework of the multilateral organizations, the details of regimes such as those concerning climate change, intellectual property and banking rules?[11] How far could they be held responsible to these international organizations for the compliance of their members with such new regimes?

On the *global level* the major question is how far the constitutions of the existing multilateral organizations could be adapted so as to accommodate regions rather than nations. Also important is the question of the distribution of power: the votes of each region would have to be established according to a certain principle (population? GDP?). Assuming that a satisfactory answer can be found to all these questions, the question arises as to what the world would gain by realizing this new grand design. What would be the balance between advantages and disadvantages?

The potential *advantages* of the option are twofold. First, it might permit progress by offering flexibility; groups could start contributing to the provision of global public goods by providing more on the regional level.[12] Second, it could limit the cost of the present stalemate in IOs by stimulating grand arbitrages between the interests of developing and developed regions.

The *disadvantages* are considerable. Regions add an extra layer in the institutional structure as a whole, which complicates coordination and adds cost. It would be difficult to prove the value added by this additional layer and to make sure that the risk of another level of bureaucracy is overcome.

12.3.2 Factors preventing realization of such a grand design

The many unanswered questions raised in the previous subsection already give an idea of the enormous obstacles standing in the way of the realization of this grand design. However, this is not all: there are quite a few more important obstacles. Opposition to the idea comes from several sides. International organizations (the WTO, World Bank, IMF) tend to look upon regional integration ventures as a threat to their power and influence. They are supported by many academics who consider that regionalism implies a second-best solution while the first best (multilateralism) is still within reach. This is also the view of quite a few countries that do not want to divert attention from the improvement of the global government system because they find that their interests are better served by enhanced integration in the world economy than in a cumbersome regional integration.[13]

But there are also powerful forces at work in favour of enhanced regionalism. In the past these have led to the creation of many regional integration schemes; the European Union stands out in this respect. The Union has always been convinced of the merits of the regional form of integration, including in areas outside Europe (e.g. Memedovic *et al.* 1999). It has supported the creation of regional trade arrangements in several parts of the world by giving technical advice on the way they should be set up and by giving financial support to the ensuing restructuring of the economy. The Union is convinced that enhanced regional cooperation is in the interest of better world government. The Union's success in solving a wide spectrum of cooperation problems has prompted many countries in other regions of the world to consider seriously the regional option. In the Americas the United States (which was initially opposed to regionalism) has switched position and has created NAFTA. In other regions of the world, cooperation schemes have developed as well (MERCOSUR in Latin America, ASEAN in Asia, the SADC in Africa (see section 3.5)). These groupings have increased their coverage in terms of subjects (public goods) and members; moreover, they have developed interregional relations, thereby partly integrating traditional bilateral relations.

Under the pressure of these developments, most international organizations have gradually accepted regional integration as a convenient middle station on the road to worldwide integration. Some (such as the United Nations) have even started to stimulate regions. Quite a few IOs have developed elementary forms of cooperation by regular staff meetings and by attributing observer status to regions.

However, the distance between the present situation and the full-fledged integrated set-up sketched earlier in the chapter is very large; the remit of most regional organizations is still very limited. Box 12.2 shows clearly that this is why many specialist regimes on the global level do not have counterparts on the regional level.

Only for trade would there be a match, as all regional organizations have developed some strength in matters of trade. We can see that most of the regions have no competences in several of the major policy areas discussed in this book and are unlikely to acquire them in the foreseeable future. Only a few of them are likely

BOX 12.2 THE MATCH BETWEEN GLOBAL AND REGIONAL REGIMES

The match between the global and regional regimes is very different for each policy area.

Trade

The WTO has a relatively strong institutional set-up; in particular, its dispute settlement procedure stands out in this respect. It is familiar with the concept and practice of regionalism. Indeed, most regional ventures deal with trade and related matters that come under the surveillance task of the WTO. The WTO, moreover, has experience with regions in its various negotiating and decision-making organs. Limiting the number of actors in these organs to the representatives of the regions while excluding nations might facilitate the reaching of agreements.[14]

Finance

The IMF as a global organization uses a direct line in its contact with nations. There is no equivalent structure dealing with monetary and macroeconomic matters on the regional level. The Economic Commissions of the United Nations are far from assuming a role as relay between the global and national levels. The European Union is the only regional organization having competence in these fields. Moreover, most authors have doubts about the capacity of regional organizations such as ASEAN to reform themselves quickly enough to be able to cope effectively with financial crises.[15]

Aid

The very large number of heterogeneous organizations that provide grants for development precludes a clear hierarchy in the global/regional/national framework. In the field of loans the situation is clearer. At present the World Bank deals directly with all countries involved, while a number of regional development banks deal with projects in countries in their own area. Recently the coordination between these institutions has been improved. The setting up of a confederate structure for these institutions would imply a clear division of roles: regional banks would be the main operational arms while the World Bank would have to limit itself to a role in the worldwide balancing of funds and the exchange of information. It would reduce the US bias in the World Bank's staff and practices (Kingah and Salimzhuarova 2012). The problem of coordination between donors would be lessened.

The environment

UNEP deals in a somewhat disparate manner with a list of global environmental problems, which has resulted in a series of individual international agreements. Kyoto on climate change is a case in point. Next to it are a host of regional agreements. These are all specific legal constructs and regimes, showing great diversity as to geographic coverage, forms, instruments, etc. The European Union is again the exception here, in the sense that as a regional organization it has extensive powers in matters of the environment. The value that would be added by regional institutions for the environment newly created to assume responsibility for harmonizing regional matters consistent with global regimes is far from self-evident.

Labour

The ILO is undisputedly the organization dealing with labour-related matters on the global level. On the regional level it has very few counterparts. The main one is the European Union, which has enacted a considerable body of legislation on ILO issues. In NAFTA a certain number of stipulations have also been agreed on. In other areas of the world, however, national governments have had great difficulty in reaching regional deals.

to become more encompassing in terms of public goods and assume responsibility not only for trade but also for issues related to finance, environment, labour, etc.

The *ambitions of the major regional cooperation schemes* are fairly limited. They range over trade- and competitiveness-related issues to early stages of socio-economic and monetary cooperation. Even these limited ambitions will not be easy to realize. The factors that permitted the European Union to reach the highest form of integration in only two generations (think of unity of purpose, limited diversity and strong institutions: Molle 2006, 2011) will not obtain in other regions of the world.[16] One need but look at the situation of the diversity of interests and cultural backgrounds in a region such as Asia to take the measure of the differences that will persist in the future.

So, the *conclusion* is that it is very unlikely that a new institutional architecture will emerge in which the regions are a constituent element of a layered set-up characterized by restricted multilateralism and enhanced regionalism.

12.3.3 Incremental improvements

Does this imply that we can dismiss the possibilities of a larger role for regions in the future world government architecture? The answer is probably no; there are many factors that drive collective action on the regional level and that are likely to push towards an enhanced role for regions in the near future. But this enhanced regionalism is likely to take the form of piecemeal complements to the present institutions – in effect, a continuation of the development trends that prevailed in the past.

The incremental developments can be seen in several aspects: increased coverage (the setting up of new organizations where they are lacking at the moment), and development of existing institutions in terms of more members, higher stages of integration and stronger instruments. I will limit myself here to two aspects of the move to higher stages of integration.[17]

With respect to the *monetary domain* the crisis that began in 2007 has stimulated thinking, as it has underscored the need for stability. On the other hand, it has also revealed the very large problems that need to be solved in order to achieve robust regional solutions to the problems (witness the internal difficulties of the eurozone). So, monetary unions are very unlikely to develop in the foreseeable future. However, we are likely to see many trials of cooperation devices that take into account both the specific situations of the cooperating countries and the challenges of the global financial markets.

The *social* domain is a particularly sensitive one. The progress in common social policy-making in the past has been slow and the various regions have shown very distinct paths as to the subjects dealt with in these common policies. To some extent, progress has been a function of the depth of the trade integration and the strength of regional institutions; concerns of fair competition probably do play a role here. Other aspects, such as cultural differences, do not seem to play a role (Deacon *et al.* 2011). So, the future will also show much diversity in the development of the social dimension of regional integration.[18]

12.3.4 Consistency

The regional option increases the consistency problem. In the multilateral situation (section 12.2) the consistency problem concerned the potentially conflicting objectives of independent international sectoral organizations. This horizontal coordination problem on the global level remains in the three-layer governance architecture we discuss here. To this is added a double coordination problem on the regional level. First, there is horizontal coordination between the different policy domains on the regional level. Moreover, there emerges a vertical coordination problem – that is, the arbitrage between the potentially conflicting policies at the global and regional levels.

Horizontal consistency problems occur in regional integration schemes when the objectives of different policy areas come into conflict. This problem becomes bigger the more areas of policy will be covered by the regions. The risk of conflicts occurring is fairly high: the forces that lead to a pillarization of the sectoral structures are as strong on the regional level as they are on the national and global levels. On the national level, frameworks have been put in place to arrive at solutions. One is the prioritization of objectives, for instance economic growth. Several free trade agreements (FTAs) have done so too; they consider that enhanced growth will facilitate the reaching of other objectives such as equitable distribution, or care for the environment. However, most rely on the coordination method; they favour stipulations on labour standards (possibly with threats of trade penalties and monetary penalties for those that do not observe them).

Vertical consistency problems occur at present only in those policy fields where both the regional and global levels have acquired competences (see Box 12.2). The number of these fields is rather limited but is likely to increase in future with the passing into higher stages of integration of several regional schemes.[19] The theoretical solution to vertical coordination problems lies either in hierarchization or in coordination. The *hierarchization* option implies the subordination of the regional schemes to global regimes by the setting of rules and standards on the global level with which regions have to comply. The situation would resemble the situation depicted in section 12.2, where national states have to comply with such rules. An example of such an arrangement is the acceptance of regional trade agreements under the WTO on the condition that they do not increase external protection levels (see Box 5.4). Similar arrangements can be envisaged for a hierarchical set-up of regional and global development banks (see Box 12.2). They could solve a few of the problems that are likely to emerge in the future. However, given the difficulties involved it is more likely that the alternative method – coordination – will be developed. It implies the establishment of frameworks for mutual information, consultation, etc. (see section 4.3.3), minimally avoiding conflicts and possibly promoting synergy between the global and regional levels.

The *double coordination problem* depicted is particularly difficult to solve even in well-developed multilevel governance structures (for instance in a federation like the United States or a supranational organization like the European Union; see, for example, Molle 2011). At the global–regional interface, where legal and administrative structures are not highly developed, the chances of solving the problem are even more limited. Moreover, improvements are difficult to make, owing to the reluctance of both national and global institutions to empower regions. So, change is likely to occur only where a certain convergence of interests of partners is emerging anyway; it is difficult to foresee on which issues this will be the case.

12.3 Summary and conclusions

- Most persistent fundamental problems of the international architecture could be solved by integrating the present disparate international organizations into a consistent new Grand Design architecture. However, none of the conditions for the realization of such a new Grand Design seems likely to be fulfilled in the near future.
- So, in the future, developments will be of an incremental nature, much as they were in the past. They will be limited to cases where benefits clearly exceed costs for the different partners involved. The "when", "where" and "what" of such developments are highly unpredictable.

- There are not many alternatives to multilateralism. The one that has some chances of being realized is regionalism. Regional cooperation schemes have the advantage of limited numbers, which makes collective action easier.
- A new architecture can be envisaged, consisting of three layers: nations, regions and the world. The regions could be charged both with the provision of a series of public goods for the member nations and with the representation of the national level in the organizations active on the global level. However, neither the national level nor the global level is ready to empower the regional level in order to let it play such a role.

So, regions are likely to develop in an incremental way, adding to the existing heterogeneity of the phenomenon. This will give rise to an increasing number of coordinated actions between multilateral and regional organizations.

NOTES

Preface

1 The overwhelming supply of Anglo-Saxon literature is reflected in the list of references. This leaves many other contributions from smaller language groups and from institutions and authors that have less access to international publishers underrepresented (such as universities in LDCs). I invite the reader to send me any relevant publications that can help to provide a more balanced view.

1 Introduction

1 Brazil, Russia, India, China and South Africa.

2 Creating institutions to deliver global public goods

1 See in this respect Kaul *et al.* 1999. In the extensive literature the term global public good (GPG) tends to get extended on two dimensions. First the *means to realize the GPG*. This is for instance the case with stability of conditions for doing international business. Second *anything that is politically desirable e.g.* poverty reduction, health improvement, gender equality, etc. We will not go along with this extended view as it would imply a loss of analytical specificity leading to a loss of clarity of policy conclusions (Bezanson 2002; Long and Wooley 2009).

2 This does not mean all parts of the world. We can give an example: the international financial system is very vulnerable to crises, the effects of which may be felt in very different parts of the world (see Chapter 6). Indeed, there is a higher potential for contagion, as problems in one country may spread to other countries (for instance the financial crises). This is a global problem even if not all countries are affected in the same way.

3 See in this respect the discussion about global commons in Hollick and Cooper (1997) and for the environment Tietzel (2001).

4 One is the International Telecommunication Union, which has set rules for allocating the global capacity of radio and other communications among countries.

5 In an imperfect world the cost of information, search and decision may be very high. The costs come from "uncertainties that arise as a consequence of both the complexity of the

problems to be solved and the limitations of the problem solving software (to use a computer analogy) possessed by the individual" (North 1990: 25).

6 Although Olson wrote his classic book on this subject some time ago and many refinements have been made since, his main conclusions are still valid.

7 Game theory has contributed much to answering this question. For the environment, see for example Folmer *et al.* (1993) and Hanley and Folmer (1998).

8 The text of this section draws heavily on Williamson (1998), notably p. 26.

9 North won a Nobel Prize for his work on the role of institutions. For other concepts used later in the chapter, I will refer to the textbooks of Kasper and Streit (1998) and Furubotn and Richter (2000), among others.

10 "What is universal to the West is imperialism to the rest" (Huntington 1997: 184).

11 Recently the term "governance" has increasingly been used in the sense of a network of interaction of regimes and organizations. According to this definition the term covers international organizations, national governments, firms and non-governmental organizations (NGOs). The whole system of interaction of these private and public bodies on the world level is then referred to as "global governance" (e.g. CGG 1995). The word "governance" has yet a different meaning in development economics: there, good governance is defined as the provision of public institutions that are effective in enhancing economic and social development. Note that the term "governance" differs in all instances from the term "government". The latter refers to a hierarchical set of public admini-strations that pursue policies for the solving of societal problems. So, government is about political leadership to reach societal goals, whereas governance is more about the deployment of instruments in implementing policies.

12 This section is based on Alt *et al.* (1988: 446), Krasner (1983: 2) and Furubotn and Richter (2000: 429–430).

13 The term "regime" has acquired its aura of nobility in political science (e.g. Krasner 1983). The term also has old roots in the work of eminent economists such as the Nobel Prize winner Jan Tinbergen (1959). Moreover, the term "regime" has received acceptance in other disciplines such as international relations, business and public administration. It has somewhat different but similar meanings in the various disciplines.

14 Compare in this respect the four levels of the scheme given in Figure 2.2; the categories of norms would correspond to the first level, the principles would correspond to the second level and the rules and procedures to levels 3 and 4.

15 For the complex interdependence of forces that contribute to regime creation and development, see among others Cooper (1985), Keohane (1993), Young and Osherenko (1993) and Efinger *et al.* (1993).

16 Based on Keohane (1993), who uses the term "institution" with the same meaning as I use the term "regime".

3 International organizations

1 See for a number of cases in which the tensions between exogenous factors and institutional aptitude have led to different outcomes Young (2010).

2 The first reason was that the USA (that emerged from the war as a leading power) refused to become a member. The League developed some activity in the negotiation of loans for countries that needed to stabilize the exchange rates of their currencies. It tried to promote the liberalization of world trade by calling a World Economic Conference, the effects of which were however limited and short lived. Finally the League entered into social affairs by creating the International Labour Organization (ILO).

3 This description will only cover some basic features; more detail on the structure and workings of the major organizations is given in the Chapters 5-10.

4 The G7 functions since 1976 as a platform of concertation among the most industrialized countries in the Americas (USA and Canada) and Europe (Germany, France, UK, Italy) and Asia (Japan). As of 1998 many meetings have taken the form of a G8, where Russia

takes part as well. However, separate meetings of the G7 are still held from time to time. See for a more detailed description of the role of the G8 Hodges, Kirton and Daniels (1999) and for the more recent account of the interrelations between the G8 and other international institutions Kirton *et al.* (2010); for the emergence of the G20 see: Kirton (2001) and for its present role Cooper and Thakur (2012). See for an account on the debates on the roles of the G8 and G20: Hajnal (2007).

5 This unlike many other meetings of heads of government, that were added as the apex to existing organizations, with well-developed decision making structures at ministerial, ambassador or other levels. Compare for instance the European Union, where the European Council of heads of State and Government was added to the institutional structure.

6 For an introduction, see Woodward (2009).

7 For a review, see Iwasaki and Prakash (2002).

8 On its development, see for example Simatupang (1998), Chirathivat *et al.* (1999), Menon (2000) and Davidson (2002).

9 Countries take very different positions as to participation of NGOs and business in official delegations. In some cases they may in this way use the informational advantage of experts; however in many other cases formal rules and financial constraints make countries decide not to go along this road. See for a case in environmental negotiations Boemelt (2012).

10 There are some specific cases where the strong involvement of the public sector has actually led to a worldwide organization of business; this is the case for the civil aviation sector, which is organized as the International Air Transport Association (IATA). However, for most sectors of activity these conditions do not hold.

11 This organization was already active by the end of the 1940s, when it issued an "International code of the fair treatment of foreign investments", containing suggestions for host governments. This was followed in the 1970s by an International Chamber of Commerce (ICC) guideline for international investment. This document contained recommendations for both enterprise and governments. The ICC has made other recommendations in related fields on corruption, the environment, etc. Particularly relevant in the face of the increased fragmentation of the production and distribution processes is the recommendation on supply chain responsibility obliging the main firm to check on suppliers' performance in terms of observance of fundamental labour rights, environment etc. (ICC/WBO 2007).

12 An example is the participation of NGOs in the UN Framework Convention on Climate Change meetings (UN/FCCC 2003).

4 Governance and compliance: methods and instruments

1 This chapter is largely composed of parts of different chapters of Molle (2011).

2 The choice of this definition has a bearing on the way I will treat certain issues in the following chapters. First, the definition excludes the word "efficiency", which has an important place in many discussions of good governance. However, as I have found very little empirical evidence on the question of the efficiency of global governance, I will go into it only sparsely. Second, in Chapter 2 I introduced Williamson (1998), who distinguishes four levels of institutions. The third level (the governance level) is heavily influenced by the choices made on the first and notably the second level. For that reason, Chapters 5–10 will pay due attention to such factors before entering into the heart of the matter: governance. Third, I will pay attention to the formal aspects and refer in subsequent chapters to treaties, principles, international organizations, etc., as these determine to a large extent the choices made in matters of governance.

3 In the literature one finds both the terms "modes" and "methods"; I have opted for the latter and will henceforth use that term.

4 The text of this subsection is partly based on World Bank (1992: 154).

5 A good example of this hierarchy is to be found in Chapter 8 on climate change. The United Nations Framework Convention on Climate Change (UNFCCC) constitutes a

fairly light form of regulation in the sense that it contains few binding commitments of a verifiable or specific nature. The latter have been given in a later treaty (the Kyoto Protocol) that fixes concrete targets for the parties to the agreement. Even Kyoto is not very specific, as it leaves the parties to the protocol much flexibility as to the means to reach the targets.

6 The international standards and codes issued by different international organizations have created a rather complicated set of regulations that must be observed by firms if they want to be part of international value chains. Doing so may be particularly difficult for firms in developing countries. Yet specific cases of MNFs that had to change their outsourcing as a result of NGO pressure give an indication of the effectiveness of this approach (see, for instance, Nadvi 2008).

7 Coordination is more difficult if it has to take place in an open negotiating setting, where the rules of the game – the agenda-setting – are often part of the negotiation. This will often imply cooperation to set up a new regime or a new organization.

8 Inspired by Metcalfe (1994).

9 This subsection is largely based on Hodson (2004).

10 There are many different definitions of "network" (see, for example, Boerzel 1997; Eising and Kohler-Koch 1999a, b; Thompson 2003). They all share the idea of a cluster of actors that have a stake in a given policy area and are prepared to cooperate to define and monitor policy.

11 "The crucial question for evaluating implementation success is to what extent a certain policy did allow for processes of learning, capacity building and support-building in order to address policy problems in a decentralized way, consistent with the interest of the actors involved" (Knill and Liefferink 2007, 153).

12 This section is largely based on Knill and Liefferink (2007: 173–176) and Knill and Lenschow (2004: 228–232). See for a good overview of the issues Joachim et al. (2007).

5 Trade

1 For the classical contributions to this field, see Molle (2008b).

2 Only in specific cases can other principles be optimal; see, for instance, Grimwade (2000).

3 There are also some specialist sectoral organizations such as the International Maritime Organization and International Air Transport Association.

4 A complete overview of the objectives, rules and operational problems of the WTO is given in the book by Hoekman and Kostecki (2009). Students will also find there a number of interesting case studies of international trade disputes.

5 For services, see for example Hoekman (2012).

6 Most of these functions will be elaborated further in the coming sections.

7 A decade ago China became a member; recently Russia has also joined.

8 All WTO members may participate in all councils, committees, etc. except the Appellate Body, Dispute Settlement panels and plurilateral committees.

9 It reads as follows: "[A]ny advantage, favour, privilege or immunity granted by any contracting party to any product originating in or destined for any country shall be accorded immediately and unconditionally to the like product originating in or destined for the territories of all other contracting parties" (from Article I of GATT).

10 See, for example, Molle (2006) and Panagariya and Krishna (2002).

11 This reflects the theoretical preference that we discussed in Chapter 3 for small-group solutions to collective action problems. It also reflects the use some members make of PTAs to strengthen their position in the WTO negotiations. This point is made by Mansfield and Reinhart (2003); however, the evidence they find to support their view is relatively weak.

12 One such instrument is the Enhanced Integrated Framework, a multi donor programme administered by the WTO for enhancing the capacity of LDCs to play a more active role in the global trading system.

13 The GSP showed up as highly relevant (Rose 2004).

14 The remaining barriers to imports originating from the LDCs are still very significant. They include sensitive sectors such as agriculture and labour-intensive manufactured products such as apparel. It is of the utmost importance to stimulate duty-free and quota-free market access for all products of LDCs. However, reaching an agreement on these issues is difficult, as the remaining trade barriers are defended by single-issue pressure groups, whereas the general interest for such measures in highly developed countries is difficult to organize.

15 In formal terms the General Council takes the decision. However, this body can only unanimously reject the findings.

16 For a good overview, see the *World Trade Report* for 2007 (WTO 2007), celebrating the sixtieth anniversary of the birth of the WTO. See for the complex issues involved in the reduction of the remaining non-tariff barriers WTO (2012).

17 This trade development went hand in hand with large increases in foreign direct investment. Here a similar shift in origin and destination occurred: in 2010 the developing countries received more than 50 per cent of total FDI. It is interesting to note that the emerging and developing countries are increasingly also the origin of FDI and that South–South investments are increasing very fast (UNCTAD 2011).

18 This is the effect of the creation of increasingly complex production chains. A case in point is the iPhone, which is assembled in China. However, most of its parts are made in other countries of the Asian basin but also in developed countries such as the United States and EU countries.

19 Theory does not indicate a clear-cut negative effect of openness on inequality of income (see, for example, Aghion 1998; Feenstra 1998; Bhagwati 1998; Wood 2002). In *empirical terms* the results of investigations are not clear-cut either. Some find that openness does not lead to inequality (e.g. Lawrence 1996; Ghose 2000); others find such an effect for developed countries (Dasgupta and Osang 2002). The effects on developing countries of increased openness are also very mixed (e.g. Meschi and Vivarelli 2009; Anderson 2012).

20 See, for example, Capling and Higgott (2009) and the other contributions to the same special issue of the journal *Global Governance*.

21 Two of these subjects, namely investment and competition, will be discussed in Chapter 10. We shall not discuss the other two subjects, as they seem obvious cases for WTO activity. Public procurement represents a considerable market. If local companies benefit from preferential treatment, the principles of the WTO will be a dead letter. Trade procedures concern administrative obligations, certificates, cautions, etc. They are of considerable relevance in the daily practice of international traders and can add significantly to transaction costs.

22 This should lead to development-friendly multilateralization of such PTAs (Hoekman and Winters 2009).

23 Negotiations in the past have often been initiated by a small group of major trading nations. Other countries have been associated with the outcome of these dealings only at a late stage. This has been efficient from a transaction cost point of view, but unfair from a distributional point of view. Present negotiations are more complicated because LDCs are involved in the early stages so that they can defend their interests better.

24 A number of publications have expressed this concern, including Bhagwati (2000), Oyejide (2000), Hertel *et al.* (2002) and the special issue of April 2000 of *The World Economy*.

25 For a critical assessment, see Mitchell and Voon (2009).

26 See in this respect the Sutherland Report (2004) and Warwick Commission (2007).

27 The idea is to see the WTO as a club that may accommodate sub-clubs (see, for example, Lawrence 2006) that go further on some issues.

28 The EU internal fair trade system works like this; see Box 11.4. The proposal to introduce it in the WTO is contested; most observers consider that it would not work.

6 Finance

1 Many authors have contributed to establishing a sound basis for the choice of the best form of such a regime. For the classical contributions to this literature, see Molle (2008c).
2 Scientific progress is made (e.g. Burkart and Coudert 2002) and one hopes that markets integrate the results of these efforts instead of reacting to superficial similarities.
3 This definition is from Crockett (1996); other authors have used similar ones.
4 Such crises have often found their origin in the real estate and housing sector. Many examples exist for developing countries (e.g. the Thailand crisis in the 1990s) but such crises also emerge in developed economies as witness the recent subprime crisis in the USA and the housing market crisis in Spain.
5 Contracts written in foreign currency and credit explosion were factors aggravating instability.
6 For the *theoretical* aspects of contagion, see Morris (2000), Sell (2001) and Clark and Huang (2006). *Empirical* studies on contagion tend to find strong neighbourhood effects, while trade links and similarity in pre-crisis growth also explain part of contagion (see Loisel and Martin 2001); the same holds for financial links (Caramazza *et al.* 2004). A favourable situation with respect to debt composition and exchange rate flexibility tends to limit contagion (De Gregorio and Valdés 2001; Hernández and Valdés 2001).
7 Mind that this has been IMF policy in the 1980s and 1990s. It was not always well advised; a country like Bolivia that did opt for public spending cuts and stabilization of the currency did recover better from a crisis than many others.
8 Theoretically, the cost of such crises could have been much reduced had countries adopted flexible exchange rates (Osakwe and Schembri 2002). However, the adoption of such a regime has other problematic sides, which is why many countries have not had recourse to this option.
9 Examples are the Basel Committee on Banking Supervision (BCBS) for banking, the International Association of Insurance Supervisors (IAIS) for insurance, the International Organization of Securities Commissions (IOSCO) for securities and the International Accounting Standards Board (IASB) for accounting. See Buthe (2008) for a further discussion of their role in matters of international financial stability.
10 See Angeloni (2008) for the reasons why so many European governments have a preference for this channel of cooperation. See also Ho (2002).
11 See for instance the slow development in Latin America (Baer *et al.* 2002) and in Asia (Box 6.2). Mind that for each continent there is a regional development bank, such as the Inter-American Development Bank. However, these banks' functions are similar to those of the World Bank and they do not assume functions on the regional level comparable to those of the IMF on the global level. See Chapter 7 for further details.
12 In matters of exchange rate stabilization the IMF plays now only a very modest role. The finance ministers (and sometimes the heads of state) of the G8, supported by central bank governors, play the role of coordinating body in this matter. The implementation of the ensuing recommendations as to coordinated macro policy-making has been put in the hands of the national governments, while the coordinated intervention in financial markets and the accompanying monetary policy has been entrusted to the central banks.
13 Note that these constituencies are relics from a distant past; they are completely at odds with the present geopolitical reality. For instance, the twenty-three non-permanent members of the EB are split over seven constituencies.
14 The share of the United States used to be some 17 per cent and the EU member states together used to account for some 30 per cent, while the whole Asian region accounted for only some 18 per cent.
15 This is unlike the ILO (see Chapter 9), which sets clear standards for labour laws in its member countries.
16 In other words, can one establish whether the stepping up of conditionality has indeed been conducive to stability and growth or not? Many empirical studies are fairly critical and reveal that the IMF policy has in many instances been wrong (e.g. on the Asia crisis).

An overview study showed that IMF conditionality was by and large balanced with respect to specific country situations (Stone 2008).

17 A very authoritative insider criticism was made by the Nobel Prize winner Joseph Stiglitz (2002). I give here the essentials of his view. See also Eichengreen (2002).

18 This view has given rise to the nickname "It's Mainly Fiscal" for the IMF. This position is in a sense the more astonishing as all developed countries have a strong institutional framework that copes with market failures and guides the economic actions of the private sector (Rappoport 2002).

19 By the end of the last century the need for an external evaluation was felt, as the organization appeared to lack sufficient capacity to adapt to the old criticisms and the new challenges. It resulted in 2001 in the creation of the Independent Evaluation Office. The results of this change seem to be fairly limited; the learning capacity of the Fund still seems inadequate (e.g. Weaver 2010).

20 The crisis has, however, created the *conditions for making a change in the modes of operation* of the IMF. There have been a number of adaptations. First, as regards the background of staff, recruitment is now oriented towards people from countries where the IMF is active and with a more diversified background in terms of experience (e.g. national supervisors) (*Financial Times*, 28 May 2009). Second, in terms of ideology the IMF has seen that in a number of cases the free movement of capital can actually create bubbles in emerging economies and has reluctantly accepted the idea of controls on incoming capital (*Le Figaro*, 20 February 2010). Third, the case of Greece has shown to the IMF that austerity measures can actually go too far and prevent the economy from recovering.

21 Throughout the history of the IMF, proposals for change have been made. For a structured overview of the proposals on the table around the turn of the century, see Eichengreen (1999). See also a special issue of the *Journal of Economic Perspectives* (vol. 13, no. 4, notably Mishkin 1999 and Rogoff 1999), the various contributions in Teunissen (2000) and the evaluation of a number of individual proposals as discussed in Kaiser *et al.* (2000). Moreover, many analyses of the problem also contain suggestions for improvement (see, for example, Chu and Hill 2001; Sell 2001).

22 These concern not only its informal character but mainly a basic controversy about the global effects of the national macro and financial policies of major players (easy money in the US; balance of payments surplus of China, etc.) (see Hazakis 2012).

23 There is an abundant literature on the subject that has recently been revived. I base the discussion, however, on two "classics", namely ul Haq *et al.* (1996) and Artesis and Sawyer (1997).

24 See for the example the special issue of *The World Economy*, (2012) Vol. 35.4 for the case of Asia.

7 Development aid

1 The Quality of Life index and the Human Development index take also such factors as health and literacy into account. Some recent official studies take these alternative dimensions into account (see, for instance, UN 2011a). In general, there is a strong correlation between the various indicators as to the distribution over country groups.

2 If we group the basic data by population deciles, we find that the richest 20 per cent of the world population has about 80 per cent of total global wealth.

3 If we look at the very long term (1820–1990), we see divergence: the ratio between the rich countries and the poor countries went from 2:1 in 1820 to 7:1 in 2000 (Maddison 2001). Diverging tendencies dominated the whole twentieth century (see IMF 2000), in particular the second part (see Stewart 1995; UNDP 1998; World Bank 1992, 2009). However, some studies (e.g. Park 2001) gave inconclusive results. For more details on the large diversity in patterns of growth see: Rao and van Ark (2013).

4 The growth of disparity in some countries has notably come from the increase in the share of the top 1 per cent. This erodes solidarity. The OECD is much concerned about

this (2011b, 2012) and suggests measures that are conducive both to growth and to less disparity.

5   These difficulties concern both data and methodology (e.g. Bhalla 2002, Anand and Segal 2008). The latter authors conclude that there is insufficient evidence to determine the direction of change in global interpersonal inequality in recent decades. See for some methodological innovations on the very long term analysis of income inequality (1820–1990) Atkinson and Brandolini 2010). Note finally that the results of studies that try to measure directly poverty are less optimistic, but still show a positive trend.

6   Simulation exercises also show that the LDCs as a group can gain considerably from trade liberalization. A new round of multilateral broad-based tariff cuts is estimated to have considerable net benefits (Brown *et al.* 2001; Francois 2001). See further Chapter 4 of OECD (2010a) for recent views on the relation between trade and development.

7   The theoretical work on the effects of trade liberalization on inequality in general (Fischer 2001) and on poverty in particular (see for an overview of the latter issue Winters *et al.* 2004) shows that much depends on the specific case whether the effect will be negative or not. The results of empirical case studies are very difficult to generalize. Some studies on the relation between trade and internal inequality (e.g. Bensidoun *et al.* 2011) conclude that income inequality within countries has increased and that this depends on the factor content of trade. High labour content raises income inequality in poor countries and reduces it in rich countries. The reverse is true for the capital content of trade.

8   FDI has in a number of cases had very positive effects on the economy of the host country (see the case of China in Graham and Wada 2001, for example); in a number of other cases, however, it has had very negative effects. The positive impacts are basically due to increased competition, technology transfer and increased access to world markets. They are enhanced by spill-overs to local firms, worker training and management development (Lipsey and Muchielli 2001). See Moran 1998; UNCTAD 1999: 152.

9   The *World Investment Report* (WIR) from which this text is cited (UNCTAD 1999: 156) describes for each of these points the way in which MNFs and FDI can actually support the development of the LDCs. These points have been further elaborated in the 2002 *World Investment Report* (UNCTAD 2002).

10   This subsection is taken from Molle (2011).

11   See notably the OECD (2005) series on enhancing coherence between development policy and other policies such as macro, trade, migration and agriculture, taking geographical and institutional aspects into account. The OECD systematically reviews the development policies of its members. Its Development Assistance Committee has issued several guidelines on best practices and on policy coherence.

12   Aid flows are not the only – or even the largest – flows of income for developing countries. Over time, remittances of people residing abroad have been an equally large factor, while in recent decades FDI has overtaken ODA as a source of finance.

13   Excluded are financial flows related to military equipment, peacekeeping, nuclear energy and cultural programmes (definitions from the Development Assistance Committee of the OECD).

14   The OECD tracks the increase in financing (ODA) and supports partnerships and catalyses political support for strategic change and good governance.

15   Text partly borrowed from www.worldbank.org.

16   AAA status is due to the huge reserves deposited with the Bank and to the fact that bonds are under-written by members in event of collapse.

17   This small margin is possible as the World Bank covers most of its operating expenses from the returns on its capital.

18   See the similar debate in section 6.5.4.

19   "Aid dependence can potentially undermine the quality of governance and public sector institutions by weakening accountability, encouraging rent-seeking and corruption, fomenting conflict over control of aid funds, siphoning off scarce talent from the bureaucracy, and alleviating pressures to reform inefficient policies and institutions. Analyses of cross-country data in this paper provide evidence that higher aid levels erode

the quality of governance, as measured by indices of bureaucratic *quality, corruption, and the rule of law*"(Knack 2000). See also Djankov *et al.* (2008).

20 As in other aspects of development, the World Bank is not alone in trying to deal with this problem: many individual donors have started to make their own assessments. This has given rise to a considerable problem for recipients. The OECD has tried to bring some order to the diversity of assessment methods (see different documents available from www.oecd.org/dac/governance/govassessment; see also the documents on capacity development at www.oecd.org/dac/capacitydevelopment).

21 E.g. Dalgaard *et al.* (2004).

22 See, for example, Riddell (2007) for an overview. In a meta-study of the aid–growth relation (Doucougliagos and Paldam 2008), a small positive effect was found for the relation but it appeared very difficult to pin down the explanatory factors of the controversial results of the basic studies. In order to obtain better results, propositions have been made to break down the total chain of causality in several links (for instance the last link: from policies via programmes and projects to outcomes; Bourguignon and Sundberg 2007). The break-down of aid by type of aid did permit Clemens *et al.* (2004) to conclude to a significant positive effect of aid for the economic sectors on growth. A similar exercise of breakdown by type (Ouatara and Strobl 2008) found positive effects for project aid, no effects for technical assistance and negative effects for food aid.

23 For the goals see UN MDG website; see also MDG progress chart (several years) of the UN statistics division and UN (2011).

24 www.worldbank.org.

25 There is evidence that donor fragmentation erodes the quality of the government in recipient countries (Knack and Rahman 2007).

26 From www.oecd.org/document/18/0,3746.

8 The environment

1 The economics of climate change have since been thoroughly analyzed in the Stern Report; for a summary, see Stern (2008). The figures cited hereafter are taken from that report. See for an assessment of the results of various studies Tol (2012).

2 Many authors have contributed to the literature on finding the basic characteristics of global regimes that would be most effective in dealing with the major problems. For an overview of the classical contributions, see Molle (2008d).

3 So, it is important to achieve sustainable management of the use of the global commons (Hardin and Baden 1977; Nordhaus 1994; see also Siebert 1998).

4 They tend to be environmental illustrations of the general problem discussed in Chapter 2 (see also Perman *et al.* 1999; Barrett 1990, 1999; Rao 2002).

5 The principle of common but differentiated responsibility, however, would imply that rich countries accept a less advantageous deal for themselves. However, empirical research shows that their own interest is the main driver of negotiators (Dannenberg *et al.* 2010).

6 The precautionary principle, although applied in a number of international environmental agreements, has not found universal acceptance. There is much discussion as to whether the principle is part of international law. LDCs are particularly concerned about the possibility of the principle's being used as a disguise for protectionist measures by the highly developed countries.

7 Compare the discussion in Chapter 2 and Black *et al.* (1993) and Bertram (1992).

8 For a good overview of the pros and cons of the various instruments, see Goulder and Parry (2008); for a more detailed description of the taxation, see Hoel (1992); for the international aspects of the design of emission trading, see Carraro (2000); and for private litigation, see Bertram (1992). For a comparison of different proposals for the climate change instruments, see Aldy *et al.* (2003).

9 For the interaction between the national and international spheres, see Wijen *et al.* (2012).

10 This boils down to the putting of property rights on these goods, which indicates the relevance of the discussion of this item in Chapter 2.

11 Much of the effectiveness of environmental policy actually starts with the removal of the opposite of taxes, as in many countries the use of polluting goods is actually subsidized.

12 For a detailed description of the causes and dynamics of the changes in roles of the various actors, see Chapter 12 of the book by Braithwaite and Drahos (2000) and part 1 of Biermann and Pattberg (2008). For NGOs, see McCormick (1999).

13 For an overview of the genesis of UNEP and the factors that have determined its design, see Ivanova (2007, 2010). The *remit* of UNEP is to support sustainable development through sound environmental practices everywhere. The various *roles* of the organization are distributed as follows. The Governing Council is the supreme decision-making body of UNEP. This Council has some sixty members, and a limited number of them are members of the Bureau. The Governing Council can meet in the form of a Global Ministerial Environmental Forum, in which also delegates from NGOs can participate. The Executive Director leads the work of the organization, supported by a staff numbering about 700. The *instruments* of the UNEP are mostly conventions (or multilateral environmental agreements); after ratification, these are binding on member states. For more details, see the basic texts and other documents available from www.unep.org, and the annual document *Global Environment Outlook*.

14 In 1987 care for the environment got its constitutional foundation (Treaty Title XVI).

15 Compare this fragmentation with the situation for development aid in Chapter 7, notably Easterly and Pfutze (2008).

16 The arguments put forward by the United States are twofold. The first is largely political; it says that the Kyoto Protocol (KP) leads to an unequal sharing of the burden. (Note that the United States has been, and is, the largest single contributor to the problem.) The second argument used is of an economic nature: it says that the KP instruments are largely ineffective and lead to very high costs for those that have to implement them. The point has been expressed most clearly by McKibbin and Wilcoxen: "All in all the Kyoto Protocol is an impractical policy focused on achieving an unrealistic and inappropriate goal" (2002: 127). However, as Aldy *et al.* (2003) show, all alternative schemes have major drawbacks as well.

17 The mechanism of joint implementation is indeed subject to a number of problems. The major ones are that the system is subject to corruption and fraud and that measuring compliance is very costly. So, much attention is now given to the putting emission trading into operation.

18 The removal of this restriction in the regime would lead to a substantial reduction of the cost (by half, according to Manne and Richels 2000 and Buonanno *et al.* 2000).

19 The WTO is here an exception, but even for trade the instrument of retaliation is besieged with problems (see Chapter 5).

20 Another relation with development is the support that the World Bank can give to projects in LDC s that improve the environment.

21 There are some rules that WTO accepts such as the ban on trade in endangered species and in dangerous toxic materials. However, the use of trade measures by importers against countries that violate international agreements on the environment is a very complex matter. Many issues are unsettled giving rise to much uncertainty as to their legal and economic consequences.

22 Bierman *et al.* (2009b) discuss various options for the new organization and conclude that the best one is to use UNEP as the core of the new structure.

23 See also pleas for a different system that does not focus on emission rights but focuses on technical improvements and programmes to stimulate this (e.g. Verzirgiannidou 2009; Lomborg 2010).

9 Labour and social protection

1 In Chapter 5 we have dealt with the movement of products (goods and services). In Chapter 6 we have dealt with the conditions for and consequences of the movement of the production factor capital. The subject of the present chapter follows in a sense the latter logic by focusing on the effects of globalization on the production factor labour and the regimes to protect labour. The international regimes that deal with the movement of production factors as such are the subject of Chapter 10.

2 Much of this section is based on earlier work in this field by the author, published in Molle (2002). Parts of the text have been borrowed from Molle (2003: section 3.3).

3 See also the earlier literature (OECD 1994; Fitoussi et al. 2000). The effects are different for different parts of the regulation. As an example, we may take the effects of the minimum wage on unemployment; here both in theoretical and empirical terms the effects are highly uncertain, for example, Dolado et al. (1996), Cahuc et al. (2001) and Broadway and Cuff (2001). An example of a more straightforward negative influence is labour-related taxes (see studies cited in text and also Stanford (1998) and Daveri and Tabellini (2000).

4 In 2012 the G20 extended the "global public good" definition to employment. It has asked the relevant international organizations (the IMF, OECD, IMF, ILO) to come up with a global employment outlook to be fitted into the reform agenda for strong, sustainable and balanced growth.

5 This section has benefited much from the contribution of Feis to the ILO publication on international labour standards (Sengenberger and Campbell, 1994). For an overview of the theoretical and empirical arguments for imposing minimum labour standards, see Kis-Katos and Schulze (2002).

6 A variant of this dynamism is known as the strategy of raising rivals' cost; see in this respect the analysis of Boockmann and Vaubel (2009).

7 More recent studies include those of Mah (2002), who found a low negative relation only for low-income countries; Hasnat (2002), who found a negative relation only for one standard (collective bargaining); and Busse (2002), who found a negative relation for unskilled labour-intensive goods exports from developing countries.

8 See the International Trade Union Confederation website (www.ituc-csi.org).

9 See the OECD website (www.oecd.org) for *Reviews of Labour Market and Social Policies*, for *Key Employment Statistics* and for *Social, Employment and Migration Working Papers*.

10 For the text, see www.business-humanrights.org/media/documents/ruggie/ruggie-guiding-principles-21-mar-2011.pdf.

11 This even resulted in the formal statement that the 1998 ILO Declaration on Fundamental Principles and Rights at Work is not to be used as a means to justify protectionist trade measures.

12 For more details, see the basic texts and other documents, available from www.ilo.org/public/english/.

13 For a more precise description of these processes and the role of the various actors in these processes, see ILO (2009: 81–91).

14 Bear in mind that the selection of these four is not based on very clear legal, economic or philosophical criteria (de Wet 2010). Many regret the lack of a clear relation between principles and standards and the selection of core labour standards because they have relegated the other standards to a sort of second class (Alston 2004).

15 This convention has had some influence on the gradual improvement of systems, but falls short of providing any minimum social floor (Kulke 2007).

16 Some authors have analyzed specific conventions. A case in point is the ban on child labour. Unfortunately the figures do not show that the problem is less in countries that have ratified than in countries that have not ratified. Neither can one find indications of a decrease of the problem over time (Boockman 2010).

17 Econometric exercises show that the former relation is true (e.g. Bazillier 2008). See also Bonnal (2010) who finds that countries with higher standards trade more; and openness to trade is supposed to enhance growth.

18 Standing (2008), for example, gives a harsh judgement on the ILO's record: he considers that the past evolution towards ever weaker governance methods, the erosion of the professional quality of the staff and its antiquated organizational structure make it ill-equipped to face the challenges of globalization.
19 Moreover it would add to the conditionality problem discussed in Chapters 6 and 7.
20 For the anatomy of RTAs, see for example Horn *et al.* (2010); for effects, see for example Cordella and Grilo (2001).
21 Some bilateral or regional arrangements impose actual fines if a country does not observe labour standards (see Elliott 2001).
22 Empirical research has shown that such corporate codes are only effective under specific conditions. See in this respect Kolk *et al.* (1999).

10 Complements

1 This section is partly based on Dymond (2000), Johnston (2000) and OECD (1998).
2 A case in point is sovereign wealth funds that have been created, which deploy the earnings of oil and gas exports. They had a capital of more than $5,000 billion in 2010. That money is increasingly invested in private firms instead of in public bonds.
3 One can see that these are very similar to the ones used by the WTO for the trade regime. Central here too is the non-discrimination principle.
4 The International Chamber of Commerce has complemented this work. The ICC is a private enterprise organization that as early as 1972 produced *Guidelines for International Investors*, giving recommendations for both investors and host governments. The turbulent relations between host governments and MNFs also induced the United Nations to work out a Code of Conduct on Transnational Corporations. The code gives recommendations with respect to issues such as ownership, taxation, industrial relations and technology transfer.
5 For a more detailed description of the structure and a comment on the position of various actors (such as developed countries), see UNCTAD (1999: 126–137).
6 These three scenarios are comparable to three of the four scenarios discussed in Sauve (2006). His fourth scenario is a remake of the MAI and as such is unlikely to be realized; hence we do not pay attention to it.
7 For the first view, see among others Carens (1987).
8 In *economic terms* the migration of labour is seen as a mechanism for the improvement of the allocation of labour. In labour-exporting countries the benefits are largely in the easing of the unemployment situation and the income from remittances; the costs are more long-term and involve the loss of human resources and investment in education. For a labour-importing country the main benefit is higher production. There are several cost factors. The first is an increase in public expenditure, as many types of immigrants are thought to put higher demands on social services than indigenous persons. The second is non-monetary costs in terms of social disruption and internal (in)security. Finally, in-migration of workers tends to slow the adaptation of the sectoral structure of the economy to new technologies and world prices (see, for example, Straubhaar 2000; Ghosh 2000; Nayyar 2002a, b).
9 For a review for the EU case in general, see Chapter 7 of Molle (2006); and for insecurity, see Huysmans (2000).
10 Immigration also has a number of distributional effects. Some claim that it drives down domestic wages (and even capital income; Lundborg and Segerstrom 2002) and that it increases unemployment. However, others (e.g. Agiomirgianakis and Zervoyianni 2001) show that this need not be true and that labour can actually benefit. The available empirical evidence both from the European Union (see, for instance, Tapinos and de Rugy 1993; Zimmermann 1995) and from the United States (for a review, see De Freitas 1998) is that the negative effects on wages and unemployment are very small. For a collection of papers on the subject see Chiswick and Miller (2012).

11 The 1990 UN International Convention on the protection of all migrant workers and members of their families.

12 See the special issue of *International Migration Review* (1991: 25–737).

13 A plea for the setting up of such a regime and ideas for the rules it should apply and how it should be organized is given in the various contributions to the book edited by Ghosh (2000) and more recently in a special issue in volume 16 of *Global Governance*, introduced by Koser (2010).

14 What would be the *objectives of a new multilateral system*? It would have to make sure that the flows of migration are indeed beneficial instead of disturbing. So, the global public good in matters of migration is of an economic rather than of a humanitarian order – in practice, the prevention of negative economic effects of migration. As these effects are not the same for all types of countries, the rationale for setting up such a regime is not self-evident. There is a parallel here with capital movements: they are in principle welfare enhancing but under certain circumstances they lead to disturbances that can cause such damage that the *principle of free movement* cannot be accepted. That means that there is no similarity with the approach for trade, so there is no use for anything like the most favoured nation treatment. It also means that a WTO type of agreement is not the way forward (Hatton 2007). However, in most countries there will be a rule for "national treatment" of foreign labour that has legally been accepted into the country.

15 Recall that the international organizations responsible for the implementation of the regime in finance (Chapter 6) consisted of an intervention force (an improved and enlarged role for the UN refugee organization?) and that interventions were based on the *principle of conditionality* (equivalent to improving the conditions in the source country).

16 Migration pressure has increased and, in view of the prevalence of increasingly selective and restrictive policies, this leads to considerable illegal migration. In their host countries illegal migrants are in more vulnerable situations than legal ones, and all migrants are in less favourable situations than indigenous workers. National protection systems often fail to identify the scope of the problem and to provide the necessary funds and administrative capacity to do something about it. An international regime might be considered but is unlikely to materialize, given the highly sensitive character of the issue.

17 Such a tax was proposed in the 1970s by Bhagwati (1976); for a good overview of the discussion, see Bhagwati and Wilson (1989).

18 In this sense this proposal is comparable to the so-called Tobin tax on international movements of capital.

19 This would have some resemblance to the idea of tradable emission rights (see Chapter 8).

20 For this, readers should refer to other parts of the literature, in particular Ghosh (2000).

21 Anti-dumping is obsolete as soon as competition policy is executed adequately. So, the introduction of a multinational competition policy should limit the use of retaliation by trade policy measures.

22 The middle one is particularly important in an international context as European Union competition authorities can actually forbid mergers and acquisitions that may lead to such a dominant position. In cases where MNFs are involved this gives rise to disputes about the extra-territorial application of national (European Union) competition rules.

23 The OECD Joint Group on Trade and Competition found that the evidence for discrimination against foreign competitors in competition policy was very weak. Most countries tend to apply the same procedures to foreign and domestic companies alike.

24 See the UNCTAD website, which gives a whole list of studies on competition law.

25 In the Havana Charter of 1947 it was envisaged that the International Trade Organization should have powers to investigate business practices that restrict competition and to recommend counter-measures. However, none of these powers has been bestowed on GATT or its successor, the WTO. Some of the agreements arrived at in the framework of the WTO contain elements of competition. These relate notably to trade in services (see Chapter 5).

26 According to some proposals the WTO should address all competition problems; others (e.g. Mattoo and Subramanian 1997) say that the WTO should only safeguard the

enforcement of national competition law so as to safeguard equal access to markets of foreign competitors.

27 For an insider's view of the discussions in the WTO working group on competition, see Anderson and Jenny (2005); for a consumer's view on the issue and alternative institutional solutions, see Evenett *et al.* (2003).

28 Proposals for free-standing organizations have a long history. Some have been made by competition policy experts from academia (e.g. Scherer 1994; Graham and Richardson 1997). See also IATCWG 1993.

29 See in this respect the various contributions to the special issue of the *Journal of European Integration*, 2012, Vol. 34, 6.

30 The public good character of the Internet (looked at as a system) is a matter of debate (see, for example, Spar 1999).

31 A first start in this sense was made for the European Union as early as 1998 with a data protection directive laying down very stringent rules about the collection and transmission of personal data.

32 Indeed, the Internet is in a state of considerable flux. It is undergoing massive technical change. It entails large changes in industrial structure and ownership. The types of services change very rapidly.

33 In practice, however, there is a very strong US influence, owing to three factors. First, the Net was developed in that country, so has been based on US law. Second, the major firms that have shaped the use of the Internet (e.g. Google, Apple) are US based. Finally, the US government does tap into it for security reasons.

34 Soon after the emergence of the computer the need was felt for an exchange of data and information between computers. To that end, networks were created. Unsurprisingly, perhaps, the first application was in military matters. Linking the various networks (to form the Internet) largely facilitated the exchange of military (strategic and operational) information and saved costs in computer time. The advantages of a network soon became apparent to the research community. Later, other organizations (such as multinational firms) saw the strategic interests of intra-company linking of national computers. With the spread of the personal computer the network became used more and more for private purposes. Next, the business sector started to recognize its potential for information exchange (including inter-company exchange) and for commercial purposes. Now the Internet is used not only for information and communication but also for trading (so-called B2B, business to business), shopping (so-called B2C, business to consumer), banking, studying, voting, etc.

11 Evaluation

1 Such a move is still due for the market-related aspects of the regimes dealing with sea and air transport, such as the International Maritime Organization (IMO) and the International Civil Aviation Organization (ICAO).

2 These may also reflect bureaucratic interests; an example is the IMF, which started to look into poverty problems when it thought that the macro problems were over.

3 Apart from these disadvantages there are also some advantages of competition among international organizations; for instance, the emergence of regional banks has stimulated the World Bank to become more effective.

4 State aid (subsidies) can have important negative effects. So, both the WTO and the European Union have policies that regulate the use of state aid. There are, however, important differences between the two, on many scores. The *objective* of the WTO regime is to prevent subsidies from nullifying the abolishment of protectionist measures such as tariffs. For the European Union the objective is the protection of fair competition on the internal market. The *procedure* of the WTO following the lodging of a complaint involves setting up a panel (much along the lines described in Box 5.7) that checks whether there has been injury to the complaining partner. When the European Union gets a complaint,

the Commission investigates the case; findings of the Commission can be challenged before the European Court of Justice. *Compliance* in the WTO has to be ensured by negotiation first and retaliation next. In the European Union the Commission can oblige the member state to stop the aid and oblige the beneficiary of a non-permissible subsidy to pay it back. The EU system is more economically sound as it removes the origin of the problem, whereas the WTO system permits retaliation, which creates another distortion. Moreover, the institutions of the European Union are more likely to arrive at economically sound conclusions. The Union relies on permanent staff in the specialist Directorate-General of the Commission, whereas the WTO relies on trade diplomats who take on alternative roles on the Subsidy Committee (Messerlin 1999: 167–174).

5 Moreover, the United States is less and less willing to bear the cost of hegemony.
6 A very clear example here is the agricultural regime of the European Union (see, for example, Molle 2006, 2011).
7 Problems in their access to markets for agricultural and labour-intensive goods explain in part the stalemate that currently exists in the WTO over progress in the Doha Round.
8 Brazil, Russia, India, China, South Africa.
9 This cooperation may even encompass private organizations; see, for instance, Renner *et al.* (2008).
10 Some countries have actually resisted improved coordination because they did not feel that the new, coordinated agendas and priorities were in their interest.

12 Outlook

1 Other alternatives that one could imagine are, for instance, enhanced roles for non-governmental organizations. However, these have not been worked out, as they can only be complementary to governmental ones, given their legitimacy problem.
2 This second option is based on the detailed analyses made in the various chapters on individual regimes.
3 Alternatively, a World Environment Organization (WEO) that would oversee all regimes in the environmental field (see Chapter 8).
4 Some diversity could be accepted to accommodate the details of the various regimes. An example of such a plea is Moshirian (2002).
5 This will not be easy. Let us recall a few important factors in this respect. First, there is a multitude of parties with different interests that, taken individually, are small. Second, the collective good is often not very clearly defined. Third, there is a strong inclination for countries to opt for free-riding on the efforts that other parties make. Fourth, there is built-in resistance to change on the part of existing organizations. Indeed, once regimes exist and show a certain level of effectiveness, it is difficult to adapt them, let alone to supplant them by others.
6 However, there are ways to capture a few basic notions in comparative form, as evidenced notably in the chapter on development aid. Note that these can be further developed according to certain principles, taking into account the complexity of the issues involved (DFID 2011).
7 Recall that some elements have been discussed in the conclusions sections of the previous chapters, for instance the changing of UNEP to a World Environment Organization. Many other proposals that have been made have not been discussed in this book. An example is the reform of the Special Drawing Rights (SDR) of the IMF to make them better reflect the changed importance of major currencies (an increased place for the renminbi) and prepare the ground for an increased role of SDR in monetary and financial relations (see, for example, Benassy-Quere *et al.* 2011). It would be too big a step to try to order them by urgency and relevance and discuss them here. The reader is referred to the abundant literature.
8 An example is the new role of the FSB; see Chapter 6.
9 In order to restore effectiveness, countries with strict measures want to install border tax

adjustment measures that take away the relative cost differences. The issue is very involved and leads to a considerable trade and climate agenda. See for instance Brewer (2010); Messerlin (2010) and the special issue of *The World Economy* (2011; Vol. 34.11).

10 An overview of the literature on the development of this idea in circles of international organizations and academia can be found in Van Langenhove and Macovi (2011: 11); see also Thakur and Van Langenhove (2008).

11 A legal problem in this respect is that not all regional schemes have international legal personality and formally mandated representatives. This would not be a problem for an informal grouping such as the G20, but it is a problem for all formal IOs.

12 Take, for instance, the problem of competition. A regional competition authority or the regional cooperation of national enforcement agencies can deal with the behaviour of firms on its internal regional market. However, it will be ineffective against major worldwide cartels (e.g. in pharmaceuticals) or de facto monopolies (e.g. Google).

13 This argument is already fairly old: see, for example, Langhammer (1992).

14 The lack of agreement in the WTO is partly due to institutional features such as the rule of consensus on a single undertaking. Limiting the number of partners in the negotiations to a few representatives of regions and acceptance of partial deals would make it easier to come to agreements (Gavin 2007).

15 See the discussion on the Chiang Mai Initiative in Chapter 6 and further, for example. Park and Wang (2000) and Moon and Rhee (2012).

16 Moreover, the model of the European Union is neither desirable nor feasible in developing countries (Winters 1997).

17 As the European Union has in the meantime reached the highest stage of regional integration, let us focus our attention on developments in other parts of the world.

18 In practice the improvement on the scores of labour and social policy will be very dependent on the evolution of local institutions.

19 One such avenue of development concerns direct investment. Here the regional schemes tend to come on top of the existing tangle of bilateral deals, adding to complexity (UNCTAD 2013).

REFERENCES

Aghion, P. (1998) Inequality and economic growth, in P. Aghion and J.G. Williamson (eds) *Growth, Inequality and Globalization: Theory, History and Policy*, Cambridge: Cambridge University Press, 6–102.

Agiomirgianakis, G. and Zervoyianni, A. (2001) Globalization of labor markets and macroeconomic equilibrium, *International Review of Economics and Finance*, 10(2): 109–133.

Aldashev, G. and Verdier, Th. (2009) When NGOs go global: competition on international markets for development donations, *Journal of International Economics*, 79: 198–210.

Aldy, J.E. and Stavins, R.N. (2008) Climate policy architectures for the post-Kyoto world, *Environment*, 50(3): 6–17.

Aldy, J.E., Barrett, S. and Stavins, R.N. (2003) Thirteen plus one: a comparison of global climate change policy architectures, *Climate Policy*, 3: 373–397.

Allegret, J.-P. and Dulbecco, Ph. (2007) The institutional failures of International Monetary Fund conditionality, *Review of International Organizations*, 2: 309–27.

Allianz (2011) *Global Wealth Report 2011*. Available at: https://www.allianz.com/v_1339 498650000/media/current/en/economic_research/images_englisch/pdf_downloads/specials/agwr_2011e.pdf (accessed June 2012).

Alston, P. (2004) "Core labour standards" and the transformation of the international labour rights regime, *European Journal of International Law*, 15(3): 457–521.

Alt, J.R., Calvert, R. and Humes, B. (1988) Reputation and hegemonic stability: a game theoretic analysis, *American Political Science Review*, 82: 445–466.

Anand, S. and Segal, P. (2008) What do we know about global income inequality? *Journal of Economic Literature*, 46(1): 57–94.

Anderson, E. (2012) Openness and inequality in developing countries: a review of theory and recent evidence, *World Development*, 33(7): 1045–1063.

Anderson, K. and Winters, L.A. (2009) The challenge of reducing international trade and migration barriers, in B. Lomborg (ed.) *Global Crises, Global Solutions*, 2nd ed., Cambridge: Cambridge University Press, 451–503.

Anderson, R. and Jenny, F. (2005) Competition policy, economic development and the possible role of a multilateral framework on competition policy: insights from the WTO working group on trade and competition policy, in E.M. Medalla (ed.) *Competition Policy in East Asia*, London: Routledge, 61–85.

Andresen, S. (2007a) The effectiveness of UN environmental institutions, *International Environmental Agreements: Politics, Law and Economics*, 7: 317–336.

Andresen, S. (2007b) Key actors in UN environmental governance: influence, reform and leadership, *International Environmental Agreements: Politics, Law and Economics*, 7: 457–468.

Angeloni, I. (2008) Testing times for global financial governance, Bruegel Essay and Lecture Series, Brussels.

Antweiler, W., Copeland, B.R. and Taylor, M.S. (2001) Is free trade good for the environment? *American Economic Review*, 91(4): 877–908.

Artesis, P. and Sawyer, M. (1997) How many cheers for the Tobin tax? *Cambridge Journal of Economics*, 21: 753–768.

Atkinson, A.B. and Brandolini, A. (2010) On analyzing the world distribution of income, *World Bank Economic Review*, 24(1): 1–37.

Bacchetta, M. and Jansen, M. (eds) (2011) *Making Globalization Socially Sustainable*, Geneva: WTO/ILO.

Baldwin, R. (2011) 21st century regionalism: filling the gap between 21st century trade and 20th century trade rules, *CEPR Policy Insights* 56.

Barrett, S. (1990) The problem of global environmental protection, *Oxford Review of Economic Policy*, 6(1): 68–79.

Barrett, S. (1999) Montreal versus Kyoto: international cooperation and the global environment, in I. Kaul, I. Grunberg and M. Stern (eds) *Global Public Goods*, Geneva: UNDP, 192–219.

Batabyal, A.A. and Beladi, H. (eds) (2001) *The Economics of International Trade and the Environment*, Boca Racon, FL: Lewis.

Bazillier, R. (2008) Core labour standards and development: impact on long-term income, *World Development*, 36(1): 17–38.

Benarroch, M. and Weder, R. (2006) Intra-industry trade in intermediate products, pollution and internationally increasing returns, *Journal of Environmental Economics and Management*, 52(3): 675–689.

Bénassy-Quéré, A., Pisani-Ferry, J. and Yu Yongding (2011) Reform of the International Monetary System: some concrete steps, *Bruegel Policy Contribution*, 2011/03.

Bensidoun, I., Jean, S. and Sztulman, A. (2011) International trade and income distribution: reconsidering the evidence, *Review of World Economics*, 147(4): 593–619.

Berthélemy, J.-C. (2006) Aid allocation: comparing donors' behaviours, *Swedish Economic Policy Review*, 13: 75–109.

Bertram, G. (1992) Tradable emission permits and the control of greenhouse gases, *Journal of Development Studies*, 28(3): 423–466.

Beverelli, C. and Mahlstein, K. (2007) Outsourcing and competition policy, HEI Working Paper 11, Geneva.

Bezanson, K. (2002) Global public goods: opportunities and threats, *EU LDC Network Newsletter*, July, 2–5.

Bhagwati, J.N. (ed.) (1976) *The Brain Drain and Taxation: Theory and Empirical Analysis*, Amsterdam: North-Holland.

Bhagwati, J. (1998) Trade and wages: a malign relationship? In O. Memedovic, A. Kuyvenhoven and W. Molle (eds) *Globalization of Labour Markets: Challenges, Adjustments and Policy Response in the European Union and Less Developed Countries*, Dordrecht: Kluwer, 31–66.

Bhagwati, J. (2000) After Seattle: free trade and the WTO, *International Affairs*, 77: 15–30.

Bhagwati, J. (2008) *Termites in the Trading System: How Preferential Agreements Undermine Free Trade*, New York: Oxford University Press.

Bhagwati, J.N. and Wilson, J.D. (1989) *Income Taxation and International Mobility*, Cambridge, MA: MIT Press.

Bhalla, S.S. (2002) *Imagine There's No Country: Poverty, Inequality, and Growth in the Era of Globalization*, Washington, DC: Institute of International Economics.

Bhattacharjea, A. (2006) The case for a multilateral agreement on competition policy: a developing country perspective, *Journal of International Economic Law*, 9(2): 293–323.

Biermann, F. and Bauer, S. (eds) (2005) *A World Environmental Organization: Solution or Threat for Effective International Environmental Governance?* Aldershot, UK: Ashgate.

Biermann, F. and Pattberg, Ph. (2008) Global environmental governance: taking stock, moving forward, *Annual Review of Environment and Resources*, 33: 277–294.

Biermann, F. and Siebenhüner, B. (eds) (2009) *Managers of Global Change: The Influence of International Environmental Bureaucracies*, Cambridge, MA: MIT Press.

Biermann, F., Siebenhüner, B. and Schreyögg, A. (eds) (2009a) *International Organizations in Global Environmental Governance*, London: Routledge.

Biermann, F., Davies, O. and van der Grijp, N. (2009b) Environmental policy integration and the architecture of global environmental governance, *International Environmental Agreements: Politics, Law and Economics*, 9(4): 351–369.

BIS (1997) Financial stability in emerging market economies, *Draghi Report of the Working Party on Financial Stability in Emerging Market Economies*, Basel.

Black, J., Levi, M.D. and de Meza, D. (1993) Creating a good atmosphere: minimum participation for tackling the "greenhouse effect", *Economica*, 60: 281–293.

Blanchard, O. (2009) The crisis: basic mechanisms and appropriate policies, IMF Working Paper WP09/89.

Blanchard, O. and Milesi-Ferretti, G.-M. (2011) (Why) Should current account balances be reduced? IMF Staff Discussion Note SDN11/11/03.

Boehmelt, T. (2012) A closer look at the information provision rationale; civil society participation in states' delegations at the UNFCCC, *Review of International Organizations*, DOI 10.1007/s11558-012-9149-6.

Boehmelt, T. and Betzold, C. (2013) The impact of environmental interest groups in international negotiations; Do ENGOs induce stronger environmental commitments? *International Environmental Agreements; Politics, Law, Economics*, 13.2, no page indications.

Boerzel, T. (1997) What's so special about policy networks? An exploration of the concept and its usefulness in studying European governance, *European Integration Online Papers*, 1(16): 8–25.

Bonnal, M. (2010) Export performance, labour standards and institutions: evidence from a dynamic panel data model, *Journal of Labour Research*, 31: 53–66.

Boockman, B. (2010) The effect of ILO minimum age conventions on child labor and school attendance: evidence from aggregate and individual level data, *World Development*, 38(5): 679–692.

Boockmann, B. and Vaubel, R. (2009) The theory of raising rivals' costs and evidence from the International Labour Organization, *The World Economy*, 32(6): 862–887.

Bordo, M., Eichengreen, B., Klingebiel, D. and Soledad, M. (2001) Financial crises: lessons from the last 120 years, *Economic Policy: A European Forum*, 32: 53–82.

Bosello, F., Roson, R. and Tol, R. (2007) Economy-wide estimates of the implications of climate change: sea level rise, *Environmental and Resource Economics*, 37(3): 549–571.

Bouet, A. and Laborde, D. (2010) Why is the Doha agenda failing? And what can be done? A computable general equilibrium–game theoretical approach, *The World Economy*, 33(11): 1486–1516.

Bourguignon, F. and Sundberg, M. (2007) Aid effectiveness: opening the black box, *American Economic Review*, 97(2): 316–321.

Boyd, R. and Ibarraran, M.E. (2002) Cost of compliance with the Kyoto Protocol: a developing country perspective, *Energy Economics*, 24: 21–39.

Braithwaite, J. and Drahos, P. (2000) *Global Business Regulation*, Cambridge: Cambridge University Press

Brealey, R., Clark, A., Goodhart, C., Healey, J., Hoggarth, G., Llewellyn, D.T., Chang Shu, Sinclair, P. and Soussa, F. (2001) *Financial Stability and Central Banks*, London: Routledge.

Brewer, T. (2010) Trade policies and climate change policies: a rapidly expanding joint agenda, *The World Economy*, 33(6): 799–809.

Brewer, T. and Young, S. (1995) Towards a new multilateral framework for FDI: issues and scenarios, *Transnational Corporations*, 4(1): 69–83.

Broadway, R. and Cuff, K. (2001) A minimum wage can be welfare-improving and employment-enhancing, *European Economic Review*, 45(3): 553–576.

Brown, A.G. and Stern, R.M. (2011) Free trade agreements and governance of the global trading system, *The World Economy*, 34.3; 331–354.

Brown, D. (2000) International trade and core labour standards: a survey of the literature, Occasional Papers 43, Paris: OECD (Labour Market and Social Policy).

Brown, D.K., Deardorff, A.V. and Stern, R.M. (2001) CGE modeling and analysis of multilateral and regional negotiating options, Discussion Paper 468, University of Michigan, Ann Arbor.

Brownlie, I. (2008) *Principles of Public International Law*, 7th ed., Oxford: Oxford University Press.

Buonanno, P., Carraro, C., Castelnuovo, E. and Galeotti, M. (2000) Efficiency and equity of emissions trading with endogenous environmental technical change, in C. Carraro (ed.) *Efficiency and Equity of Climate Change Policy*, Dordrecht: Kluwer, 121–162.

Burkart, O. and Coudert, V. (2002) Leading indicators of currency crises for emerging countries, *Emerging Markets Review*, 3: 107–133.

Busse, M. (2002) Do labour standards affect comparative advantage in developing countries? *World Development*, 30(11): 1921–1932.

Busse, M. (2004) On the determinants of core labour standards: the case of developing countries, *Economics Letters*, 83(2): 211–217.

Buthe, T. (2008) Politics and institutions in the regulation of global capital: a review article, *Review of International Organizations*, 3: 207–220.

Cahuc, P., Saint Martin, A. and Zylberberg, A. (2001) The consequences of the minimum wage when other wages are bargained over, *European Economic Review*, 45(2): 337–352.

Calderon, C. and Chong, A. (2009) Labor market institution and income inequality: an empirical exploitation, *Public Choice*, 138: 65–81.

Capling, A. and Higgott, R. (2009) Introduction: the future of the multilateral trade system – what role for the World Trade Organization? *Global Governance*, 15(3): 313–325.

Caramazza, F., Ricci, L. and Salgado, R. (2004) International financial contagion in currency crises, *Journal of International Money and Finance*, 23(1): 51–70.

Carens, J.H. (1987) Aliens and citizens: the case for open borders, *Review of Politics*, 49(2): 251–273.

Carlson, L.J. (2000) Game theory, international trade conflict and cooperation, in R. Palan (ed.) *Global Political Economy: Contemporary Theories*, London: Routledge, 117–129.

Carraro, C. (ed.) (2000) *Efficiency and Equity of Climate Change Policy*, Dordrecht: Kluwer.

Carraro, C. and Siniscalco, D. (1993) Strategies for the international protection of the environment, *Journal of Public Economics*, 52: 309–328.

Carraro, C. and Siniscalco, D. (1998) International environmental agreements: incentives and political economy, *European Economic Review*, 42: 561–572.

Cave, M. and Mason, R. (2001) The economics of the Internet: infrastructure and regulation, *Oxford Review of Economic Policy*, 17(2): 188–201.

CGG (1995) *Our Global Neighborhood: The Report of the Commission on Global Governance*, New York: Oxford University Press.

Chirathivat, S., Pachusanoud, C.H. and Wongboonsin, P. (1999) ASEAN prospects for regional integration and the implications for the ASEAN legislative and institutional framework, *ASEAN Economic Bulletin*, 16(1): 28–50.

Chiswick, B. and Miller, P.W. (eds) (2012) *Recent Developments in the Economics of International Migration*, Cheltenham, UK: Edward Elgar.

Chu, Y.-P. and Hill, H. (eds) (2001) *The Social Impact of the Asian Financial Crisis*, Cheltenham, UK: Edward Elgar.

Clark, P.B. and Huang, H. (2006) International financial contagion and the Fund: a theoretical framework, *Open Economies Review*, 17(4–5): 399–422.

Clemens, M.A., Radelet, S. and Bhavnani, R. (2004) Counting chickens when they hatch, the short term effect of aid on growth, Working Paper 44, Center for Global Development.

Coase, R.H. ([1937] 1988) The nature of the firm, *Economica*, 4: 386–405; reprinted as Chapter 2 in R.H. Coase (1988) *The Firm, the Market and the Law*, Chicago: University of Chicago Press.

Collier, P., Guillaumont, P., Guillaumont, S. and Gunning, J.-W. (1997) Redesigning conditionality, *World Development*, 25(9): 1399–1407.

Convery, F.J. (2009) Origins and development of the EU ETS, *Environmental Resource Economics*, 43: 391–412.

Cooper, A.F. and Thakur, R. (2012) *The Group of 20 (G20)*, London: Routledge.

Cooper, R.N. (1985) *Economic Policy in an Interdependent World*, Cambridge, MA: MIT Press.

Cordella, T. and Grilo, I (2001) Social dumping and relocation: is there a case for imposing a social clause? *Regional Science and Urban Economics*, 31: 643–668.

Costantini, V. and Crespi, F. (2008) Environmental regulation and the export dynamics of energy technologies, *Ecological Economics*, 66(2–3): 447–460.

Crockett, A. (1996) The theory and practice of financial stability, *De Economist*, 144(4): 531–568.

Dalgaard, C.-J., Hansen, H. and Tarp, F. (2004) On the empirics of foreign aid and growth, *The Economic Journal*, 114(496): 191–216.

Dannenberg, A., Sturm, B. and Vogt, C. (2010) Do equity preferences matter for climate change negotiators? An experimental investigation, *Environmental Resource Economics*, 47: 91–109.

Dasgupta, I. and Osang, T.E. (2002) Globalization and relative wages: further evidence from US manufacturing industries, *International Review of Economics and Finance*, 11: 1–16.

Daveri, F. and Tabellini, G. (2000) Unemployment, growth and taxation in industrial economies, *Economic Policy: A European Forum*, 30: 47–104.

Davidson, P.J. (2002) *ASEAN: The Evolving Legal Framework for Economic Cooperation*, Singapore: Times Academic Press.

De Freitas, G. (1998) Immigration inequality and policy alternatives, in D. Baker, G. Epstein and R. Pollin (eds) *Globalization and Progressive Economic Policy*, Cambridge: Cambridge University Press, 337–356.

De Gregorio, J. and Valdés, R.O. (2001) Crisis transmission: evidence from the debt, tequila and Asian flu crises, *World Bank Economic Review*, 15(2): 289–314.

De Lombarde, Ph. and Puri, L. (eds) (2009) *Aid for Trade: Global and Regional Perspectives*, Berlin: Springer.

de Wet, E. (2010) Governance through promotion and persuasion: the 1998 ILO

Declaration on Fundamental Principles and Rights at Work, *German Law Journal* (Special Issue: Public Authority and International Institutions), 9(11): 1429–1452.

Deacon, R. (2007) *Global Social Policy and Governance*, London: Sage.

Deacon, R., De Lombaerde, Ph., Macovei, M.-C. and Schröder, S. (2011) Globalisation and the emerging regional governance of labour rights, *International Journal of Manpower*, 32(3): 334–365.

Deere Birkbeck, C. (2011) Development-orientated perspectives on global trade governance: a summary of proposals for making global trade governance work for development, Global Economic Governance Working Paper 2011/64.

DFID (2011) Multi-lateral aid review, available at: www.gov.uk/government/publications/multilateral-aid-review (accessed June 2013).

Dijkstra, A.G. (2002) The effect of policy conditionality: eight country experiences, *Development and Change*, 33(2): 307–334.

Djankov, S. and Ramalho, R. (2009) Employment laws in developing countries, *Journal of Comparative Economics*, 37(1): 3–13.

Djankov, S., Montalvo, J.G. and Reynal-Querol, M. (2008) The curse of aid, *Journal of Economic Growth*, 13: 169–194.

Doh, J.P. and Teegen, H. (eds) (2003) *Globalization and NGOs: Transforming Business, Government and Society*, Westport, CT: Praeger.

Dolado, J., Kramarz, F., Machin, S., Manning, A., Margolis, D. and Teulings, C. (1996) The economic impact of minimum wages in Europe, *Economic Policy: A European Forum*, 23: 317–372.

Dollar, D. and Kraay, A. (2001) *Trade, Growth and Poverty*, Development Research Group, Washington, DC: World Bank.

Doucougliagos, H. and Paldam, M. (2008) Aid effectiveness on growth: a meta study, *European Journal of Political Economy*, 24(1): 1–24.

Dreher, A. (2009) IMF conditionality: theory and evidence, *Public Choice*, 141: 233–267.

Dreher, A. and Walter, S. (2012) Does the IMF help or hurt? The effect of IMF programs on the likelihood and outcome of currency crises, *World Development*, 38(1): 1–18.

Dreher, A., Herz, B. and Karlb, V. (2006) Is there a causal link between currency and debt crises? *International Journal of Finance and Economics*, 11(4): 305–325.

Drezner, D.W. (2007) *All Politics Is Global: Explaining International Regulatory Regimes*, Princeton, NJ: Princeton University Press.

Dymond, W. (2000) The MAI: back to the future, in MINEZ (eds) *From Havana to Seattle and Beyond*, The Hague: SDU, 175–185.

Easterly, W. and Pfutze, T. (2008) Where does the money go? Best and worst practices in foreign aid, *Journal of Economic Perspectives*, 22(2): 29–52.

EC (2006) *EU Action against Climate Change: The EU Emissions Trading Scheme* (2009 edition). Available at: http://ec.europa.eu/clima/publications/docs/ets_en.pdf (accessed November 2011).

Economides, G., Kalyvitis, S. and Philippopoulos, A. (2008) Does foreign aid distort incentives and hurt growth? Theory and evidence from 75 recipient countries, *Public Choice*, 134: 463–88.

Eden, L. and Hampson, F.O. (1997) Clubs are trump: the formation of international regimes in the absence of a hegemon, in J.R. Hollingsworth and R. Boyer (eds) *Contemporary Capitalism: The Embeddedness of Institutions*, Cambridge: Cambridge University Press, 361–394.

Ederington, J. (2010) Should trade agreements include environmental policy? *Review of Environmental Economics and Policy*, 4(1): 84–102.

Efinger, M., Mayer, P. and Schwarzer, G. (1993) Integrating and contextualizing hypotheses: alternative paths to better explanations of regime formation, in V. Rittberger (ed.) *Regime Theory and International Relations*, Oxford: Clarendon Press, 252–281.

Eggertsson, T. (1990) *Economic Behavior and Institutions*, Cambridge: Cambridge University Press.

Eichengreen, B. (1999) *Toward a New International Financial Architecture: A Practical Post-Asia Agenda*, Washington, DC: Institute for International Economics.

Eichengreen, B. (2002) *Financial Crises and What to Do about Them*, Oxford: Oxford University Press.

Eichengreen, B. (2008) *Globalizing Capital: A History of the International Monetary System*, 2nd ed., Princeton, NJ: Princeton University Press.

Eising, R. and Kohler-Koch, B. (1999a) Introduction: network governance in the European Union, in B. Kohler-Koch and R. Eising (eds) *The Transformation of Governance in the European Union*, London: Routledge, 1–29.

Eising, R. and Kohler-Koch, B. (1999b) Governance in the European Union: a comparative assessment, in B. Kohler-Koch and R. Eising (eds) *The Transformation of Governance in the European Union*, London: Routledge, 267–285.

Ellerman, A.D. (2008) The EU's emissions trading scheme: a prototype global system? Harvard Kennedy School Discussion Paper 08-02.

Elliott, K.A. (2001) Fin(d)ing our way on trade and labor standards? International Economics Policy Briefs 01.5, Washington, DC: Institute for International Economics.

Esty, D.C. (2009) Revitalizing global environmental governance for climate change, *Global Governance*, 15: 427–434.

Evenett, S.J. (2007) Five hypotheses concerning the fate of the Singapore issues in the Doha round, *Oxford Review of Economic Policy*, 23(3): 392–414.

Evenett, S. *et al.* (2003) *Consumers, Multilateral Competition Policy and the WTO: Technical Report*, Consumers International. Available at: www.wto.org/english/tratop_e/dda_e/symp03_ci_tech_report_e.pdf (accessed June 2013).

Evrensel, A.Y. (2002) Effectiveness of IMF-supported stabilization programs in developing countries, *Journal of Money and Finance*, 21: 565–587.

Faure, M. and Lefevere, J. (1999) Compliance with international environmental agreements, in N.J. Vig and R.S. Axelrod (eds) *The Global Environment: Institutions, Law and Policy*, Washington, DC: CQ Press, 138–156.

Feenstra, R.C. (1998) Integration of trade and disintegration of production in the global economy, *Journal of Economic Perspectives*, 12(4): 31–50.

Feldmann, H. (2009) The unemployment effects of labor regulation around the world, *Journal of Comparative Economics*, 37(1): 76–90.

Fischer, R.D. (2001) The evolution of inequality after trade liberalization, *Journal of Development Economics*, 66(2): 555–579.

Fitoussi, J.-P., Jestaz, D.P., Phelps, E.P. and Zoega, J. (2000) Roots of the recent recoveries: labour reforms or private sector forces? Documents de travail de L'OFCE no. 2000.4, Paris.

Florini, A.M. (2000) Who does what? Collective action and the changing nature of authority, in R.A. Higgott, G.R.D. Underhill and A. Bieler (eds) *Non-state Actors and Authority in the Global System*, London: Routledge, 15–30.

Folmer, H., van Mouche, P. and Ragland, S. (1993) Interconnected games and international environmental problems, *Environmental and Resource Economics*, 3: 313–335.

Francois, J.F. (2001) *The Next WTO Round: North–South Stakes in New Market Access Negotiations*, Adelaide: Centre for International Economic Studies/Tinbergen Institute.

Fratianni, M. and Pattison, J. (1982) The economics of international organization, *Kyklos*, 35: 244–266.

Freeman, R.B. (2010) Labor regulations, unions, and social protection in developing countries: market distortions or efficient institutions? *Handbook of Development Economics*, 5(70): 4657–4702.

Frey, B.S. (1984) The public choice view of international political economy, *International Organization*, 38(1): 199–223.

Frieden, J.A. (2009) Global governance of global monetary relations: rationale and feasibility, *Economics*, 3: article 2009–2006.

Furubotn, E.G. and Richter, R. (2000) *Institutions and Economic Theory: The Contribution of the New Institutional Economics*, Ann Arbor: Michigan University Press.

Gavin, B. (2007) Regional representation in the WTO: a new role for regional trade clubs? UNU/CRIS Working Papers W2007/13.

George, C. (2010) *The Truth about Trade: The Real Impact of Liberalization*, London: Zed Books.

Ghose, A.K. (2000) Trade liberalization, employment and global inequality, *International Labour Review*, 139(3): 281–305; the full study is Trade liberalization and manufacturing employment, Employment Paper 2000/3, ILO. Available at: www.ilo.org/employment/Whatwedo/Publications/WCMS_142284/lang—en/index.htm (accessed June 2013).

Ghosh, B. (ed.) (2000) *Managing Migration: Time for a New International Regime?* Oxford: Oxford University Press.

Goldberg, P.M. and Kindleberger, C.P. (1970) Towards a GATT for investment: a proposal for supervision of the international corporation, *Law and Policy in International Business*, 2(2): 295–325.

Goldstein, M. (2000) *IMF Structural Conditionality: How Much Is Too Much?* Washington, DC: Institute for International Economics.

Goulder, L.H. and Parry, W.H. (2008) Instrument choice in environmental policy, *Review of Environmental Economics and Policy*, 2(2): 152–174.

Graham, A. (2001) The assessment: economics of the internet, *Oxford Review of Economic Policy*, 17(2): 145–158.

Graham, E.M. and Richardson, J.D. (1997) *Global Competition Policy*, Washington, DC: Institute for International Economics.

Graham, E.M. and Wada, E. (2001) Foreign direct investment in China, in P. Drysdale (ed.) *Achieving High Growth: Experience of Transition Economies in East Asia*, Oxford: Oxford University Press.

Grether, J.-M., Mathys, N.A. and de Melo, J. (2012) Unravelling the worldwide pollution haven effect, *Journal of International Trade and Economic Development*, 21(1): 131–162.

Griffith-Jones, S., Montes, M.F. and Nasution, A. (eds) (2001) Managing capital surges in emerging economies, in S. Griffith-Jones, M.F. Montes and A. Nasution (eds) *Short-Term Capital Flows and Economic Crises*, Oxford: Oxford University Press, 263–290.

Grimes, W.W. (2011) The Asian Monetary Fund reborn? Implications of Chiang Mai Initiative Multilateralization, *Asia Policy*, 11: 79–104.

Grimwade, N. (2000) *International Trade: New Patterns of Trade, Production and Investment*, 2nd ed., London: Routledge.

Gstoehl, S. (2007) Governance through government networks; the G8 and international organizations, *The Review of International Organizations*, 2(1): 1–37.

Gutterman, B. (ed.) (2011) *Developing the Future Together*, Fifth Meeting of the Internet Governance Forum, Vilnius, 14–17 September 2010, Geneva: United Nations.

Hagemann, F., Diallo, Y., Etienne, A. and Mehran, F. (2006) *Global Child Labour Trends 2000–2004*, Geneva: ILO IPEC.

Hajnal, P.I. (2007) *The G8 system and the G20: Evolution, Role and Documentation*, Aldershot, UK: Ashgate.

Hanley, N. and Folmer, H. (eds) (1998) *Game Theory and the Environment*, Cheltenham, UK: Edward Elgar.

Haq, M. ul, Kaul, I. and Grunberg, I. (eds) (1996) *The Tobin Tax: Coping with Financial Volatility*, Oxford: Oxford University Press.

Hardin, G. and Baden, J. (eds) (1977) *Managing the Commons*, San Francisco: Freeman.

Hartlapp, M. (2007) On enforcement, management and persuasion: different logics of implementation policy in the EU and the ILO, *Journal of Common Market Studies*, 45(3): 653–674.

Hasnat, B. (2002) The impact of core labour standards on exports, *International Business Review*, 11(5): 563–575.

Hatton, T. (2007) Should we have a WTO for international migration? *Economic Policy*, 22(50): 339–383

Hazakis, K. (2012) Analyzing the logic of international monetary cooperation in the Group-Twenty (G20) summits, UNU/CRIS Working Papers W2012/2.

Heal, G. (1999) New strategies for the provision of global public goods: learning from international environmental challenges, in I. Kaul, I. Grunberg and M. Stern (eds) *Global Public Goods*, Geneva: UNDP, 220–239.

Helm, D. and Hepburn, C. (eds) (2009) *The Economics and Politics of Climate Change*, Oxford: Oxford University Press.

Hermes, N. and Lensink, R. (2001) Changing the conditions for development aid: a new paradigm? *Journal of Development Studies*, 37(6): 1–16.

Hernández, L.F. and Valdés, R.O. (2001) What drives contagion: trade, neighborhood or financial links? *International Review of Financial Analysis*, 10: 203–218.

Hertel, T.W., Hoekman, B.M. and Martin, W. (2002) Developing countries and a new round of WTO negotiations, *World Bank Research Observer*, 17(1).

Hertz, B. and Wagner, M. (2011a) Regionalism as building block for multilateralism, *Global Economy Journal*, 11(1): article 3.

Hertz, B. and Wagner, M. (2011b) The real impact of GATT/WTO: a generalized approach, *The World Economy*, 34(6): 1014–1041.

Ho, D.E. (2002) Compliance and international soft law: why do countries implement the Basle accord? *Journal of International Economic Law*, 5: 647–688.

Hodges, M.R., Kirton, J.J. and Daniels, J.P. (eds) (1999) *The G8's Role in the New Millennium*, Aldershot, UK: Ashgate.

Hodson, D. (2004) Macroeconomic co-ordination in the euro area: the scope and limits of the open method, *Journal of European Public Policy*, 11(2): 231–248.

Hoekman, B. (ed.) (2012) *The WTO and Trade in Services*, Cheltenham, UK: Edward Elgar.

Hoekman, B.M. and Kostecki, M.M. (2009) *The Political Economy of the World Trading System: The WTO and Beyond*, 3rd ed., Oxford: Oxford University Press.

Hoekman, B. and Özden, Ç. (2006) *Trade Preferences and Differential Treatment of Developing Countries*, Cheltenham, UK: Edward Elgar,

Hoekman, B. and Winters, L.A. (2009) Multilateralizing preferential trade agreements: a developing country perspective, in R. Baldwin and P. Low (eds) *Multilateralizing Regionalism: Challenges for the Global Trading System*, Cambridge: World Trade Organization and Cambridge University Press, 636–680.

Hoel, M. (1992) Carbon taxes: an international tax or harmonized domestic taxes? *European Economic Review*, 36(2–3): 400–406.

Hollick, A.L. and Cooper, R.N. (1997) Global commons: can they be managed? In P. Gasgupta, K.G. Maler and A. Vercelli (eds) *The Economics of the Transnational Commons*, Oxford: Clarendon Press, 141–171.

Hope, E. and Maeleng, P. (eds) (1998) *Competition and Trade Policies: Coherence or Conflict?* London: Routledge.

Horn, H. and Mavroidis, P.C. (2001) Economic and legal aspects of the Most-Favored-Nation clause, *European Journal of Political Economy*, 17: 233–279.

Horn, H., Mavroidis, P.C. and Sapir, A. (2010) Beyond the WTO? An anatomy of EU and US preferential trade agreements, *The World Economy*, 33: 1565–1588.

Huppes, G. and Simonis, U.E. (2009) Environmental policy instruments, *Principles of Environmental Science*, II: 239–280.

Huntington, S.P. (1997) *The Clash of Civilizations and the Remaking of the World Order*, London: Touchstone.

Huysmans, J. (2000) The European Union and the securitization of migration, *Journal of Common Market Studies*, 38(5): 751–778.

IATCWG (International Antitrust Code Working Group) (1993) Draft international antitrust code: a GATT–MTO plurilateral trade agreement, *World Trade Materials* 5 (September): 126–196; also published as *BNA Antitrust and Regulation Report*, 64, no. 1628, Washington, DC.

ICC/WBO (2007) ICC policy statement on supply chain responsibility. Available at: www.iccwbo.org/Advocacy-Codes-and-Rules/Document-centre/2007/ICC-Policy-Statement-on-Supply-Chain-Responsibility/ (accessed June 2013).

IDA (2007) *Selectivity and Performance: IDA's Country Assessment and Development Effectiveness*, IDA 15, Washington, DC.

IDA (2010) *IDA's Performance Based Allocation System: Review of the Current System and Key Issues for IDA 16*, IDA 16, Washington, DC.

ILO (2008) *Declaration on Social Justice for a Fair Globalization*, Geneva: ILO.

ILO (2009) *Rules of the Game: A Brief Introduction to International Labour Standards*, Geneva. Available at: www.ilo.org/global/publications/WCMS_108393/lang-en/index.htm (accessed June 2013).

IMF (2000) *World Economic Outlook* (May), 149–163; and supporting studies, 1–19, Washington, DC: IMF.

IMF (2004) Capital account liberalization and economic performance: survey and synthesis, IMF Staff Papers 51.

IMF (2008a) *Governance of the IMF: An Evaluation*. Available at: www.ieo-imf.org/ieo/pages/IEOPreview.aspx?img=i6nZpr3iSlU%3d&mappingid=K1g%2bWj0GTnY%3d (accessed June 2013).

IMF (2008b) *Current Developments in Monetary and Financial Law*, vol. 5, Washington, DC: IMF.

IMF (2009) *Committee on IMF Governance Reform: Final Report*. Available at: www.imf.org/external/np/omd/2009/govref/032409.pdf (accessed June 2013).

IMF (2011a) *Annual Report 2011: Pursuing Equitable and Balanced Growth*, Washington, DC: IMF.

IMF (2011b) *Global Financial Stability Report: Grappling with the Crisis Legacies*, Washington, DC: IMF.

IMF (2012) *Liberalizing capital flows and managing outflows – background paper*, Washington, DC: IMF.

Ivanova, M. (2007) Designing the United Nations Environment Programme: a story of compromise and confrontation, *International Environmental Agreements: Politics, Law, Economics*, 7: 337–361.

Ivanova, M. (2010) UNEP in global environmental governance: design, leadership, location, *Global Environmental Politics*, 10(1): 30–59.

Iwasaki, Y. and Prakash, B. (2002) ASEAN economic cooperation: a review, *Journal of Asian Economics*, 13(3): 319–335.

Jaffe, J., Ranson, M. and Stavins, R.N. (2010) Linking tradable permit systems: a key element of emerging international climate change policy architecture, *Ecology Law Quarterly*, 36: 789–808.

Jansen, M., Peters, R. and Salazar-Xirinax, J.-M. (eds) (2011) *Trade and Employment: From Myths to Facts*, Geneva: ILO.

Jeanne, O. and Zettelmeyer, J. (2001) International bailouts: the IMF's role, *Economic Policy: A European Forum*, 33: 407–432.

Jeanne, O., Ostry, J. and Zettelmeyer, J. (2008) A theory of international crisis lending and IMF conditionality, IMF Working Paper 236, Washington, DC.

Joachim, J., Reinalda, B. and Verbeek, B. (2007) *International Organizations and Policy Implementation; Enforcers, Managers, Authorities*, London: Routledge.

Johnston, D. (2000) Fostering international investment and corporate responsibility, in MINEZ (eds) *From Havana to Seattle and Beyond*, The Hague: SDU, 159–166.

Kaiser, K., Kirton, J.J. and Daniels, J.P. (2000) *Shaping a New International Financial System: Challenges of Governance in a Globalizing World*, Aldershot, UK: Ashgate.

Kapur, D. (2002) Processes of change in international organizations, in D. Nayyar (ed.) *Governing Globalization: Issues and Institutions*, Oxford: UNU/WIDER and Oxford University Press, 334–355.

Kasper, W. and Streit, M. (1998) *Institutional Economics: Social Order and Public Policy*, Cheltenham, UK: Edward Elgar.

Kaufmann, D., Kraay, A. and Zoido-Lobaton, P. (1999a) Aggregate governance indicators, Policy Research Department Working Paper 2195, Washington, DC: World Bank.

Kaufmann, D., Kraay, A. and Zoido-Lobaton, P. (1999b) Governance matters, Policy Research Department Working Paper 2196, Washington, DC: World Bank.

Kaufmann, D., Kraay, A. and Mastruzzi, M. (2009) Governance matters VIII: aggregate and individual governance indicators, 1996–2008, Policy Research Working Paper 4978, Washington, DC: World Bank.

Kaul, I., Grunberg, I. and Stern, M.A. (eds) (1999) *Global Public Goods*, Geneva: UNDP.

Keohane, R.O. (1993) The analysis of international regimes: towards a European–American research programme, in V. Rittberger (ed.) *Regime Theory and International Relations*, Oxford: Clarendon Press, 23–45.

Kilby, C. (2009) The political economy of conditionality: an empirical analysis of World Bank loan disbursements, *Journal of Development Economics*, 89: 51–61

Killick, T. (1995) *IMF Programmes in Developing Countries: Design and Impact*, London: Routledge.

Kim, D.-H. and Lin, S.-C. (2009) Trade and growth at different stages of economic development, *Journal of Development Studies*, 45(8): 1211–1224.

Kim, J.A. and Chung, S.-Y. (2012) The role of the G20 in governing the climate change regime, *International Environmental Agreements; Politics, Law and Economics*, 12(4): 361–374.

Kimura, H., Mori, Y. and Sawada, Y. (2012) Aid proliferation and economic growth: a cross-country analysis, *World Development*, 40(1): 1–10.

Kingah, S. and Salimzhuarova, A. (2012) Enhanced coordination between the World Bank and regional development banks as a means to reduce perceived inequalities at the World Bank, UNU/CRIS Working Paper W2012/4.

Kirton, J.J. (2001) The G20: representativeness, effectiveness and leadership in global governance, in J.J. Kirton, J. Daniels and A. Freytag (eds) *Guiding Global Order: G8 Governance in the Twenty-first Century*, Aldershot, UK: Ashgate, 143–172.

Kirton, J.J. and von Furstenberg, G.M. (2001) *New Directions in Global Economic Governance: Managing Globalization in the Twenty-first Century*, Aldershot, UK: Ashgate.

Kirton, J.J., Larionova, M. and Savona, P. (eds) (2010) *Making Global Economic Governance Effective: Hard and Soft Law Institutions in a Crowded World*, Aldershot, UK: Ashgate.

Kis-Katos, K. and Schulze, G. (2002) Labour standards and international trade, *World Economics Journal*, 3(4): 101–129.

Klodt, H. (2001) Conflicts and conflict resolution in international anti-trust: do we need international competition rules? *The World Economy*, 24(7): 877–888.

Knack, S. (2000) Aid dependence and the quality of governance: a cross-country empirical analysis, World Bank Policy Research Working Papers 2396; also published in an adapted form in *Southern Economic Journal* (2001) 68(2): 310–329.

Knack, S. and Rahman, A. (2007) Donor fragmentation and bureaucratic quality in aid recipients, *Journal of Development Economics*, 83: 176–197.

Kneller, R., Morgan, C.W. and Kanchanahatakij, S. (2008) Trade liberalization and economic growth, *The World Economy*, 31(6): 701–719.

Knill, C. and Lenschow, A. (2004) Modes of regulation in the governance of the European Union: towards a comprehensive evaluation, in J. Jordana and D. Levi-Faur (eds) *The Politics of Regulation: Institutions and Regulatory Reforms for the Age of Governance*, Cheltenham, UK: Edward Elgar, 218–244.

Knill, C. and Liefferink, D. (2007) *Environmental Politics in the European Union: Policy-Making, Implementation and Patterns of Multi-level Governance*, Manchester: Manchester University Press.

Kodama, M. (2012) Aid unpredictability and economic growth, *World Development*, 40(2): 266–272.

Kolk, A., van Tulder, R. and Welters, C. (1999) International codes of conduct and corporate social responsibility: can transnational corporations regulate themselves? *Transnational Corporations*, 8(1): 143–180.

Kooiman, J. (2003) *Governing as Governance*, London: Sage.

Koser, K. (2010) Introduction: international migration and global governance, *Global Governance*, 16: 301–315.

Krasner, S.D. (ed.) (1983) *International Regimes*, Ithaca, NY: Cornell University Press.

Kremer, M., Van Lieshout, P. and Went, R. (eds) (2009) *Doing Good or Doing Better: Development Policies in a Globalizing World*, Amsterdam: Amsterdam University Press.

Kruger, J., Oates, W.E. and Pizer, W.A. (2007) Decentralizing in the EU emissions trading scheme and lessons for global policy, *Review of Environmental Economics and Policy*, 1(1): 112–133.

Kucera, D. (2008) Introduction and overview, in D. Kucera (ed.) *Qualitative Indicators of Labour Standards: Comparative Methods and Applications*, Dordrecht: Springer, 1–26.

Kuik, O., Aerts, J., Berkhout, F., Biermann, F., Bruggink, J., Gupta, J. and Tol, R.S.J. (2008) Post-2012 climate policy dilemmas: a review of proposals, *Climate Policy*, 8(3): 317–336.

Kulke, B. (2007) The present and future role of ILO standards in realizing the right to social security, *International Social Security Review*, 60(2–3): 119–141.

Langhammer, R.J. (1992) The developing countries and regionalism, *Journal of Common Market Studies*, 30(2): 211–232.

Lavigne, R. and Schembri, L. (2009) Strengthening IMF surveillance: an assessment of recent reforms, Bank of Canada Discussion Papers 2009/10, Ottawa. Available at: econstor.eu.bitstream/10419/66936/1/618939075.pdf (accessed June 2013).

Lawrence, R.Z. (1996) *Single World, Divided Nations? International Trade and OECD Labor Markets*, Paris: OECD.

Lawrence, R.Z. (2006) Rulemaking amidst growing diversity: a club-of-clubs approach to WTO reform and new issue selection, *Journal of International Economic Law*, 9(4): 823–835.

Lee, J.-W., Park, I. and Shin, K. (2008) Proliferating regional trade arrangements: why and whither? *The World Economy*, 31(12): 1525–1557.

Lewer, J. and Van den Berg, H. (2003) How large is international trade's effect on international growth? *Journal of Economic Surveys*, 17(3): 363–396.

Lewis, D. and Kanji, N. (2009) *Non-governmental Organizations and Development*, London: Routledge.

Lipsey, R.E. and Muchielli, J.-L. (eds) (2001) *Multinational Firms and Impact on Employment, Trade and Technology: New Perspectives for a New Century*, London: Routledge.

Loisel, O. and Martin, Ph. (2001) Coordination, cooperation, contagion and currency crises, *Journal of International Economics*, 53: 399–419.

Lomborg, B. (ed.) (2010) *Smart Solutions to Climate Change: Comparing Costs and Benefits*, Cambridge: Cambridge University Press.

Long, D. and Woolley, F. (2009) Global public goods: critique of a UN discourse, *Global Governance*, 15: 107–122.

Lücke, M. (2009) IMF reform in the aftermath of the crisis: let the IMF speak truth to power, in H. Klodt and H. Lehment (eds) *The Crisis and Beyond*, Kiel Institute for the World Economy, 83–92. e-Book. Available at: www.ifw-kiel.de/think-tank/policy-support/pdf/the-crisis-and-beyond (accessed June 2013).

Lundborg, P. and Segerstrom, P.S. (2002) The growth and welfare effects of international mass migration, *Journal of International Economics*, 56(1): 177–204.

McCalman, P. (2002) Multilateral trade negotiations and the Most Favoured Nation clause, *Journal of International Economics*, 57: 151–176.

McCormick, J. (1999) The role of environmental NGOs in international regimes, in N.J. Vig and R.S. Axelrod (eds) *The Global Environment: Institutions, Law, and Policy*, Washington, DC: CQ Press, 52–71.

McGillivray, M. and Markova, N. (2010) Global inequality in well-being dimensions, *Journal of Development Studies*, 46(2): 371–378.

McKibbin, W.J and Wilcoxen, P.J. (2002) The role of economics in climate change policy, *Journal of Economic Perspectives*, 16(2): 107–129.

Maddison, A. (2001) *The World Economy*, vol. 1, *A Millennial Perspective, Development Centre Studies*, Paris: OECD.

Mah, J.S. (2002) Core labour standards and export performance in developing countries, *The World Economy*, 20(6): 773–785.

Malan, P. *et al.* (2007) *Report of the External Review Committee on Bank-Fund Collaboration*, Washington, DC. Available at: www.imf.org/external/np/pp/eng/2007/022307.pdf (accessed June 2013).

Manne, A.S. and Richels, R.G. (2000) The Kyoto Protocol: a cost-effective strategy for meeting environmental objectives? In C. Carraro (ed.) *Efficiency and Equity of Climate Change Policy*, Dordrecht: Kluwer, 43–62.

Mansfield, E.D. and Reinhart, E. (2003) Multilateral determinants of regionalism: the effects of GATT/WTO on the foundation of preferential trading arrangements, *International Organization*, 57(4): 829–862.

Marsiliani, L., Rauscher, M. and Withagen, C. (eds) (2003) *Environmental Policy in an International Perspective*, Dordrecht: Kluwer.

Mathieson, D.J. and Schinasi, G.J. (2000) *International Capital Markets: Developments, Prospects and Key Policy Issues*, Washington, DC: IMF.

Matsui, Y. (2002) Some aspects of the principle of "common but differentiated responsibilities", *International Environmental Agreements: Politics, Law and Economics*, 2: 151–171.

Mattli, W. and Woods, N. (eds) (2009) *The Politics of Global Regulation*, Princeton, NJ: Princeton University Press.

Mattoo, A. and Subramanian, A. (1997) Multilateral rules on competition policy: a proposal for early action? *Journal of World Trade*, 31(5): 95–115.

Mayer, W. and Mourmouras, A. (2008) IMF conditionality: an approach based on the theory of special interest politics, *Review of International Organizations*, 3: 105–121.

Meiklejohn, R. (1999) An international competition policy: do we need it? Is it feasible? *The World Economy*, 22(9): 1233–1249.

Memedovic, O., Kuyvenhoven, A. and Molle, W.T.M. (eds) (1999) *Multilateralism and Regionalism in the Post-Uruguay Round Era: What Role for the EU?* Dordrecht: Kluwer.

Menon, J. (2000) The evolving ASEAN free trade area: widening and deepening, *Asian Development Review*, 18(1): 49–72.

Meschi, E. and Vivarelli, M. (2009) Trade and income inequality in developing countries, *World Development*, 37(2): 287–302.

Messerlin, P. (1999) External aspects of state aids, *European Economy*, 3: 161–195.

Messerlin, P. (2010) Climate change and trade policy: from mutual destruction to mutual support, World Bank Policy Research Working Paper Series 5378, Washington, DC: World Bank.

Metcalfe, L. (1994) International policy coordination and public management reform, *International Review of Administrative Science*, 60: 271–290.

Metha, P. and Evenett, S.J. (2006) Promoting competition around the world: a diversity of rationales and approaches, in P. Metha (ed.) *Competition Regimes in the World: A Civil Society Report*, Jaipur: CUTS.

Mishkin, F.S. (1992) Anatomy of a financial crisis, *Journal of Evolutionary Economics*, 2(2): 115–130.

Mishkin, F.S. (1999) Global financial instability: framework, events, issues, *Journal of Economic Perspectives*, 13(4): 3–20.

Mitchell, A.D. and Voon, T. (2009) Operationalizing special and differential treatment in the World Trade Organization: game over? *Global Governance*, 15: 343–357.

Molle, W. (2002) Globalization, regionalism and labour markets: should we recast the foundations of the EU regime in matters of regional (rural and urban) development? *Regional Studies*, 36(2): 163–174.

Molle, W. (2003) *Global Economic Institutions*, London: Routledge.

Molle, W. (2006) *The Economics of European Integration: Theory, Practice, Policy*, 5th ed., Aldershot, UK: Ashgate.

Molle, W. (ed.) (2008a) *Global Economic Institutions*, vol. 1, *General*, London: Routledge.

Molle, W. (ed.) (2008b) *Global Economic Institutions*, vol. 2, *Trade*, London: Routledge.

Molle, W. (ed.) (2008c) *Global Economic Institutions*, vol. 3, *Finance*, London: Routledge.

Molle, W. (ed.) (2008d) *Global Economic Institutions*, vol. 4, *Environment*, London: Routledge.

Molle, W. (2011) *European Economic Governance: The Quest for Consistency and Effectiveness*, London: Routledge.

Moon, W. and Rhee, Y. (2012) *Asian Monetary Integration: Coping with a New Monetary Order after the Global Crisis*, Cheltenham, UK: Edward Elgar.

Moran, T.H. (1998) *Foreign Direct Investment and Development: The New Policy Agenda for Developing Countries and Economies in Transition*, Washington, DC: Institute for International Economics.

Morris, S. (2000) Contagion, *Review of Economic Studies*, 67: 53–78.

Morrissey, O. (2004) Conditionality and aid effectiveness re-evaluated, *The World Economy*, 27(2): 153–171.

Moshirian, F. (2002) New international financial architecture, *Journal of Multinational Financial Management*, 12: 273–284.

Mueller, M.L. (2010) *Networks and States: The Global Politics of Internet Governance*, Cambridge, MA: MIT Press.

Murphy, H. (2010) *The Making of International Trade Policy: NGOs, Agenda-Setting and the WTO*, Cheltenham, UK: Edward Elgar.

Murray, J. (2004) Corporate social responsibility: an overview of principles and practice, International Labour Office Working Paper 34, Geneva: ILO.

Nadvi, K. (2008) Global standards, global governance and the organization of value chains, *Journal of Economic Geography*, 8(3): 323–343.

Nayyar, D. (2002a) The existing system and the missing links, in D. Nayyar (ed.) *Governing Globalization: Issues and Institutions*, Oxford: UNU/WIDER and Oxford University Press, 356–384.

Nayyar, D. (2002b) Cross-border movements of people, in D. Nayyar (ed.) *Governing Globalization: Issues and Institutions*, Oxford: UNU/WIDER and Oxford University Press, 144–76.

Neumann, M. (2001) *Competition Policy: History, Theory and Practice*, Cheltenham: Edward Elgar.

Nordhaus, W.D. (1994) *Managing the Global Commons*, Cambridge, MA: MIT Press.

North, D.C. (1990) *Institutions, Institutional Change and Economic Performance*, Cambridge: Cambridge University Press.

North, D.C. (1991) Institutions, *Journal of Economic Perspectives*, 5(1): 97–112.

OECD (1987) *Competition Policy and International Trade*, Paris: OECD.

OECD (1994) *Jobs Study: Evidence and Explanations*, 2 vols, Paris: OECD.

OECD (1995) *New Dimensions of Market Access in a Globalising World Economy*, Paris: OECD.

OECD (1996) *Trade, Employment and Labour Standards: A Study of Core Workers' Rights and International Trade*, Paris: OECD.

OECD (1998) *The Multilateral Agreement on Investment* (draft consolidated text), Paris: OECD.

OECD (1999a) *Action against Climate Change: The Kyoto Protocol and Beyond*, Paris: OECD.

OECD (1999b) *International Emissions Trading under the Kyoto Protocol*, Paris: OECD.

OECD (2000) *A Multi-gas Assessment of the Kyoto Protocol*, Paris: OECD.

OECD (2005) *Using Performance Information for Managing and Budgeting: Challenges, Lessons and Opportunities*, GOV/PGC/SBO.2005.3, Paris: OECD.

OECD (2006) *Policy Framework for Investment: A Review of Good Practices*, Paris: OECD.

OECD (2009a) *Building Blocks for Policy Coherence for Development*, Paris: OECD.

OECD (2009b) *2009 OECD Report on Division of Labour: Addressing Fragmentation and Concentration of Aid across Countries*. Available at: www.oecd.org/development/effectiveness/44318319.pdf (accessed June 2013).

OECD (2010a) *Development Co-operation Report 2010*, Paris: OECD.

OECD (2010b) *Perspectives on Global Development 2010: Shifting Wealth*, Paris: OECD.

OECD (2011a) *The OECD Guidelines for Multinational Enterprises*, 2011 ed. Available at: www.oecd.org/daf/inv/mne/oecdguidelinesformultinationalenterprises.htm (accessed June 2013).

OECD (2011b) *Perspectives on Global Development 2010: Shifting Wealth*, Paris: OECD.

OECD (2011c) *Divided We Stand: Why Inequality Keeps Rising*, Paris: OECD.

OECD (2011d) *2011 Report on Division of Labour: Addressing Cross-country Fragmentation of Aid*. Available at: www.oecd.org/dac/49106391.pdf (accessed June 2013).

OECD (2012) *Going for Growth: II*, Paris: OECD.

Olson, M. Jr. (1965) *The Logic of Collective Action: Public Goods and the Theory of Groups*, Cambridge, MA: Harvard University Press.

Onida, F. (2008) Labour standards and ILO's effectiveness in the governance of globalization, KITes Working Papers 25.

Osakwe, P.N. and Schembri, L.L. (2002) Real effects of collapsing exchange rate regimes: an application to Mexico, *Journal of International Economics*, 57: 299–325.

Ouattara, B. and Strobl, E. (2008) Aid, policy and growth: does aid modality matter? *Review of World Economics*, 114(2): 347–365.

Oyejide, T (2000) Interests and options of developing countries and LDCs in a new round of multilateral trade negotiations, G24 Discussion Paper 2, New York: United Nations.

Panagariya, A. and Krishna, P. (2002) On necessarily welfare-enhancing free trade areas, *Journal of International Economics*, 57: 353–367.

Park, D. (2001) Recent trends in the global distribution of income, *Journal of Policy Modeling*, 23: 497–501.

Park, S. and Vetterlein, A. (2010) *Owning Development: Creating Policy Norms in the IMF and the World Bank*, New York: Cambridge University Press.

Park, Y.C. (2002) Beyond the Chang Mai initiative: rationale and need for a regional monetary arrangement in East Asia, in J.J. Teunissen (ed.) *A Regional Approach to Financial Crisis Prevention: Lessons from Europe and Initiatives in Asia, Latin America and Africa*, The Hague: Fondad, 121–147.

Park, Y.C. and Wang, Y. (2000) Reforming the international financial system: prospects for regional financial cooperation in East Asia, in J.J. Teunissen (ed.) *Reforming the International Financial System: Crisis Prevention and Response*, The Hague: Fondad, 70–84.

Parry, I., de Mooy, R. and Keen, M. (2012) *Fiscal Policy to Mitigate Climate Change; A Guide for Policymakers*, Washington, DC: IMF.

Pearce, D. and Turner, K. (1990) *Economics of Natural Resources and the Environment*, London: Harvester Wheatsheaf.

Pelzman, J. and Shoham, A. (2007) WTO enforcement issues, *Global Economy Journal*, 7(1): article 4.

Perman, R.Y.M., McGilvray, J. and Common, M. (1999) *Natural Resources and Environmental Economics*, Harlow, UK: Pearson.

Peters, B.G. and van Nispen, F.K.M. (1998) *Public Policy Instruments: Evaluating the Tools of Public Administration*, New York: Edward Elgar.

Petrakis, E. and Xepapadeas, A. (1996) Environmental consciousness and moral hazard in international agreements to protect the environment, *Journal of Public Economics*, 60: 95–110.

Pigman, G.A. (2007) *The World Economic Forum: A Multi-stakeholder Approach to Global Governance*, London: Routledge.

Pizer, W.A. (2002) Combining price and quantity controls to mitigate global climate change, *Journal of Public Economics*, 85: 409–434.

Pop-Eleches, G. (2009) *From Economic Crisis to Reform: IMF Programs in Latin America and Eastern Europe*, Princeton, NJ: Princeton University Press.

Rajan, R.G. and Subramanian, A. (2008) Aid and growth: what does the cross-country evidence really show? *The Review of Economics and Statistics*, 90(4): 643–665.

Rao, D.S.P. and van Ark, B. (eds) (2013) *World Economic Performance: Past, Present and Future*, Cheltenham, UK: Edward Elgar.

Rao, P.K. (2002) *International Environmental Law and Economics*, Malden, MA: Blackwell.

Rappoport, L. (2002) Global governance and poverty reduction: the lessons of the Argentina case, Paper for the EU LDC Network Conference on Global Governance, Chiang Mai.

Reinhart, C.M. and Rogoff, K.S. (2009) *This Time Is Different: Eight Centuries of Financial Folly*, Princeton, NJ: Princeton University Press.

Reinhart, C.M. and Smith, R.T. (2002) Temporary controls on capital inflows, *Journal of International Economics*, 57: 327–351.

Reisen, H. (2010) The multilateral donor non-system: towards accountability and efficient role assignment, *Economics*, 4: article 2010-2015.

Renner, M., Sweeney, S. and Kubit, J. (2008) *Green Jobs: Towards Decent Work in a Sustainable, Low-Carbon World*, Geneva: UNEP/ILO/IOE/ITUC.

Rhodes, R.A.W. (2000) Governance and public administration, in J. Pierre (ed.) *Debating Governance: Authority, Steering and Democracy*, Oxford: Oxford University Press, 54–90.

Riddell, R.C. (2007) *Does Foreign Aid Really Work?* Oxford: Oxford University Press.

Rodrik, D., Subramanian, A. and Trebbi, F. (2004) Institutions rule: the primacy of institutions over geography and integration in economic development, *Journal of Economic Growth*, 9: 131–165.

Rogoff, K. (1999) International institutions for reducing global financial instability, *Journal of Economic Perspectives*, 13(4): 21–42.

Rose, A.K. (2004) Do we really know that the WTO increases trade? *American Economic Review*, 94(1): 98–114.

Rudra, N. (2002) Globalization and the decline of the welfare state in less developed countries, *International Organization*, 56(2): 411–445.

Ruffing, K.G. (2010) The role of the Organization for Economic Cooperation and Development in environmental policy making, *Review of Environmental Economics and Policy*, 4(2): 199–220.

Sapir, A. (2009) The crisis of global governance, in A. Hemerijck, B. Knapen and E. van Doorne (eds) *Aftershocks: Economic Crisis and Institutional Choice*, Amsterdam: Amsterdam University Press, 177–184.

Sauve, P. (2006) Multilateral rules on investment: is forward movement possible? *Journal of International Economic Law*, 9(2): 325–355.

Scharpf, F. (2002) Globalization and the welfare state: constraints, challenges and vulnerabilities, in R. Sigg and C. Behrendt (eds) *Social Security in the Global Village*, New Brunswick, NJ: Transaction Publishers, 85–117.

Scherer, F.M. (1994) *Competition Policies for an Integrated World Economy*, Washington, DC: Brookings Institution.

Sell, F.L. (2001) *Contagion in Financial Markets*, Cheltenham, UK: Edward Elgar.

Sending, O.J. and Neumann, I.B. (2006) Governance to govermentality: analyzing NGOs, states, and power, *International Studies Quarterly*, 50(3): 651–672.

Sengenberger, W. and Campbell, D. (eds) (1994) *International Labour Standards and Economic Interdependence*, Geneva: ILO.

Siebert, H. (1998) *Economics of the Environment: Theory and Policy*, 5th ed., Berlin: Springer.

Siebert, H. (2009) *Rules for the Global Economy*, Princeton, NJ: Princeton University Press.

Simatupang, B. (1998) Association of the South-East Asian Nations' (ASEAN) Free Trade Area (AFTA): the changing environment and incentives, in A.E. Fernández Jilberto and A. Mommen (eds) *Regionalization and Globalization in the Modern World Economy: Perspectives on the Third World and Transitional Economies*, London: Routledge, 307–327.

Singh, A. (2004) *Multilateral Competition Policy and Economic Development: A Developing Country Perspective on the EC Proposals*, New York and Geneva: UNCTAD.

Singh, T. (2010) Does international trade cause economic growth? A survey, *The World Economy*, 33(11): 1517–1564.

Slaughter, A.M. (2004) *A New World Order?* Princeton, NJ: Princeton University Press.

Smith, S. (1992) Taxation and the environment: a survey, *Fiscal Studies*, 13(4): 21–57.

Somanathan, E. (2010) Effects of information on environmental quality in developing countries, *Review of Environmental Economics and Policy*, 4(2): 275–292.

Spar, D.L. (1999) The public face of cyberspace, in I. Kaul, I. Grunberg and M. Stern (eds) *Global Public Goods*, Geneva: UNDP, 344–362.

Standing, G. (2008) The ILO: an agency for globalization? *Development and Change*, 39(3): 355–384.

Stanford, J. (1998) Openness and equity: regulating labor market outcomes in a globalized economy, in D. Baker, G. Epstein and R. Pollin (eds) *Globalization and Progressive Economic Policy*, Cambridge: Cambridge University Press, 245–270.

Stern, N. (2008) The economics of climate change, *American Economic Review*, 98(2): 1–37.

Stewart, F. (1995) Biases in global markets: can the forces of inequity and marginalization be modified? In M. ul Haq, R. Jolly, P. Streeten and K. Haq (eds) *The UN and Bretton Woods Institutions: New Challenges for the Twenty-first Century*, New York: St Martin's Press, 164–184.

Stiglitz, J.E. (2002) *Globalization and Its Discontents*, New York: W.W. Norton.

Stiles, K.W. (2000) Grassroots empowerment: states, non-state actors and global policy formulation, in R.A. Higgott, G.R.D. Underhill and A. Bieler (eds) *Non-state Actors and Authority in the Global System*, London: Routledge, 32–47.

Stone, R.W. (2008) The scope of IMF conditionality, *International Organization*, 62(4): 589–620.

Stone, R.W. (2011) *Controlling Institutions; International Organizations and the Global Economy*, New York: Cambridge University Press.

Straubhaar, T. (2000) Why do we need a general agreement on movements of people (GAMP), in B. Ghosh (ed.) *Managing Migration: Time for a New International Regime?* Oxford: Oxford University Press, 110–136.

Straubhaar, T. (2006) Labour market relevant migration policy, *Zeitschrift für Arbeitsmarktforschung*, 39(1): 149–158.

Subramanian, A. and Shang Jin, W. (2007) The WTO promotes trade, strongly but unevenly, *Journal of International Economics*, 72(1): 151–175.

Sutherland Report (2004) *A Report by the Consultative Board to the Director-General*, Geneva: WTO.

Swanston, T. and Johnston, S. (1999) *Global Environmental Problems and International Environmental Agreements: The Economics of International Institution Building*, Cheltenham, UK: Edward Elgar.

Tabb, W.K. (2004) *Economic Governance in the Age of Globalization*, New York: Columbia University Press.

Tapinos, G. and de Rugy, A. (1993) The macroeconomic impact of immigration: review of the literature published since the mid-1970s, in SOPEMI, *Trends in European Migration*, 1993 report, Paris: OECD, 157–177.

Tavares, J. (2003) Does foreign aid corrupt? *Economic Letters*, 79: 99–106.

Taylor, I. and Smith, K. (2007) *The United Nations Conference on Trade and Development*, London: Routledge.

Te Velde, D.-W. (2008) The impact of codes and standards on investment flows to developing countries, Employment Sector Working Paper 25, Geneva: ILO.

Teunissen, J.J (ed.) (2000) *Reforming the International Financial System: Crisis Prevention and Response*, The Hague: Fondad.

Thakur, R. and Van Langenhove, L. (2008) Enhancing global governance through regional integration, in A.F. Cooper, C. Hughes and De Lombaerde, P. (eds) *Regionalisation and Global Governance: The Taming of Globalisation?* London: Routledge, 17–42.

Thirlwall, A.P. and Pacheco-López, P. (2009) *Trade Liberalisation and the Poverty of Nations*, Cheltenham, UK: Edward Elgar.

Thompson, G.F (2003) *Between Hierarchies and Markets: The Logic and Limits of Network Forms of Organisation*, Oxford: Oxford University Press.

Tietenberg, T. (2006) *Emissions Trading: Principles and Practice*, 2nd ed., Washington, DC: Resources for the Future.

Tietzel, M. (2001) In praise of the commons: another case study, *European Journal of Law and Economics*, 12: 159–171.

Tinbergen, J. (1959) The theory of the optimum regime, in L.H. Klaasen, L.M. Koyck and H.J. Witteveen (eds) *Jan Tinbergen: Selected Papers*, Amsterdam: North-Holland, 264–304.

Tol, R.S.J. (2012) On the uncertainty about the total economic impact of climate change, *Environmental and Resource Economics*, 53, 97–116.

Treib, O., Baehr, H. and Falkner, G. (2007) Modes of governance: towards a conceptual clarification, *Journal of European Public Policy*, 14(1): 1–20.

Tussie, D. and Whalley, J. (2002) The functioning of a commitment based WEO: lessons from experience with the WTO, *The World Economy*, 25(5): 685–695.

UN (2011a) *World Development Indicators*, New York: UN.

UN (2011b) *Millennium Development Goals Report*, 2011, New York: UN.

UN (2012) *The Future we Want, Outcome of the Conference Rio + 20*, United Nations Conference on Sustainable Development, agenda item 10, A/Conf.216/L.I. New York: United Nations.

UN (n.d.) *Glossary*. Available at: http://treaties.un.org/Pages/Overview.aspx?path=overview/glossary/page1_en.xml (accessed June 2013).

UNCTAD (1993, 1999, 2000, 2001, 2002, 2011) *World Investment Report*, Geneva: UN.

UNCTAD (2012) *Addressing the Policy Challenges for Sustainable Investment and Enterprise Development*, Round Table II, Doha, UNCTAD XII.

UNCTAD (2013) *The rise of regionalism in international investment policy making; consolidation or complexity?* Available at: www.unctad.org/diae (accessed June 2013).

UNDP (1998) *Overcoming Human Poverty*, New York: UNDP.

UNDP (2008) *Human Development Report: Fighting Climate Change: Human Solidarity in a Divided World*, New York: UNDP.

UN/UNFCCC (2003) Guidelines for the participation of representatives of non-governmental organizations at meetings of the bodies of the UNFCCC. Available at: www.unfcc.int/files/partiesand_observers/ngo/application.pdf/coc_guide.pdf (accessed June 2013).

van den Bossche, P. (2008) *The Law and Policy of the World Trade Organization: Text, Cases and Materials*, 2nd ed., Cambridge: Cambridge University Press.

Van Langenhove, L. and Macovi, M.C. (2011) Regional formations and global governance, in B. Deacon, M.C. Macovei, L. Van Langenhove and N. Yeates (eds) *World-Regional Social Policy and Global Governance: New Research and Policy Agendas in Africa, Asia, Europe and Latin America*, London: Routledge, 9–26.

Vaubel, R. (1986) A public choice approach to international organization, *Public Choice*, 51: 39–57.

Vezirgiannidou, S.-E. (2009) The climate change regime post-Kyoto: why compliance is important and how to achieve it, *Global Environmental Politics*, 9(4): 41–63.

Vijge, M. (2013) The promise of new institutionalism; explaining the absence of a World or United Nations Environment Organisation, *International Environmental Agreements; Politics, Law, Economics*, 13.2, no page indications.

Voigt, S. (2009) The effects of competition policy on development: cross–country evidence using four new indicators, *Journal of Development Studies*, 45(8): 1225–1248.

Walmsley, T.L., Winters, A. and Ahmed, A. (2011) The impact of the movement of labour; results from a model of bi-lateral migration flows, *Global Economy Journal*, 11(4): 1524ff.

Warwick Commission (2007) *The Multilateral Trade Regime: Which Way Forward?* Coventry: University of Warwick.

Wavermann L., W.S. Comanor and A. Goto (1997) *Competition Policy in the Global Economy: Modalities for Cooperation*, London: Routledge.

WBCSD (2010) *Vision 2050: The New Agenda for Business*. Available from: www.wbcsd.org/pages/edocument/edocumentdetails.aspx?id=219 (accessed June 2013).

Weaver, C. (2010) The politics of performance evaluation: independent evaluation at the International Monetary Fund, *Review of International Organizations*, 5: 365–385.

Weisband, E. (2000) Discursive multilateralism: global benchmarks, shame, and learning in the ILO labor standards monitoring regime, *International Studies Quarterly*, 44(4): 643–666.

Whalley, J. and Zissimos, B. (2002) An internationalization-based World Environmental Organization, *The World Economy*, 25(5): 619–642.

Wijen, F., Zoeteman, K., Pieters, J. and van Seters, P. (eds) (2012) *A Handbook of Globalisation and Environmental Policy: National Government Intervention in a Global Arena*, 2nd ed., Cheltenham, UK: Edward Elgar.

Williamson, O.E. (1998) Transaction cost economics: how it works, where it is headed, *De Economist*, 146(1): 23–58.

Winters, L.A. (2004) Trade liberalization and economic performance; an overview, *The Economic Journal*, 114(493): 4–21

Winters, L.A., McCulloch, N. and McKay, A. (2004) Trade liberalization and poverty: the evidence so far, *Journal of Economic Literature*, 42: 72–115.

Witherell, W.H. (1995) The OECD Multilateral Agreement on Investment, *Transnational Corporations*, 4(2): 1–14.

Wood, A. (1995) How trade hurt unskilled workers, *Journal of Economic Perspectives*, 9(3): 57–80.

Wood, A. (2002) Globalization and wage inequalities: a synthesis of three theories, *Weltwirtschaftliches Archiv*, 138(1): 54–82.

Woodward, R. (2009) *The Organisation for Economic Cooperation and Development*, London: Routledge.

World Bank (1992) *World Development Report*, Washington, DC: World Bank.

World Bank (1997) The state in a changing world, in *World Development Report*, Washington, DC: World Bank.

World Bank (2002) Building institutions for markets, in *World Development Report*, Washington, DC: World Bank.

World Bank (2009) *Repowering the World Bank for the 21st century: Report of the High Level Commission on Modernization of Word Bank Group Governance*, Washington, DC: World Bank.

WTO (1998) Globalization and Trade, *WTO Annual Report*, Geneva: WTO.

WTO (2007) Sixty years of the multilateral trading system: achievements and challenges, *World Trade Report 2007*, Geneva: WTO.

WTO (2011a) The WTO and preferential trade agreements: from co-existence to coherence, *World Trade Report 2010*, Geneva: WTO.

WTO (2011b) *Overview of Developments in the International Trading Environment*, WT/TPR/OV/14, Geneva: WTO.

WTO (2012) Trade and public policies; a closer look at non-tariff measures in the 21st century, *World Trade Report 2012*, Geneva: WTO.

Young, O.R. (2010) *Institutional Dynamics, Emergent Patterns in International Environmental Governance*, Cambridge, MA: MIT Press.

Young, O.R. and Osherenko, G. (1993) Testing theories of regime formation, in V. Rittberger (ed.) *Regime Theory and International Relations*, Oxford: Clarendon Press, 223–251.

Yunker, J.A. (2011) *The Idea of World Government: From Ancient Times to the Twenty-first Century*, London: Routledge.

Zimmermann, K.F. (1995) Tackling the European migration problem, *Journal of Economic Perspectives*, 9(2): 45–62.

Zlatko, N. (2011) Impact of financial crises on poverty in the developing world: an empirical approach, *Journal of Development Studies*, 47(11): 1757–1779.

INDEX

Locators to figures and tables are in *italics*; and the letter 'n' refers to an end note.